DISORDER
in the
COURT

Judge Lawrence Waddington

TABLE OF CONTENTS

ACKNOWLEDGEMENT

The author acknowledges the work of law students enrolled in Pepperdine University School of Law for their research and review of the text. The range of cases covers the years 2002 through 2012, but some of the cases have been changed or added by the courts after the final proofing of the book.

The book could not have archived finality without the assistance of Mike Winkelmann and the infusion of his computer skills. During the composition of the text, his advice and guidance were incomparable.

DEDICATION

To Jane, my life

READER NOTES

This book was written without "legal lingo" for those unfamiliar with the process of the courts and for them to understand the impact of judicial decisions on the public. The text focuses on cases decided in the last decade by two courts: the U.S. 9th Circuit Court of Appeals and the Supreme Court. Cases in the text include those decided between 2000 and 2013 but do not include the term of the Supreme Court ending in June 2013 and 9th Circuit cases decided on the same date.

Each case is identified by the volume, page number, and year reported in the Federal Reports for those who opt to do additional research at law schools or on the Internet. Lawyers and judges may also find the text interesting although edited for the public.

The chapters can be read independently for those familiar with the background of both courts. This accounts for occasional repetition of basic principles to those who read consecutively.

PREFACE

To restrict the scope of judicial authority, the U.S. Constitution confers on federal judges the power to resolve "Cases" or "Controversies" - not "questions and issues." The American people in general, and the citizens of several western states in particular, wonder how a federal judiciary can impose its power to resolve innumerable "questions and issues" undermining the vote of the people. Judicial imposition of its "policy," rather than allocating responsibility to the citizenry to vote on controversial issues, has resulted in the same anger of people today *as in 1787 when the Constitution was signed*. No court has ignored its role of restricting judicial power to resolve "Cases and Controversies", as distinct from "questions and issues," more than the U.S. 9th Circuit Court of Appeals (hereinafter the 9th Circuit).

When drafting the Constitution prior to its adoption, all representatives from the thirteen colonies had lived in the shadow of religious and political persecution perpetrated by English monarchs. The newly created Constitution specifically restricted the power previously exercised by kings and queens with whom the American colonists had fought and quarreled. By separating executive, legislative, and judicial functions, the Constitution intentionally diluted federal governmental power. The authors, to confirm their convictions, wrote the first ten amendments to the Constitution imposing further restrictions specifically in response to the grievances of English people who had suffered at the hands of royalty.

In support of the Constitution and the limitations of judicial power, three of its authors, Alexander Hamilton, John Jay, and James Madison wrote a document entitled *The Federalist Papers*. As Hamilton noted in "Federalist No. 78,"

> "Whoever attentively considers the different departments of power must perceive, that, in a government in which they are separated from each other, the judiciary, from the nature of its functions, will always be the least dangerous to the political rights of the Constitution; because it will be least in a capacity to annoy or injure them." The Executive not only dispenses the honors, but holds the sword of the community. The legislature not only commands the purse, but prescribes the rules by which the duties and rights of every citizen are to be regulated. The judiciary, on the contrary, has no influence over either the sword or the purse; no direction either of the strength or of the wealth of the society; and can take no active resolution whatever. It may truly be said to have neither FORCE nor WILL, but merely judgment; and must ultimately depend upon the aid of the executive arm even for the efficacy of its judgments. It proves incontestably that the judiciary is beyond comparison the weakest of the three departments of power; that it can never attack with success either of the other two."

The Constitution also provides that "[t]he power reserved to the states under the Constitution to provide for the determination of 'controversies' in their courts, may be restricted only by action of Congress in conformity to the Judiciary Articles of the Constitution." And the U.S. Supreme Court has said in *Arizona Christian School Tuition Organization v. Winn* of the judicial role that "[i]n granting relief, we [the Supreme Court] try not to nullify more of a legislature's work than is necessary, for we know that a ruling of unconstitutionality frustrates the intent of the elected representatives of the people."

That quotation from the Supreme Court undergirds the theme of this book reviewing the legal history of the 9th Circuit Court of Appeals, a controversial federal appellate court exercising jurisdiction over federal trial courts (district courts) and, under certain circumstances, the courts of several western states. The 9th Circuit is not a trial court, but one of several federal courts of appeal throughout the United States. The role of an appellate court is confined to reviewing the district court trial record, determining whether the trial judge committed any legal errors, listening to the legal arguments of counsel for all sides, and ultimately writing a decision published in public records. Decisions of all federal appellate courts are subject to review by the Supreme Court.

The judges who sit on the 9th Circuit have written extremely controversial, and often lengthy and verbose decisions, but the Supreme Court has reversed a substantial proportion of them. Because many of the decisions impact the American people living within the jurisdiction of the 9th Circuit but unfamiliar with the legal process, this book attempts to inform nonlawyers of the consequences of these judicial decisions in their lives. Discussion of 9th Circuit rulings is not specifically directed to lawyers, and not written in standard legal format, but hopefully of interest to members of the legal profession.

The principle issues in Part I of the text reviews 9th Circuit decisions on criminal law and procedure during the last decade, and their statutory and Constitutional application in state and federal courts. The text reviews 9th Circuit decisions on the doctrine of habeas corpus; due process; jury trials; the death penalty; the effectiveness of defense lawyers; prisoner rights; and civil liability of public officials. These decisions affect public safety, one of the principle objectives of government.

Part II reviews 9th Circuit decisions impacting American culture: racial preferences; voting rights; education; religious expression; freedom of speech; the military; international relations; and abortion. The 9th Circuit has left no judicial stone unturned in constructing its aberrant jurisprudence, undermining state law and defying Supreme Court precedent. The American people have a right to know how these decisions affect their lives.

Cases recently decided by the Supreme Court may have changed the results written in the text due to the lapse of time between those decisions and publication.

INTRODUCTION

In the 2003-2004 court term of the Supreme Court, the 9th Circuit was reversed nineteen times. In the 2004-2005 term the 9th Circuit was reversed sixteen times. In the 2005-2006 term the 9th Circuit was reversed fifteen times. In the 2006-2007 term the 9th Circuit Court was reversed twenty-one times, far exceeding the record of any other Circuit Court of Appeals in the country. The *Los Angeles Daily Journal*, a daily newspaper, headlined the 9th Circuit record in decisions of the Supreme Court between 2008 and 2011 as "Champions of Reversal." The span of cases range from reversals of death penalty sentences; Fourth Amendment cases on search and seizure, the Fifth Amendment Miranda rule and its privilege against self-incrimination, state educational systems, prisoners' rights, freedom of speech and religion, and elections and voting rights.

The texts in Part I and II review Supreme Court and 9th Circuit cases decided during the last decade to provide the reader not only with context but to avoid unfairly isolating a single decision or citing only a handful of recent examples. In innumerable Supreme Court decisions the justices reversed or vacated 9th Circuit decisions summarily, unanimously, and caustically, often dispensing with courtroom argument by lawyers. The 9th Circuit record of twenty reversals out of twenty-one cases in the 2010-2011 Supreme Court term differs insignificantly from that of previous years. The 2011-2012 and 2012-2013 terms provide another record of reversals.

Because Supreme Court decisions generate media publicity in greater proportion than those of any of the federal appellate courts, many of the 9th Circuit opinions slumber unnoticed until their decisions strike the collective heart of the citizenry or are reversed by the Supreme Court. Public indignation exploded when the 9th Circuit buried the California Initiative entitled Proposition 187, passed by voters barring the distribution of public benefits to illegal aliens. Opponents to the Proposition had challenged its provisions, and 9th Circuit judges submitted the case to mediation (a private method of negotiating a dispute between parties), and concealed any explanation of its reason for the decision to the public.

In other decisions angering California citizenry, the 9th Circuit has repeatedly refused to allow display of the Latin Cross privately erected by veterans on public property and dedicated as a memorial to men who died in war. The court also denied enforcement of the California statutory requirement mandating all state prisoners on parole to consent to warrantless searches of their person; upheld racial preferences; ordered public schools to discontinue reciting the words "under God" in the Pledge of Allegiance; approved same sex marriage. In all of these cases the U.S. Supreme Court reversed the 9th Circuit. In the Latin Cross decision, Congress promptly responded by enacting legislation to overrule the 9th Circuit.

The death penalty unquestionably remains one of the most controversial issues in American society. Unsurprisingly, the Supreme Court repeatedly reverses 9th Circuit decisions on this issue. Whatever the moral dimension of the death penalty, voters in western states have approved capital punishment for first degree murder, and jurors regularly vote to impose the sentence despite judicial roadblocks erected by the 9th Circuit. The Supreme Court has never outlawed the death penalty, but California has rarely executed any of prisoners on death row who were convicted decades ago. This delay is substantially attributable to the 9th Circuit.

To achieve this dilatory conduct in executions, at least in part, the 9th Circuit reverses state court death penalty convictions and sentences by frequently criticizing defense lawyers as "ineffective" in representing defendants in murder cases despite overwhelming and irrefutable evidence of guilt. To be sure, the Supreme Court has unquestionably ruled that defendants in criminal cases are entitled to "effective representation by counsel." But the 9th Circuit, on review of state court convictions and death penalty sentences at trial, and despite a previous finding by state appellate courts that counsel properly represented the defendant, routinely reviews and criticizes defense counsel strategy. Instead, 9th Circuit judges explain their own strategy that defense counsel could have devised at trial to avoid conviction or imposition of the death penalty. The Supreme Court has repeatedly reversed those decisions, often in harsh and critical language.

Perhaps the most disturbing issue lies in the conflict between federal and state courts. The 9th Circuit routinely sets aside state court decisions either by invoking the federal review power of habeas corpus or by expanding an application of a legal concept labeled "due process" contained in the Fourteenth Amendment to the Constitution. But more alarming is the increasing use of federal courts to institute "structural reform" of state or local government agencies. In some cases, state officials supinely accept federal intervention into state jurisdiction to achieve political goals unattainable in the legislature or among the citizenry. The 9th Circuit has ordered "structural reform" of police departments, county jails, state prisons, hospitals, schools, and election policies.

What accounts for these controversial judges of the 9th Circuit whose opinions are the subject of repeated Supreme Court censure for ignoring Constitutional, statutory, and decisional law? A suggested hypothesis: several members of the 9th Circuit are determined to impose "policy," not law. In their written decisions, the underlying social, political, religious, and economic policy issues in a particular case are cloaked in legal language, written in prolix and lengthy decisions, and sometimes buried in public records. On issues of race, gender, age and disability, a reader of 9th Circuit decisions can predict a result by reading the "identity" or the "status" of parties who initiated or defended litigation.

In criminal prosecutions, state and federal law enforcement agencies and prosecutors are suspect in 9th Circuit reversal of convictions in cases rendered decades ago and often preventing any retrial. With the passage of time, witnesses have died, forgotten details, are no longer available, or refuse to relive the courtroom experience. The 9th Circuit continues to rule on cases twenty to twenty-five years old.

Not all the 9th Circuit judges are engaged in the imposition of "policy," and the dissenting judges in many of their court decisions unhesitatingly, and often sharply, express their disagreement. But the policy predispositions of many 9th Circuit judges are easily recognized when they write controversial decisions undeterred by their dissenting colleagues or Supreme Court criticism.

Several judges of the 9th Circuit have voiced support for geographically splitting the court and adding another circuit court, contending the size of its jurisdiction over eight states and two U.S. territories is excessively large and cumbersome. The former chief judge and other judges of the 9th Circuit disagree on the grounds that the court maintains its case load consistent with other circuit courts. But the quantity of written decisions is not the issue. The content and consequences of a decision to the public are the core of the argument. Aside from managerial disagreement among the judges, those who support splitting the court allege the opponents of change are attempting to retain ideological decisions previously written by 9th Circuit judges.

Supporters of splitting the court gained two important allies in Supreme Court Justices Anthony Kennedy and Clarence Thomas. Kennedy, formerly a 9th Circuit judge familiar with the workload of the circuit, noted, "The size of the Ninth Circuit created a 'command and control' problem for [trial] court judges who don't know who is going to be on this ever-changing galaxy that are on the three- judge [appellate] panels reviewing a decision. So you can actually take a chance and call the law as you see it." This quote from a Supreme Court justice who knows the members of the 9th Circuit received no public reply from his former colleagues.

An example of judicial disconnect among 9th Circuit judges is illustrated by the difference between majority and minority opinions in the case of *United States v. Fort*. The dissenting judge wrote: "In addition to deciding an exceptionally important issue in a way that directly conflicts with every controlling authority, the [9th Circuit] panel majority's opinion is just plain wrong. It gets the textual interpretation wrong. It gets the policy analysis wrong. It deviates from Supreme Court and circuit law... It hamstrings district court judges [trial court judges]. It condones trial by ambush in a capital [death penalty] case."

This quote does not represent the first time judicial denunciation of a decision has occurred among 9th Circuit judges. For this judge in the *Fort* case to publicly assert that her colleagues are out of sync with other Circuit Courts of Appeal and Supreme Court precedent is not unusual. The 9th Circuit is frequently cited by the other eleven Circuit Courts of Appeal as the solitary dissenter from their collective agreement in appellate opinions. One circuit court recently characterized a decision of the 9th Circuit as an "outlier."

Displeasure with 9th Circuit decisions by other federal courts is shared by those in the public at large who do read its controversial decisions. State court judges surely bristle when their decisions are overruled by the 9th Circuit. In the Supreme Court, the justices confirm their disagreement with 9th Circuit decisions by issuing summary reversals, often unanimously and unaccompanied by any explanation. The constitutional injunction to consider "Cases and Controversies" limits jurisdiction of federal courts to Congress but its scope repeatedly undermined by the 9th Circuit.

As noted earlier, most members of the public are only familiar with controversial decisions written by the 9th Circuit. Aside from California Initiative Proposition 187 sent by the 9th Circuit into the limbo of "mediation," mention the court's prohibition of the election recall of former governor Gray Davis (subsequently reversed by a different panel of judges) despite approval by the California Supreme Court; the pledge of allegiance case; death penalty cases; the Latin Cross case, and a groundswell of public indignation ignites. In many of these cases the 9th Circuit prevents any retrial of a criminal case as a practical matter some cases by "constitutionalizing" the result thereby making it immune from change by the electorate.

Perhaps Alexander Hamilton said it best in "Federalist No. 78," a document written in the formative years of this country: "The courts must declare the sense of the law; and if they should be disposed to exercise WILL [capitalized in original] instead of judgment, the consequence would equally be the substitution of their pleasure to that of the legislative body."

PART I

CHAPTER 1

THE CONSTITUTION
AND THE COURTS

To understand the role of the 9th Circuit and its unenviable record of decisions reversed by the Supreme Court, a brief legal background of both courts is necessary. The Constitutional powers of the federal judiciary are outlined in Article III of the U.S. Constitution and include this language: "The Supreme Court is clothed with original jurisdiction over certain cases, but in all other cases the Supreme Court has only appellate jurisdiction . . . with such exceptions, and under such regulations as the Congress shall make." In other words, the Supreme Court does not conduct trials and only hears appeals from decisions of other state and federal courts.

For our purposes, the Constitution and federal statutory law (the Judiciary Act, (1789) provides three levels of federal courts: trial courts (U.S. District Courts), intermediate appellate courts (Circuit Courts of Appeal) and the Supreme Court. Although the Supreme Court is most widely known, its justices decide only a handful of cases each year, yet geographically divided federal circuit courts of appeal decide innumerable appeals from U.S. district court trials. The Supreme Court reviews not only decisions rendered by federal circuit courts of appeal but also state appellate courts' ruling on federal issues. The Circuit Courts, in their role as federal intermediate courts of appeal, as well as state courts on certain issues, are legally bound to adhere to Supreme Court decisions in their rulings.

The Constitution sets forth the scope of jurisdictional limits in federal courts restricted to interpretation of three categories: federal statutes, constitutional principles, and treaties. All federal trials begin in a district court, but appeals from those decisions are heard in the 9th Circuit Court of Appeals or other federal appellate courts. Final review of appellate court decisions are heard in the Supreme Court, but only if the justices elect to accept the case.

When a party appeals a district court decision to one of the federal courts of appeal, the process is labeled a "direct appeal." But the Constitution also empowers a federal court to issue "writs of habeas corpus" which "shall not be suspended, unless when in cases of rebellion or invasion the public safety may require it." The term *"habeas corpus"* is a Latin phrase that legally translates into "bring the body for a hearing in court to determine the right of a government to restrain a person in custody."

The doctrine of habeas corpus in the United States is derived from English common law enabling courts to determine governmental justification for imprisonment or detention of a person. In the United States, prisoners file a petition for habeas corpus after their trial, conviction, sentence, and imprisonment despite denial of an earlier direct appeal from a federal or state court. The writ of habeas corpus contained in the Constitution originally applied only to federal courts although many states permitted the writ within their own courts. In 1867, after the Civil War ended, Congress enacted a statute providing that federal courts "shall have the power to grant writs [orders] of habeas corpus in all cases where any person may be restrained of liberty in violation of the Constitution or . . . laws of the United States." Thus, Congress expanded the jurisdictional source of federal court power to include federal review.

This federal statute was initially limited to questions of jurisdiction in "sentencing" an individual by state courts, but ultimately the Supreme

Court expanded the scope of habeas corpus to include allegations that state courts had violated federal constitutional claims. Not all trial court legal or constitutional errors warrant issuance of habeas corpus, only those "that undermine confidence in the fundamental fairness of state court adjudication." This language, written by the Supreme Court, is obviously capable of subjective interpretation. Habeas corpus is a *collateral* challenge to a consummated trial and appeal of a case already decided in a state or federal court.

Congress also amended the Constitution after the Civil War ended. At the time the Constitution was originally enacted creating federal courts, individual states maintained their own court systems for the trial of criminal and civil cases, a system that remains to this day. These State courts conducted the vast majority of criminal cases without significant interference by federal courts. When the Civil War ended, Congress passed several Constitutional amendments applicable to states in addition to the statutory expansion of habeas corpus.

The most important clause, the Fourteenth Amendment, entitled everyone to "Due Process of Law" and to the "Equal Protection of the Law." Although added to statutory changes of the role of habeas corpus, not until a century later did the Supreme Court undertake significant review of state court decisions in criminal law using the Fourteenth Amendment as the basis for Constitutional revision and superintendence of state courts. As a consequence of these statutory and constitutional changes, prisoners convicted and sentenced initially in state court can not only file an appeal from that decision, but if the appeal is denied by a state appellate court, can file a petition for habeas corpus in state court. These petitions allege violation not only of state law but of the Fourteenth Amendment or any other federal Constitutional right. If the state court denies the petition, the prisoner can file another petition in U.S. district court alleging violation of federal law.

The federal judge in district court reads the same record of the previous state trial court and a state appellate court to determine whether any federal legal errors occurred. If the district court judge denies the petition, the prisoner files an appeal to a federal circuit court of appeals. That court, without ever having seen the trial lawyers, witnesses, jurors, or the prisoner, reviews the records in the state trial court, state appellate court, and the district court (all these judges having denied the petition). As the Supreme Court noted in its decision in *Uttecht v. Brown*, trial court judges are those most knowledgeable of the trial record, and therefore appellate courts require deference to their decisions.

Because these habeas corpus petitions filed in federal court challenging state court convictions and sentences are "collateral" (separate) attacks on the judgment in the state court, the rules differ from those on a direct appeal to the 9th Circuit from a district court. In either case, a panel of three judges, purportedly selected randomly, listens to the arguments of counsel who identify the alleged legal errors. One judicial panelist writes the appellate court decision for all three judges, either affirming the district court decision or reversing it.

In some cases, one of the 9th Circuit panelists disagrees with the others and writes a dissenting opinion. Lawyers representing a party who did not prevail on the appeal from the district court judge may ask the 9th Circuit court to reconsider (rehear) its decision by filing papers in support of their argument. In most cases, the panel rejects a rehearing, but one of the judges may again dissent from that request. The unsuccessful party may also request a rehearing of the three- panel decision by the other members of the court (called an *en banc* decision). Or, if one of the other 9th Circuit judges requests a rehearing, additional judges may elect to either agree, or not, to rehear the decision. If a majority agrees, these judges will rehear the case and publish their decision agreeing or disagreeing with the original panel. This decision is the controlling law of the 9th Circuit.

To summarize: in reviewing petitions seeking habeas corpus, whether in federal or state courts, the pattern is essentially the same as "direct" appellate review of trials except the federal court of appeals reviews "collaterally" a state court trial. In other words, a federal appeals court reviewing a trial and conviction in district court applies its rules for convictions in criminal cases of direct appeals from that court, whereas a petition for habeas corpus filed in federal court for a state court conviction is a *collateral appeal* and governed by stricter rules.

The Supreme Court has always distinguished the rules applicable to directly reviewing a federal court decision in cases filed in federal court, and those cases reviewed collaterally by habeas corpus in federal court after a state court trial and conviction. In 1996 Congress attempted to rein in federal court habeas corpus review of state court convictions by enacting the Antiterrorism and Effective Death Penalty Act (AEDPA) "to prevent, in effect, a retrial in federal courts, [confirm] state court convictions to the extent possible under the law, and to further the principles of comity, finality and federalism."

A cursory review of 9th Circuit case load reveals an abundance of habeas corpus cases in criminal cases overruling, or at least reviewing, state court decisions. Only the dismal record of the 9th Circuit on immigration cases numerically compares with these numbers in criminal cases. Under AEDPA, a federal court hearing federal habeas corpus cases must defer to state court decisions in criminal cases unless that adjudication "on the merits of the case resulted in a decision contrary to, or involved an unreasonable application of clearly established Federal law, as determined by the Supreme Court of the United States." Or, the state court decision must have been "contrary to Supreme Court precedent or have unreasonably determined the facts in light of the record."

AEDPA also provides: "In . . . an application for a writ of habeas corpus by a state prisoner, determination of factual issues made by a State court shall be presumed to be correct. The applicant shall have the burden of rebutting the presumption of correctness by clear and convincing evidence." In reversing the 9th Circuit decision in *Wiggins v. Smith*, the Supreme Court wrote: "The [Ninth Circuit failed] to observe the statutory requirement that a federal habeas court respect state-court factual determinations [by the statutory standard of AEDPA]. The decision [of the 9th Circuit in *Wiggins*] sets at naught the statutory scheme [of AEDPA] we once described as 'highly deferential' in evaluating state court rulings."

The 9th Circuit itself wrote this comment at one time: "Federal habeas relief should not be granted lightly. Rather, [AEDPA] 'imposes a highly deferential standard for evaluating state court rulings[;] demands that state court decisions be given the benefit of the doubt[;] and mandates 'our full respect' for rulings of our 'coequal judiciary.'" This language is cited frequently in subsequent 9th Circuit decisions but ignored by the judges deciding a case.

A federal court cannot grant a petition for habeas corpus on the ground that the state court judgment is incorrect. The decision must be an *unreasonable* application of clearly established Supreme Court law or an *unreasonable* application of the facts.

In the chapters that follow, the majority of cases involve federal courts reviewing state court judgments on habeas corpus. To evade the statutory limitations of AEDPA, the 9th Circuit judges resort to the Due Process Clause of the Fourteenth Amendment or another Constitutional issue, review the case on their own initiative, and label the state court decision "unreasonable." As early as 2002, two cases illustrate the frustration and impatience of the Supreme Court in reviewing convictions previously affirmed by state courts and reversed by the 9th Circuit on habeas corpus.

Early v. Packer, 537 U.S. 3 (2002)
Reversing the 9th Circuit decision in *Packer v. Hill,* 291 F.3d 569 (9th Cir. 2002).

The Supreme Court language in the case *Early v. Packer* ought to serve as the touchstone for the 9th Circuit in reviewing state court cases. Unfortunately, this has not been the result. According to the Supreme Court, the 9th Circuit judges in the *Packer* case applied the wrong law and invented their own version of the law. Almost a decade later the pattern has not changed, as illustrated by the decisions in this chapter and in following chapters.

The Supreme Court in *Early v. Packer* criticized the integrity of the 9th Circuit judges who wrote the original decision (*Packer v. Hill*). In reviewing the 9th Circuit habeas court decision reversing an earlier California state court decision upholding a jury verdict in a criminal case, the Justices wrote this:

> "The contention [by the Ninth Circuit] that the California court "failed to consider' facts and circumstances had it taken the trouble to recite strains credulity. The Ninth Circuit may be of the view that the [state] Court of Appeal did not give certain facts and circumstances adequate weight (and hence adequate discussion), but to say that it did not consider them is an exaggeration. There is, moreover, nothing to support the Ninth Circuit's claim that the [California] Court of Appeal did not consider the 'cumulative impact of all the recorded events , , , It suffices that was the fair import of the [Cal.] Court of Appeals opinion.
>
> [The Ninth Circuit], having determined that the California Court of Appeal 'failed to apply clearly established Supreme Court law,' and [terms] of the Anti Terrorism and Effective Death Penalty law (AEDPA) that the decision is 'contrary to clearly established Supreme Court law,' the Ninth Circuit then proceeded to address the question 'whether [the California Court of Appeal's] decision constituted error and if so whether the error had a substantial or injurious effect on the verdict. But that inquiry would have been proper only if the Ninth Circuit had first found [pursuant to the correct standard] that the California court's decision was 'contrary to' clearly established Supreme Court law-which it did not.
>
> By mistakenly making the [AEDPA statute] 'contrary to' determination and then proceeding to a 'simple error' inquiry, the Ninth Circuit evaded the statutory requirement that decisions which are

not 'contrary to' clearly established Supreme Court law can [not] be subjected to habeas relief if they are merely erroneous, but [must be] an unreasonable application of clearly established federal law, or based on an unreasonable determination of the facts."

Note: The federal statute cited by the Supreme Court, AEDPA, will be discussed in future chapters.

McMurtrey v. Ryan (Warden), 539 F.3d 1112 (9th Cir. 2008)
This case was decided only by the 9th Circuit and never reviewed by the Supreme Court. This decision manifests the background resulting in congressional enactment of AEDPA.

In 1979, McMurtrey murdered two men and wounded a third. Fleeing to Kansas, he was subsequently arrested, tried, convicted by an Arizona court and sentenced to death in 1981. The Arizona Supreme Court affirmed his conviction on appeal and subsequently denied his petition for a state court evidentiary review of the trial.

McMurtrey then began a round of federal habeas petitions and, in 1988, eventually convinced a district court to hold a hearing on the ground his counsel rendered "ineffective assistance." He also alleged failure of the state trial court to hold a competency hearing to determine whether he was rational enough to stand trial. The federal court ordered the state court to hold an evidentiary hearing. The state court complied, and numerous doctors and nurses testified. Although the evidence was conflicting, the judge resolved the testimony against McMurtrey and denied the petition in 1994.

Dissatisfied with the state court decision, McMurtrey returned to the district court. The judge held his own hearing and granted the petition on the grounds the state trial court had failed to hold a satisfactory hearing to determine whether McMurtrey was competent to stand trial. In addition, the district court not only granted the petition but ordered release of this man sentenced to death. On appeal by the State of Arizona to the 9th Circuit, the court panel affirmed the district court in 2008, twenty years after conviction by a jury.

In the 9th Circuit decision, the panel wrote endlessly of McMurtrey's mental and physical condition previously revealed in the records by every court having reviewed and denied his petition. The 9th Circuit panel never heard the witnesses, did not observe the defendant, ignored the state trial judge ruling, dismissed the Arizona Supreme Court decision, and decades later re-reweighed the evidence and sided with McMurtrey. The 9th Circuit panel contended it resolved the legal issue of competency under "ordinary rules" rather than under AEDPA (the case was tried in 1981 prior to enactment of AEDPA in 1996)). Inexplicably, the Supreme Court denied review.

Frequent Supreme Court reproaches of the 9th Circuit for abuse of AEDPA are confirmed by a dissenting judge in a 9th Circuit 2004 decision evading AEDPA entitled Kennedy v. Lockyer.

> The judge wrote, "Our apparent inability to internalize AEDPA's strict standard of review has become a source of repeated public embarrassment. During the past two terms [of the Supreme Court] alone, we have been summarily reversed by a unanimous Supreme Court no fewer than four times for disregarding AEDPA's strict limitations on the scope of our collateral review of state court constitutional adjudications."

Citing Supreme Court decisions, the dissenting judge continued:

> "Apparently in search of a result, the [Ninth Circuit majority of the panel in *Kennedy*] yet again runs roughshod over the principles of comity and federalism underlying the Antiterrorism and Effective Death Penalty Act. '[P]remised on the fact that the state courts, as part of a coequal judiciary, are competent interpreters of federal

law deserving of our full respect, AEDPA mandates a highly deferential standard for evaluating state-court rulings . . . and adamantly 'demands that state court decisions be given the benefit of the doubt . . .'"

Notwithstanding the eminent reasonableness of their colleagues' [state court judges] analysis, two judges today inform seven others, a state trial judge, three state appellate judges, a federal magistrate judge, a district court, and a [dissenting] federal appellate judge (and that's not to mention the seven justices of the California Supreme Court who summarily denied Kennedy's state petition for review) that their understanding of the law is contrary to clearly established Supreme Court precedent."

In 2011, 9th Circuit judges continued to rule similarly on habeas corpus cases filed prior to the 1996 enactment of AEDPA, a time when the court could decide a case indifferent to the state court decision. In criminal cases filed prior to 1996, 9th Circuit judges did not hesitate to announce their decision is unaffected by the state court decision, and as late as 2014 they continued to rule on cases of defendants convicted prior to 1996 (*Robinson v. Schriro*). In 2010, the 9th Circuit panel reviewed a petition for habeas corpus for a crime committed in *1987*, and granted the petition requiring retrial of the penalty phase of the trial. What are the chances of successfully retrying the penalty phase of this case for a crime committed twenty-four years ago?

The debate over habeas corpus, and its revision in 1996, has ignited a firestorm of debate from various quarters. More recently, critics renewed the application of habeas corpus based on the imprisonment of non-citizens captured during battles between American troops and Islamic fundamentalists. In this instance, the federal government - not the state government - detained individuals without charging them with a specific crime in federal court; *Ashcroft v. Kidd*. Apparently the current administration has changed elected to use district courts for trial instead of military courts. That decision brought harsh criticism from those who saw no need to increase the district court case load to the detriment of its own citizens.

CHAPTER 2

FEDERALISM

In drafting the U.S. Constitution, the authors developed a model of government denominated "federalism." Pursuant to the origin of this title, and against a background of English history, the Constitution confirmed autonomy for existing individual states yet simultaneously formed a separate national government. The states, previously operating under the Articles of Confederation, had keenly experienced their national and international impotence and sought a sovereign authority to unify and protect the country. Colonial times demanded a national government, and necessity forged the Constitution, a document emerging out of compromise and negotiation.

In 2002 the Supreme Court wrote, "Dual sovereignty (governing authority) is a defining feature of our Nation's constitutional blueprint. States, upon ratification of the Constitution, did not consent to become mere appendages of the Federal Government. Rather, they entered the Union with their sovereignty intact." The 9th Circuit repeatedly ignores any vestige of state authority in its decisions when vacating state supreme court opinions, or in managing California prisons, supervising the Los Angeles Police Department, directing curricula of school districts, and initiating a host of other federal interventionist policies including forced release of California prison inmates.

When the authors of the Constitution undertook to write a document governing the United States as an entity not yet in existence, they were compelled to compromise with existing individual states. The states understandably insisted on their continued existence in conjunction with a national government. As a result, the Constitution carved out various limitations on the newly formed federal government, including retention of state sovereignty. Until the Civil War, individual states maintained considerable power. After 1865, the Due Process Clause and Equal Protection Clauses of the Fourteenth Amendment to the Constitution diminished state authority.

The only basis for these amendments to the Constitution was elimination of slavery. But during the heady days of the 1960s, the Supreme Court began an incursion into state authority by interpreting these two Clauses applicable to the administration of criminal law in individual states. The Supreme Court and the 9th Circuit also began deciding cases involving issues restricting state law in elections, schools, churches, free speech, and prisons. More recently the 9th Circuit has begun interfering in state, city, and county jail administration.

The authors of the Constitution wrote in the shadow of English history, readily familiar with monarchical abuse and clerical domination bequeathed by Henry VIII and Elizabeth I. Subsequent to the adoption of the Constitution, the authors added ten amendments constraining the federal government under the rubric of the Bill of Rights. Again the remnant of English history dominated, and each of the ten amendments reflected either a rejection of specific official conduct or mandatory compliance with certain precepts protecting personal or property interests.

Several amendments were fact - specific. The Second Amendment confirmed the right of the people to bear arms, and the Third Amendment forbad quartering of soldiers in private homes. The Fourth Amendment limited officials to searches and seizures conducted legally "reasonable." The Fifth Amendment prohibited the use at trial of involuntary statements taken from the accused, and mandated the federal government to proceed with "due process" of law. The Sixth Amendment guaranteed the right of an accused to an attorney and juries in criminal cases. The Seventh Amendment embodied the right to trial by jury in civil cases; the Eighth Amendment prohibited cruel and unusual punishment.

The Ninth and Tenth Amendments attempted to confirm recognition of unenumerated rights deserving protection of the states from federal interference. Other amendments in the Bill of Rights were conceptual, lacking specificity but expressing the essence of a democratic society. The First Amendment right to freedom of speech, assembly, the press, and an absence of state - sponsored religion attained numerical priority. None of the first ten amendments to the Constitution, i.e., the Bill of Rights, originally applied to the states.

Despite their predominantly anti governmental context, the Constitution and Bill of Rights are not an invitation to anarchy and license. The general public has every right to expect the government to protect it from the depredations of those who prey on others. No one disagrees with the right of a federal, state, or local government to enact laws prohibiting criminal conduct and to exact punishment for violation of the law. In some quarters this social construct is labeled "collective rights" owed by the government to the public, as distinct from "individual rights" protected against governmental abuse.

This clash between individual and collective rights resounds in courtrooms every day but nowhere more so than in the 9th Circuit, and its critics and supporters would agree to the anti-governmental bias of a majority of these judges. The Supreme Court has concurred in this observation, and many of their opinions overturning 9th Circuit decisions are written in language unconfined to mild reproaches. For the 9th Circuit, these reversals are embarrassingly common. As noted earlier, in every annual term of the Supreme Court the Justices review a disproportionate number of 9th Circuit cases compared to those of other circuit courts, and write an equally disproportionate number of reversals. The actual number of cases is not necessarily the format evaluating the work of the 9th Circuit.

The crucial issue is the political, social, economic, and religious character of these cases and their impact on society.

Equally important is the heavy price the citizenry pays for courts that ignore public safety. A judicial decision citing Constitutional grounds as the basis of its decision is virtually irreversible by legislative or executive action. When the 9th Circuit writes a decision releasing a person convicted of a crime(s), or ordering a new trial on Constitutional grounds, there is no recourse for the prosecution except to conduct a new trial confronting all the ravages that time exacts from witnesses and the retention of evidence.

The American public reads about controversial opinions written by the Supreme Court and does not understand the rationale enabling life-tenured judges to overrule decisions of federal and state legislatures in general and state courts in particular. The basis of that power is based on the role of federalism applicable to all federal judges.

Someone, or some institution, must inevitably interpret the breadth of Constitutional language and the Bill of Rights. Although neither of these documents outlined the source of this authority at the time the Constitution was adopted, the U.S. Supreme Court ultimately became the final arbiter. Given the controversial nature of cases decided by federal courts, approval of presidential nominees to these courts, most prominently to the Supreme Court, has led to contentious and unseemly congressional hearings. The genesis of the debate lies in the decisions of the Supreme Court and the 9th Circuit dismantling a social and political fabric justifiably objectionable to U.S. senators who are empowered to confirm presidential federal judicial appointments. Judges, caught in the wake of this political maelstrom, including controversial decisions written by judges of the 9th Circuit, angered Republicans who had promised the electorate they would not confirm "activist" judges nominated by Democratic presidents.

The Supreme Court, despite its own controversial decisions, has attempted to control those federal appellate court judges who expand the scope of the judicial role. The Supreme Court has also severely criticized

9th Circuit judges who have attempted to craft their own agenda. Ninth Circuit judges, driven by a controversial philosophy of the law that cites Supreme Court precedent but undermines it by misapplying the rules, mask their rationale by attempting to distinguish a Supreme Court case on the facts or the law. For this reason, the 9th Circuit reversal record in the Supreme Court reflects a repeated misapplication of the law.

Part II of this book reveals a more insidious device to undermine state sovereignty and eviscerate a democratic society under the guise of "structural reform." As will be discussed more fully in the text, the Supreme Court decided a case entitled *Horne v. Flores* in which a district court judge had issued orders administering a local school district for several years and refused to relinquish control despite repeated efforts by the local school board to introduce amendments to educational policies demanded by the court. Here is a quotation from the Supreme Court after the 9th Circuit refused to intervene on appeal from district court orders: "For nearly a decade, the orders of a U.S. district court have substantially restricted the ability of the State of Arizona to make basic decisions regarding educational policy, appropriations, and budget priorities. The record strongly suggests that some *state officials have welcomed the involvement of the federal court as a means of achieving appropriations objectives that could not be achieved through the ordinary democratic process* (emphasis in original). Because of these features, these cases implicate all of the unique features and risks of institutional reform [police departments, schools, prisons, jails]."

Brown v. Plata. A Supreme Court case reviewing a 9th Circuit case under the name *Plata v. Schwarzenegger*

To illustrate this "structural reform" deception, in 2001 several state prisoners filed a class action (numerous parties alleging similar claims) in federal court against the State of California Department of Corrections and Rehabilitation alleging the state prison system failed to provide adequate medical care to inmates. A federal judge decided the medical services in

California prisons were inadequate, and the State of California stipulated (agreed without objection) to the court order to "remedy the violation." When the state conceded its inability to expend the funds necessary to comply with the order, the judge appointed a Receiver (a person who manages an entity experiencing financial difficulties). The state failed to appeal this order requiring it to pay all remedial costs. The Receiver filed a "Plan" requiring construction of ten thousand new beds, and the state agreed, again without objection. The Plan included construction of a medical facility to which the state also did not object.

The Receiver filed a final "Plan" that he would supervise all construction and costs (equaling two million dollars). The state did not object or appeal the Receiver's order for the necessary money to fund the "Plan." Later the asked the state to expend the money, and the state finally objected. The Receiver filed a motion in court asking the judge to hold the State in contempt.

At this point, the previously italicized comment by the Supreme Court in *Horne v. Flores* of imposing "structural reform" surfaces. A federal court submits an order appointing a person who can ignore the State Department of Corrections and Rehabilitation, and who will manage the medical facilities of a state prison, responsible only to a single federal judge. Aside from compelling the State of California to expend millions of unbudgeted dollars, and obviously diverting funds from other state duties, this order not only ignores the role of federal courts but questions the failure of the state to object until the last minute, and too late.

California Attorney General (Jerry Brown) inexplicably never opposed any federal intervention until the Receiver asked for the money to be expended. At all prior hearings the state agreed with the court order and recommendations of the Receiver. The state should have objected to federal intervention from the beginning and at every step of the way. In fact, this indolence and absence of objection is the very point the California Supreme Court criticized when former Attorney General Brown refused to defend an Initiative passed by voters to require marriage between people of opposite sexes; *Perry v. Brown*.

Few cases unhinge the constitutional pattern of dual sovereignty more than the prison case. Although the Supreme Court ultimately upheld the decision, it did so over the vigorous objections of four of the nine Justices. Allowing a single federal judge to supervise the prison system by retaining a manager to replace the state Department of Corrections and Rehabilitation ignored federalism and breached state sovereignty.

Southwest Voter Registration Education v. Shelley, 344 F.3d 914 (9th Cir. 2003)

Another flagrant example of interference with state sovereignty in California occurred during the recall election of former California Governor Gray Davis. The California Supreme Court rejected challenges to the recall of Davis, but the American Civil Liberties Union (ACLU) filed a lawsuit in federal court alleging the same grounds of objection that had been raised in state court. The three-judge 9th Circuit panel issued an order enjoining (prohibiting) the election despite millions of dollars expended by the registrar of voters in preparation for the vote. The panel complained that minority voters would be disenfranchised by the use of voting machines, a fantasy dreamed up out of whole cloth, unsupported by any facts, and cloaked entirely in speculation. The injunction threatened to throw the recall into chaos.

Fortunately, other judges in the 9th Circuit reheard the case, dismissed the rationale written by the three-judge panel (all noted for their liberal opinions) and correctly reversed the original decision in a few paragraphs. That three unelected tenured judges could undermine the votes of millions of Californians on a gossamer theory is inconceivable. But these federal judges enjoining a state election after the California Supreme Court had upheld the voting process is an inexcusable abuse of judicial power. Only the 9th Circuit evisceration of Proposition 187 (withholding benefits from illegal aliens) is comparable.

Purcell v. Gonzales, 549 U.S. 1 (2006)
Supreme Court reverses a 9th Circuit order (curiously, this case was not
published in the court reports).
In *Purcell v. Gonzales,* the 9th Circuit displayed complete disregard of state
courts and legislatures. The State of Arizona enacted legislation (Proposition
200) to combat voter fraud. The statute included a provision mandating
voter identification at the time of voting, but also permitted alternatives for
voters to subsequently validate their vote in the event of non compliance
with statutory requirements at the time of election. Various community
organizations filed suit in federal court to invalidate the statute, citing federal law requiring the U.S. Attorney General to confirm that this voting
procedure did not bar a person of color from voting. The district court
denied a request for an injunction. On appeal from that decision, the 9th
Circuit invalidated the statute.

Here is the Supreme Court decision reversing the 9th Circuit:

"The district court denied the request for an injunction to prevent
the election but did not file findings of fact and conclusions of law.
The plaintiffs [parties challenging the statute] appealed the denial,
and the Clerk of the 9th Circuit Court of Appeals set a briefing
schedule (filing legal papers) due by November 21, two weeks after
the upcoming November 7 election. The (moving parties} then
requested an injunction pending appeal of the district court order
directly from the same Court of Appeals. Pursuant to the Court of
Appeals' rules, the request for an injunction was assigned to a two-
judge motions/screening panel.

On October 5, after receiving lengthy written responses from
the State and county officials, but without oral argument, the
Ninth Circuit panel issued a four-sentence order enjoining Arizona
from enforcing Proposition 200's provisions pending a decision by
the court after both sides filed [legal papers] regarding the denial of

a preliminary injunction. The two judge Court of Appeals offered no explanation or justification for its order. Four days later, the court denied a motion for reconsideration. The order denying the motion likewise gave no rationale for the court's decision.

Despite the time-sensitive nature of the proceedings and the pendency of a request for emergency relief in the Court of Appeals, the district court did not issue its findings of fact and conclusions of law until October 12. It then concluded that plaintiffs have shown a possibility of success on the merits of some of their arguments but the Court cannot say that at this stage they have shown a strong likelihood . . . [of success]. The district court then found the balance of the harms and the public interest counseled in favor of denying the injunction."

In other words, a two-judge panel of 9th Circuit judges enjoined (prevented) the State of Arizona from conducting the election despite denial of the request for an injunction in the district court and without any evidence submitted to that judge. In fact, when the district court did hear evidence, the judge denied the injunction. The Supreme Court reversed the order of the 9th Circuit.

How does one explain this decision by the two-judge panel? Without any evidence from the district court to review, with no explanation of its own decision, and based on mere speculation comparable to the original decision rendered in the *Southwest Voter Registration* case, these judges departed from any pretense of judicial reasoning, and imposed policy on the State of Arizona.

The plaintiffs, who sought the injunction after having lost in the Supreme Court, filed a second lawsuit challenging the voter registration requirements of Proposition 200. The district court denied injunctive relief, and this time the 9th Circuit affirmed that decision in *Gonzales v. Arizona*. Yet a suspicion lingers that it did not want to receive another reprimand from the Supreme Court.

Doe v. Reed, 130 S.Ct. 2811 (2010) [Doe is an anonymous name for a party allowed under certain circumstances]
The Washington State Legislature enacted legislation extending rights and benefits to state registered domestic partners. Washington law also provides a Public Records Act (P.R.A.) mandating disclosure of signatories who sign petitions in support of a referendum (voting to change existing law). Voters signed petitions to submit domestic partners legislation to a referendum restricting application of the P.R.A. on grounds that several opposition groups sought disclosure of all names of those who had signed the petitions.

To assure the integrity of an election or petition for referendum, Washington criminal law also prohibits voting by: anyone who cannot legally vote; who uses a false name in voting; or who otherwise makes a false statement in signing a petition. Washington statutes also provide a method for certification of voter signatures by the secretary of state and an appellate process seeking review of the administrative decision on the integrity of ballots or petitions.

Plaintiffs (parties who opposed the state legislation) filed a Complaint (a written document alleging certain injurious acts or misconduct committed by another party and seeking judicial relief) alleging any disclosure of signatories to the petitions violated the First Amendment "because the P.R.A. is not narrowly tailored to serve a compelling public interest." The Complaint also alleged the P.R.A. is unconstitutional because "there is a reasonable probability that signatories of the petitions . . . will be subject to threats, harassment, and reprisals. In support of that allegation, plaintiffs alleged various groups have publicly stated they intend to publish the names of signatories on the Internet . . . and have encouraged individuals to contact petition signers to have 'personal' and 'uncomfortable' conversations."

The district court ordered injunctive relief (court order prohibiting enforcement of the statue) in accord with the conventional test of finding the plaintiffs likely to succeed on the merits and likely to suffer irreparable injury in the absence of an injunction; finding a balance of equities in its favor; and finding that the an injunction served the public interest. The State of Washington (and other defendants) appealed to the 9th Circuit.

In its decision the 9th Circuit ignored the court order for injunctive relief entirely despite the trial judge's finding that the plaintiffs would suffer injury upon disclosure of their names. The 9th Circuit panel reversed the district court on the ground the trial judge used the wrong legal test for allegations of First Amendment violations. The 9th Circuit reversed only one allegation, as the district court had ruled only on that claim. Under First Amendment analysis, the court asks rhetorically what government interests are furthered by the P.R.A. The reasoning is twofold, according to the court: to preserve the integrity of the election and "providing Washington voters with information about who supports placing a referendum on the ballot." The court cites no authority for this latter "government interest" category, and the decision is patently without precedent.

The purpose of assuring the integrity of an election or validity of petitions for a referendum identified in the above statutory requirements is prevention of fraud and an assurance no false names or statements are counted in the ballots or petitions. Nothing in the 9th Circuit rationale to allegedly "inform the public about who supports the referendum" validates the need for disclosure. This supposed rationale is directly contradicted by the allegations of the Complaint alleging that the demand for disclosure of signatories to the referendum was sought to threaten or intimidate, not to inform the public.

The 9th Circuit further cited another Washington statute allowing various interested parties to observe the secretary of state staff processing the names of "qualified voters" who signed the petitions "so long as observers make no record of the names, addresses, or other information on the petitions or related records during the verification process." In other words, the Washington statute specifically prohibits observers of the certification process from recording any names signed on the petitions.

According to the 9th Circuit, this particular Washington statute is not controlling because the alleged demands for disclosure of "who is qualified" to sign petitions are insufficient to provide "information about who supports placing a referendum on the ballot." But the defendants are not concerned about qualified voters. They want disclosure to fulfill their publicly announced interest to confront signatories.

This erroneous 9th Circuit interpretation of First Amendment law and Washington state law was originally stayed (stopped) by the Supreme Court. Buried in the footnotes of *Doe v. Reed*, the 9th Circuit panel noted that its decision was stayed by Supreme Court Justice Kennedy who referred his decision to the entire Court, which confirmed the stay.

Regrettably, the Supreme Court ultimately confirmed the denial of an injunction sought by the parties. Despite evidence that opponents of the referendum demanded disclosure in order to threaten people rather than ensuring the validity of the election, the Supreme Court discounted that issue. Voter intimidation ought to be prohibited as it is in other contexts.

This raises interesting questions. Suppose the plaintiffs were a minority group and they alleged that their supporters would be threatened by disclosure. Would the 9th Circuit issue the same ruling it did in *Doe v. Reed*? Or, let's assume that state legislation mandates proof of identification (comparable to disclosure in *Doe v. Reed*) on the part of voters before voting in an election. The Supreme Court approved precisely that state legislation in Indiana; *Crawford v. Marion Co. Election Board*. Had that case been before the 9th Circuit instead of the Supreme Court, the result would have been different.

CHAPTER 3

THE SUPREME COURT

The back story to the 9th Circuit begins with the Supreme Court. The president appoints federal judges to the Supreme Court, to all federal circuit courts of appeal, and federal district courts. Over time, during the tenure of several former presidential appointees, the Supreme Court angered the electorate in deciding numerous controversial cases. Decisions on racial and sexual preferences, abortion, sodomy, burning the American flag, terrorism, and denying display of Nativity scenes all became fodder for the Supreme Court.

In 1994, the Republican Party swept congressional elections, energized by a commitment to eliminate pervasive federal court interference with state courts. A scant thirteen years later, Democrats surged into power and took control of the House and Senate. Pundits assigned this tectonic political shift to a variety of causes, but the historical record mirrors, at least in part, the shifting sands of congressional elections influenced by a variety of events including an unpopular war, infidelity, presidential scandal, and misconduct of legislators. Voters express their displeasure by exercising their franchise and replacing members of Congress or the president. In 2010 and 2012 the balance shifted again.

Conversely, judges of all federal courts are unelected, appointed by the president for life, and subject to removal only on limited grounds of impeachment. Despite the job security of federal judges, the public has also targeted the judiciary for reprisal. In the volatile decade of the 1970s, the public demanded impeachment of the chief justice of the Supreme Court. During the tumultuous tenure of Chief Justice Earl Warren, the Supreme Court eviscerated rules of state criminal procedure, excluded incriminating evidence in criminal cases by imposing an "exclusionary rule" allegedly inherent in the Fourth Amendment to the U.S. Constitution, fashioned the infamous *"Miranda"* warning attributed to the Fifth Amendment, and required lawyers at police lineups, ostensibly a doctrine included within the Sixth Amendment.

The Fourth, Fifth, and Sixth Amendments to the Constitution originally applied only to the federal government. But the Supreme Court, in a series of decisions, selectively "incorporated" these amendments, making them applicable to state courts by invoking the Fourteenth Amendment Due Process Clause enacted by Congress after the Civil War. The source of the "incorporation" doctrine lacked any precedent in Constitutional law and emerged only by judicial invention. As Justice Harlan noted in a Fourth Amendment case, . . . " [a]bsent any convincing reason for imposing federal constitutional rules on states, the court simply exercises the 'voice of power, not of reason.' And there is no practical alternative to reversing a Supreme Court decision based on constitutional grounds except through the passage of time and replacement of its personnel. Congress and the general public remain impotent."

The Due Process Clause of the Fourteenth Amendment, which reads, ". . . nor shall any State deprive any person of life, liberty, or property, without due process of law; nor deny to any person within its jurisdiction the equal protection of the laws," has laid the groundwork for decisions in criminal cases affecting public safety and social and cultural values in civil cases. The Fourteenth Amendment language of the Due Process Clause has served as the judicial vehicle for violation of "liberty interests." For example, the judicial origin of the constitutional "right of privacy," invoked by the Supreme Court in its abortion decision, and the Equal Protection

Clause sanctioning "racial preferences" in a state law school, illustrate twin examples of unbounded Constitutional language filled in by judicial rhetoric according to views of the court majority in a specific case.

In fairness, not all Supreme Court decisions have superimposed federal authority on the states, but the tenor of many of its controversial decisions inevitably left gaps in the law. The 9th Circuit, and other federal courts of appeal, published decisions filling in those gaps, yet the vast majority of American people never hear about, let alone read, these frequently prolix and lengthy decisions unless the issue touches a public nerve. In sum, Supreme Court opinions have supplied the legal fodder stimulating the 9th Circuit to broaden its jurisdiction overruling (reversing) state courts on controversial topics in California, Washington, Oregon, Arizona, Idaho, Hawaii, Alaska, Montana, and Nevada.

Subsequent years witnessed a continuing erosion of state sovereignty as the Supreme Court imposed federal constitutional rules on state court criminal cases. Not all judges shared this enthusiasm, and not all decisions were "anti state," but the court nonetheless laid the groundwork for expanding the power of federal courts. The 9th Circuit rapidly became the most aggressive appellate federal court in the country in extending jurisdiction over state courts by invoking the Constitution or the Fourteenth Amendment not only in criminal law but also in a variety of social, political, and religious contexts.

Understanding the work of courts is not only complicated but intimidating. The American people lack the time to study and read lengthy discourses written in decisions primarily directed to lawyers, judges, and law professors. The collective inability of the public in a democracy to remedy court decisions profoundly affecting their lives is frustrating and incomprehensible to them. This book attempts to explain the decisions of a single federal appellate court incrementally distorting the law to achieve a social and political agenda. In many cases, the words of judges dissenting from a controversial decision will speak for themselves.

CHAPTER 4

CRIMINAL LAW

" In reviewing criminal cases [on appeal from a conviction or sentence], it is particularly important for appellate courts to relive the whole trial imaginatively and not to extract from episodes in isolation abstract questions of evidence and procedure. To turn a criminal appeal into a quest for error no more promotes the ends of justice than to acquiesce in low standards of criminal prosecution." This sage advice from Supreme Court Justice Frankfurter written over a half century ago, if adopted, would eliminate a substantial number of cases from the 9th Circuit docket and avoid the innumerable reversals of trials caused by that court.

This chapter consists of selected decisions by the 9th Circuit in criminal cases, illustrating the adverse impact of its decisions on public safety. To confirm the validity of that allegation, the text quotes highlights from the language of Supreme Court decisions. The first sections summarize state court convictions reviewed by the 9th Circuit under the federal authority of habeas corpus and the Due Process Clause of the Fourteenth Amendment. The remaining Sections summarize cases decided initially by judges in district courts at trial and subsequently appealed to the 9th Circuit without further review by the Supreme Court.

The subject of "criminal law" is vast and includes court cases alleging violation of Constitutional rights, but the merits of an underlying case against a defendant is the prosecution of a specific crime(s). The chapters on the Death Penalty, The Lawyers, and the Fourth and Fifth Amendments all involve criminal law and procedure but are treated separately. Topics in this Chapter focus include construction of statutory language, pretrial proceedings, evidence, jury instructions, jury deliberations and verdict, questioning of jurors, and sentencing. The roles of habeas corpus and due process are interwoven.

In a related context, discussed elsewhere in the text, a party in a civil case can sue law enforcement officers and their public employer in district court for allegedly violating Constitutional or statutory civil rights, but the underlying facts in many cases are arrest and prosecution for a crime. In some cases, third parties can sue for alleged violations of civil rights. As discussed in Chapter 10, public officials can defend against this litigation under a legal doctrine immunizing them from lawsuits.

As discussed in Chapters 7 and 8 on the Fourth and Fifth Amendments respectively, a defendant can file a motion (written request) in the court prior to trial to exclude evidence on grounds the arrest or search were illegally conducted (the Fourth Amendment), or law enforcement agents failed to properly advise the arrestees of their rights to silence and counsel (the Fifth Amendment). The defendant in criminal cases can also request a release from custody by posting security or cash ("bail") conditioned on a promise to return for future hearings and trial, and in some cases, subject to other conditions. If a defendant fails to return to court or meet other conditions, the court will issue an arrest warrant.

Counsel for defendants can file other pretrial motions requiring the prosecution to produce evidence related to the crime charged, disclose personnel records of police officers, submit evidence favorable to the defense, or file other motions affecting the admissibility of evidence. When the court has ruled on all pretrial motions, the judge summons potential jurors to commence the first stage in a trial.

A. State Courts in General

State or federal prosecutors can file criminal charges in court against a suspect previously arrested by law enforcement officers. In either case, the arrestee must be "arraigned," (brought before a judge or magistrate within a short period of time after the arrest and notified of the charges filed by the prosecution. In most cases, the court appoints a defense lawyer (Public Defender) to represent the arrestee throughout the court proceedings although private lawyers represent defendants financially able to afford counsel.

Within a specified time after the defendant has been charged with a specific crime (s), the court will conduct a "preliminary hearing" to determine whether sufficient prosecution evidence warrants a trial. The hearing is usually brief and if the judge concludes the evidence is sufficient the defendant is held in custody, or remains on bail, for trial. Later, a trial date is set by the court.

The mechanism for charging the crime and subsequent conduct of certain pretrial motions in state and federal courts differs, but the basic criminal justice system begins at trial with selection of the jury presided over by a judge.

After the lawyers for prosecution and defense select a jury as discussed below, the court offers counsel for prosecution and defense an opportunity to summarize the evidence they intend to present in an "opening statement." The judge informs the jurors that these statements of counsel explaining their sides of the case are only summaries—not evidence. The trial itself ordinarily consists of a conflict between the testimony of prosecution and defense witnesses, and jurors must decide who is telling the truth. After all witnesses have testified and evidence submitted, the prosecution lawyer and defense counsel may summarize the case to the jury. These "closing statements" are also subject to the judicial restriction that comments by the lawyers are not evidence. Following summation of the evidence, the judge reads various legal rules, and these jury instructions explain the relevant law guiding jurors in their deliberations. As the Supreme Court has noted, jurors are more likely to look to the judge for assistance than either counsel for the prosecution and defense but impartiality prohibits any judicial comment from the bench

1. Juries

Prior to presentation of evidence at trial, most state and federal courts statutorily permit the judge, prosecution, and defense counsel to question potential jurors to determine whether any event, act, or condition in their backgrounds might prevent them from ruling impartially. Prosecutors and defense counsel can ask a limited number of questions and, if dissatisfied with the answers, request the court to excuse jurors without explanation. This process, known as *voir dire*, is applicable in civil and criminal trials. Minor differences exist between state and federal courts, but the process is essentially the same.

In 1986, the Supreme Court undertook the unprecedented task of forbidding prosecutors from excusing jurors on the grounds of race during *voir dire*. In the case entitled Batson v. Kentucky, the Court fashioned a three-part "test" for trial courts to use in determining whether a juror was excused on grounds of racial animus. Suffice to say that the "test" is subsequently cited by lawyers (usually defense counsel) objecting to the prosecution excusing a juror on racial grounds. The legal test is fact intensive, and subject to wide disparity in agreement.

The consequence of this new judicially imposed rule has extended the process of questioning of jurors before trial. Prosecution and defense argue over the application of the *Batson* case at trial assuring a built-in ground for appeal. If a defense lawyer objects to a prosecutor excusing a juror on grounds of race, the trial judge must hold a hearing to determine the basis for the prosecution decision. Assuming the trial judge denies the defense objection, and the trial resumes, the judge's decision is subject to appeal in state and federal courts.

*Rice (Warden) v. Collins,*546 U.S. 333 (2006)

Reversing the 9th Circuit in *Collins v. Rice*, 451 F.3d 1092 (9th Cir. 2006)

In *Rice v. Collins*, a unanimous Supreme Court decision, the Justices reviewed a California state court of appeals decision that had originally affirmed a narcotics conviction of the defendant. The state court record reflects that the prosecutor had excused a black juror, who, according to the prosecutor, had rolled her eyes in response to a question from the judge during jury selection, was youthful, potentially reluctant to punish narcotics violations, and lacked any community ties. Counsel for defendant Collins contended the prosecutor excused the juror on racial grounds in violation of the *Batson* case. The trial judge upheld the prosecution explanation and agreed with her reasons for excusing the juror.

The jury convicted the defendant, and the California Court of Appeal affirmed the conviction, as did the district court judge on Collins's petition for habeas corpus. On appeal from that decision, the 9th Circuit panel disagreed. The panel asserted that the prosecution excused the juror for racial reasons, in effect reversing the state trial court on the same trial record reviewed by the California court on appeal and the district court judge in denying habeas corpus.

The Supreme Court reversed the 9th Circuit: Justice Kennedy described the juror excused by the prosecution as "young and rootless," and concluded the 9th Circuit panel merely decided not to believe the prosecutor and instead *"substituted its own judgment."* He wrote: "In this case there is no demonstration that either the trial court or the California Court of Appeal acted contrary to 'clearly established federal law' as determined by the Supreme Court [in the *Batson* case]."

Justice Kennedy, writing on behalf of a unanimous court, continued, "Concerned that in this . . . case, the [9th Circuit] set aside reasonable state court determinations of fact in favor of its own debatable interpretation of the record, we granted [review]. Our review confirms that the Court of Appeals for the Ninth Circuit erred, misapplying settled law that limits its role and authority." Reversing the 9th Circuit, the Supreme Court sent the case back "for further proceedings."

Here is the language of the 9th Circuit decision after it received the reproach from the Supreme Court: "Pursuant to the opinion of the Supreme Court in *Rice v. Collin* . . . the judgment of the district court [denying habeas corpus] is affirmed." Without a word about the caustic remarks from a unanimous Supreme Court, the 9th Circuit having been reversed in its decision had to return the case to the district court judge. The 9th Circuit court buried its ruling in a two-line sentence.

The Sixth Circuit Court of Appeal (a different federal court of appeals) in an unrelated case wrote an excellent rebuttal to the 9th Circuit's substitution of its own judgment for the trial court by quoting the Supreme Court decision in *Arizona v. Washington*:

> "There are compelling institutional considerations militating in favor of appellate deference to the trial judge's evaluation of the significance of possible juror bias. He has seen and heard the jurors during their *voir dire* [questioning of jurors]. He is the judge most familiar with the evidence and the background of the case on trial. He has listened to the tone of the [answers to questions] as delivered during jury selection and has observed the apparent reaction of the jurors. In short, he is far more 'conversant with the factors relevant to the determination of bias than any reviewing court can possibly be."

Green v. LaMarque [Warden], 532 F.3d 1028 (9th Cir. 2008)
In this case, the 9th Circuit panel modified one sentence of its original decision and inexplicably reprinted the entire amended decision. The Supreme Court decision in *Rice v. Collins* may have stemmed the appellate reversal tide in some cases but it had not deterred the 9th Circuit in *Green v. LaMarque*. In 1998 Green was convicted in California state court, his conviction affirmed on appeal by the California Court of Appeal, a review was denied by the state supreme court, and his petition for habeas corpus was denied

in district court. The 9th Circuit, without mentioning the denial of rulings in state court and federal district court, and without even ordering an evidentiary hearing, reversed the conviction in 2008 - ten years after the original conviction - on grounds the prosecutor excused a juror on racial grounds.

In this decision on appeal from the district court ruling, the 9th Circuit repudiated the decisions of both the California Court of Appeal and the district court, writing that the trial judge in state court should have used a "comparative analysis" of similarly situated jurors to determine if that juror was excused due to race as required by "clearly established federal law." The court cited two Supreme Court cases, neither one applicable to this case, and reversed the district court.

What is a "comparative analysis of jurors?" The court is supposed to consider the reasons used by the prosecution in excusing a black juror compared to questions asked of other members of the jury who were not excused. One year after the *Green v. La Marque* decision, the 9th Circuit panel in the case *Ali v. Hickman* spent endless pages comparing the questions asked and answered of one juror and those asked of another prospective juror. The prosecutor explained the reasons for excusing one black juror, and the trial judge agreed, but the 9th Circuit panel found the rationale unacceptable, in effect, "substituting its own judgment" consistent with criticism by the Supreme Court statement in Rice v. Collins. Once again, the 9th Circuit panel ignored the trial judge's ruling in addition to dismissing the California Court of Appeal's decision.

The 9th Circuit judges in the *La Marque* and *Hickman* cases completely misunderstand jury selection and fail to consider intuition gleaned by a prosecutor when questioning jurors. The prosecutor may prefer an older jury; a female jury; a jury of married people; jurors with children; or without; those who live near the courthouse; or those who do not. Most importantly: the voice and the demeanor of the juror are impossible to duplicate on a cold appellate record.

The *Batson* case decided by the Supreme Court and interpreted by the 9th Circuit poses the most disturbing challenge to a prosecution decision to excuse a juror(s) under the following scenario: first, the trial judge, the person most knowledgeable according to the Supreme Court,   disallows the defense objection to a juror the prosecution seeks to exclude; second, the state appellate court affirms the trial judge; third, in district court the prisoner files a writ of habeas corpus and the court denies the petition. Despite all these courts, the 9th Circuit on appeal from the habeas corpus district court ruling engaged in an endless discussion of the reasons for excusing each juror, and determined which legal test to use based upon a decision the appellate court wanted to reach. The wasted time at trial and appeal is incalculable because everyone saw the case differently. Yet the 9th Circuit, ignoring all the other judges who ruled on the case, reversed all previous decisions.

Williams v. Runnels (Warden), 432 F.3d 1102 (9th Cir. 2006)
The 9th Circuit also invented the doctrine of "statistical disparity" in excusing black jurors to raise an inference of purposeful discrimination. In *Williams v. Runnels* the prosecutor in a California state court excused three black jurors after questioning them and without explanation. The jury subsequently convicted the defendant, and the California Court of Appeal confirmed the conviction as did the district court in rejecting a petition for habeas corpus. Williams appealed to the 9th Circuit.

Excusing black jurors in this case constitutes "statistical disparity," said the 9th Circuit, and reversed a conviction for robbery. The trial judge had seen no purposeful discrimination in excusing the juror. In fact, the trial court judge in *Williams v. Runnels* thought the defense objection so frivolous he did not even require an explanation from the prosecutor for excusing a juror. The California Court of Appeal similarly found no purposeful discrimination. The California Supreme Court agreed, as did the district court judge.

The 9th Circuit held that the decision of the California Court of Appeal applied the wrong legal standard of the federal statute (AntiTerrorism and Effective Death Penalty Act; AEDPA). The 9th Circuit panel in the *Runnels* case briefly noted AEDPA mandated federal courts to acknowledge "state court findings of fact are presumed to be correct unless the petitioner rebuts that presumption with clear and convincing evidence." But, said the 9th Circuit panel, "AEDPA only applies to challenges . . . to evidence presented for the first time in federal court and does not appl(y) to an intrinsic review of state court processes, or situations where petitioner challenges the state court's finding based entirely on the state record." The panel cites it own prior decision for this unique insight in *Kesser v. Cambra*. There is no authority for this proposition yet the California Attorney General [Jerry Brown] sought no review from the Supreme Court.

This 9th Circuit rationale was thoroughly repudiated in *Harrington v. Richter* and *Cullen v. Pinholster,* two Supreme Court cases decided five years later and discussed in another chapter in the text. *Williams v. Runnels,* and another decision of the 9th Circuit entitled *Paulino v. Harrison,* converted a routine felony trial into numbers games invoking arguments over whether the prosecutor had the right to excuse jurors.

These decisions in the 9th Circuit, and the Supreme Court decision in *Batson,* have turned trials into dilatory and burdensome hearings, inciting delay at trial, on appeal, and in petitions for habeas corpus. Why is a federal court, reading the same trial record as the California court of appeal (or any state appellate court), permitted after ten years (or more) to reverse a conviction previously affirmed in state courts and despite a clear congressional intent and Supreme Court concurrence in limiting the role of federal appellate courts?

As noted above, both prosecution and defense in a criminal prosecution have the right to excuse jurors without assigning any reason unless challenged by the other side, yet often one side surprises the other side by excusing, or accepting, a juror. Trial lawyers are experienced in questioning jurors and evaluating their responses, their attitudes, and their excuses unlike 9th

Circuit judges, or their clerks, who sit and read a record of printed words with none of the chemistry that marks a prosecution in general and questioning of jurors in particular. The crime charged, the witnesses, expert witnesses, police officers, the defendant, the exhibits, all these factors and others that combine to reflect human nature are missing on appeal.

Why some of the 9th Circuit judges continue to undermine trials and appeals by repeatedly disbelieving prosecutors, verbally lashing them, and finding discrimination where no one else can, is inconceivable. Call it "Social Injustice."

Aside from unduly extending a trial and encouraging appeals and writs of habeas corpus in state and federal courts, how do these decisions affect the public? First: there is the inordinate cost of the trial and the appeal and petitions in state and federal courts. Second: the prosecution is often unable to re-retry a defendant after a conviction has been reversed on appeal on grounds unrelated to the evidence. Witnesses die, are no longer living in the area, refuse to return and expose themselves to the stress of another trial; exhibits are destroyed, unavailable, or lost. Third: witnesses who do return after years have passed obviously cannot remember all the details and can be impeached (contradicted). Fourth: another appeal in the event of a conviction exists for the second time and another round of petitions for habeas corpus is possible.

Most important, the refusal of the 9th Circuit to accept the decision of state courts is in defiance of a clear federal statutory mandate and Supreme Court order to defer to state jurisdiction. As one 9th Circuit judge noted, the state courts are jurisdictional colleagues and capable of ruling on Constitutional issues as well as federal courts.

2. Trials

McDaniel (Warden) v. (Troy) Brown, 130 S.Ct. 665 (2010)
Reversing and returning the 9th Circuit decision in *Brown (Troy) v. Farwell (Warden)*, 525 F.3d 787 (9th Cir. 2008)
McDaniel v. Brown illustrates an appellate court (9th Circuit) reviewing the state court record in *Farwell v. Brown*, (same case) and concluding that

the jury came to the wrong result. In *McDaniel v. Brown*, the Supreme Court reversed the 9th Circuit.

At this Nevada state trial, the evidence was conflicting but an expert witness testified to the DNA positive match found between defendant Troy Brown and the evidence found on the victim who had been assaulted and raped in Nevada. The 9th Circuit panel, reviewing the record of this trial on habeas corpus after the conviction was affirmed on appeal by the Nevada Supreme Court and confirmed by the district court judge, surmised the results of the DNA test could also have included Brown's brothers who lived in the "vicinity." Even assuming the DNA evidence introduced at trial was erroneous, the evidence established that two of Brown's brothers lived in Utah. Another brother was thirteen years old, and the fourth brother had an airtight alibi.

At another hearing in federal court several years after the conclusion of the trial, the district court judge allowed the defense to produce evidence contradicting the DNA evidence introduced at trial and granted the habeas corpus petition. On appeal from this ruling by the state, the 9th Circuit agreed with the district court judge. In its decision, the 9th Circuit panel, by a 2-1 majority, retried the case despite the Supreme Court's repeated admonitions to federal appellate courts to review the trial "in the light most favorable to the prosecution" (citing a Supreme Court decision in an unrelated case, *Jackson v. Virginia*). The two-judge majority decision ignored the comments of the dissenting judge on the panel who criticized their decision for considering evidence *never introduced in the state court trial*, produced several years after trial, and simultaneously defying Supreme Court jurisprudence.

At no time did the 9th Circuit panel offer deference to the state court as required by AEDPA, or bothered by a district court judge considering evidence never introduced at trial in a hearing held years later. The panel also ignored an additional evidentiary hearing provided by the state to Brown after his trial concluded, at which time the state court judge denied Brown's claims.

On January 26, 2009 the Supreme Court granted review of the 9th Circuit decision, and in *McDaniel v. Brown*, reversed the 9th Circuit in a unanimous decision. Counsel for Brown, at his appearance in the Supreme Court, admitted the 9th Circuit analysis of the law was incorrect. The Supreme Court wrote: "[Brown's lawyer] correctly concedes that a reviewing court must consider all of the evidence admitted at trial . . . Even if we set that concession aside, however, and assume that the (9th Circuit] Court of Appeals could have considered the [subsequent DNA report] . . . the court made an egregious error in concluding the Nevada Supreme Court's rejection of [Brown's] insufficiency-of-the-evidence claim 'involved an unreasonable application of 'clearly established Federal law.'"

Chastising the 9th Circuit for considering evidence submitted twelve years after the trial, the Justices added:

> "The Court of Appeals acknowledged that it must review the evidence in the light most favorable to the prosecution, but the Court's recitation of inconsistencies in the testimony shows it failed to do so". . . The [Ninth Circuit] Court of Appeals had also clearly erred in concluding the Nevada Supreme Court's decision was 'contrary to' [federal law] because the Nevada court stated a legal standard that requires a 'reasonable' jury, not a 'rational one,' in assessing whether the jury could have been convinced of a defendant's guilt rather than whether it could have been convinced of each element of the crime. It is of little moment that the Nevada Supreme Court analyzed whether a 'reasonable' jury could be convinced of guilt beyond a reasonable doubt, rather than asking whether a 'rational' one could be convinced of each element of guilt; a reasonable jury could hardly be convinced of guilt unless it found each element satisfied beyond a reasonable doubt."

Unfortunately, the Supreme Court sent the case back to the 9th Circuit to review Brown's contention that his counsel was "ineffective." This is another illustration of the methodology the 9th Circuit uses: A petitioner files habeas corpus from an adverse state trial court judgment on several grounds but the 9th Circuit resolves only one. On review by the Supreme Court from that decision, the justices resolve the only issue raised. When the Supreme Court reverses and sends the case back to the 9th Circuit, in effect it allows another hearing on the unresolved issues. The parties must brief (draft written arguments) the unresolved issues, and the court holds another hearing and writes another decision, thus laying the groundwork for another appeal to the Supreme Court.

The court cited the *McDaniel v. Brown* case as grounds for reversing *Patrick v. Smith*, discussed next.

Patrick (Warden) v. Smith, 130 S.Ct. 1134 (2010)

This case was heard three times by the 9th Circuit after the Supreme Court reversed those decisions three times. *Patrick v. Smith* is another illustration of 9th Circuit usurpation of state court authority and indifference to juries. An appellate court (9th Circuit), oblivious to reality, dismissive of a state court decision, substituted its own opinion of the evidence introduced at trial. The 9th Circuit abandoned its role as an appellate court, ignored the jury verdict, misinterpreted the evidence and reversed the state Court of Appeal which had affirmed the subsequent judgment.

Smith had been charged in state court with criminal responsibility for the death of a child. The evidence between expert witnesses at trial indisputably conflicted among those who testified to different opinions attributable to the cause of death in a "baby shaking" case. The jury unanimously convicted Smith and the trial court properly sentenced her. None of the jurors was impermissibly excused, the trial judge correctly read the jury instructions, evidentiary errors were not challenged, no prosecutorial misconduct or jury issues arose. And surprisingly, Smith urged no challenge to the "ineffective assistance" of her counsel. The California Court of Appeal affirmed the verdict as did the district court judge on habeas corpus.

With no legal error to criticize, the 9th Circuit panel in reviewing the district court denial of the petition for habeas corpus reviewed the evidence at trial and elected to support the expert testimony of the defense witnesses. Aside from this unsupportable decision by an appellate court, the judges ignored the reality of a criminal trial. The defense attorney obviously made the same argument to the jury as he did when arguing his case to the panel of 9th Circuit judges. The defendant herself may have testified, (the court does not say), but the trial judge, the California Court of Appeal, the California Supreme Court (which also denied review), and the district court judge all heard the same argument and rejected the defense version.

Had it occurred to the 9th Circuit panel that the jury - who which actually heard the testimony - did not believe the defense experts? Did the prosecution experts carry more weight with the jury? This case is purely a factual dispute between expert witnesses, and the jury resolved the conflict. As the dissenting 9th Circuit judge in the decision caustically remarked, "that's why we have juries." What is the purpose of the jury if the appellate court merely decides it prefers a different version of the evidence?

The State of California immediately sought review in the Supreme Court of the 9th Circuit decision, and the Justices promptly reversed the 9th Circuit decision without any explanation, merely citing their own decision in *Carey v. Musladin* (discussed later) and returned the case to the 9th Circuit. In response, the 9th Circuit panel rearranged the language they wrote in the original case, reiterated its earlier decision, and ordered the defendant released.

The state sought review again, and the Supreme Court reversed the 9th Circuit again. The 9th Circuit panel, in its second decision had cited the Supreme Court decision in *Jackson v. Virginia*, a case warranting reversal of a different state court decision on grounds of the Fourteenth Amendment Due Process Clause. In *Jackson*, the Supreme Court had held that "no rational juror considering all of the evidence in the light most favorable to the prosecution could find guilt beyond a reasonable doubt." As the dissenting judge in *Jackson* notes"

"[The role of the federal judge is not to determine whether 'it' would find a different result . . . [I]nstead, the relevant question is whether, after viewing all the evidence in the light most favorable to the prosecution, any rational trier of fact could have found the essential elements of the crime beyond a reasonable doubt."

The 9th Circuit panel ignored this injunction in the Patrick case and again substituted its own verdict thereby rejecting the jury, the proper trier of facts.

The dissenting judge in *Jackson* added a prophecy fulfilled by the 9th Circuit in *Smith v. Patrick*: "According to the [panel] majority, the Constitution now prohibits the criminal conviction of any person, including apparently a person against whom the facts have already been found beyond a reasonable doubt by a jury, a trial judge, and one of more levels of state appellate judges, except upon proof to convince a federal judge that a 'rational trier of fact could not have found the essential elements of the crime beyond a reasonable doubt.'"

Smith v. Patrick is an egregious and dishonest decision by judges in an appellate court of appeal who never saw or heard a single witness, never examined any tangible evidence, and defied the verdict of a unanimous jury. Inexcusable, and an abuse of judicial power that did not go unnoticed by the Supreme Court in vacating the judgment and returning the case for the third time to the 9th Circuit, informing that court to read its previous case of *Brown v. McDaniel*, above, reversing the 9th Circuit.

When the 9th Circuit panel received the case again from the Supreme Court, they acknowledged reading the Supreme Court decision in *Brown v. McDaniel* as cited by the justices and found it inapplicable. For the third time, the panel reversed the conviction on grounds the evidence was insufficient to establish guilt, duplicating the same excuse it used in the *Brown* case also reversed by the Supreme Court; (*Smith v. Mitchell.* This record speaks for itself.

And then, something unusual happened. Within six weeks after the 9th Circuit third reversal the California governor (Jerry Brown) pardoned the defendant. Pardoning a defendant in that short of time suggests a phone call from someone to Brown. The press ignored any political connection between the 9th Circuit and Brown.

U.S. v. Jernigan, 492 F.3d 1050 (9th Cir. 2007)
The 9th Circuit panel reverses its earlier opinion: *U.S. v. Jernigan,* 451 F. 3d 1027 (9th Cir. 2006).
U.S. v. Jernigan is an example of another 9th Circuit panel abandoning its role as a reviewing court and re-retrying the case. A jury convicted Jernigan of bank robbery based on the testimony of five witnesses and retrieval of images from a video surveillance camera. Several months later, while Jernigan was in custody, she learned that another woman had robbed several banks in the same area, including the one she had robbed. In a motion for new trial, Jernigan argued that the government had wrongfully withheld evidence that a woman similar in appearance to her had committed robberies while she herself was in custody, and therefore her conviction should be reversed for failure of the government to disclose this evidence.

The trial judge in the district court, who also conducted an evidentiary hearing on the motion for a new trial, concluded no similarity existed between the two women and denied Jernigan's contention of a similar party committing the robberies. On her appeal to the 9th Circuit, Jernigan repeated the same objections she raised in the motion for new trial, alleging that the government had suppressed evidence that another woman had robbed the banks. The 9th Circuit panel who heard Jernigan's original appeal from the trial judge who had affirmed the conviction, quoted extensively from the trial record. The panel upheld the verdict and included in its decision the comments of the trial judge who had specifically rejected the evidence of similarity.

The 9th Circuit reheard the case as a full panel of judges and reversed the conviction, never referring to the comments of the trial judge or to his ruling on the motion. In each case, the trial judge unambiguously commented on the different appearances between the two women. The 9th Circuit panel rehearing the case also failed to consider the decision of its earlier panel describing the inaccuracy of the identification.

A dissenting judge in the *Jernigan* case issued a stinging rebuke to the majority for reweighing the evidence. More specifically, he reproached the majority panel for completely ignoring the findings of the trial judge who presided at trial and at the motion for a new trial. The dissenting judge writes: "Those of our sister [circuit courts] which have considered this question [disclosure of evidence] . . . afford deference to the district court's findings of fact. The First, Second, Third, Fifth, Seventh, Eighth, Tenth and Eleventh Circuits [Courts of Appeal] . . . all afford some level of deference to a district court's factual findings [on pretrial governmental disclosure of evidence]."

As noted in this and other contexts, the 9th Circuit has repeatedly used this tactic of ignoring the findings of the trial judge who heard all the witnesses and examined the evidence. The 9th Circuit refuses to act as a reviewing court without any deference to trial judges who observed the witnesses and supervised prosecution of the case. The dissenting judges in *Jernigan* wrote, "Similar appellate fact finding contrary to what the trial judge observed and has deduced from his own observations have recently resulted in reversals [by the Supreme Court] of our decisions in *Uttecht v. Brown* and *Rice v. Collins* (citations omitted; both cases reviewed in the text.)."

Horel (Warden) v. Valdovinos, 131 S.Ct. 142 (2011)
Reversing the 9th Circuit decision in *Valdovinos v. McGrath*, 598 F.3d 568 (9th Cir. 2010).
In a fact situation similar to the *Jernigan* case above, the witness identification of a man who had shot and killed another man was the single

issue at trial. The jury believed the conflicting testimony of witnesses on the identification of the shooter and convicted Valdovinos. The California Court of Appeal affirmed the conviction, and the district court denied the petition for habeas corpus.

The 9th Circuit panel on appeal from the district court decision literally retried the case and granted the writ of habeas corpus. The argument on the writ to the 9th Circuit panel was identical to the argument made by defense counsel and rejected by the jury at trial. On review of the 9th Circuit decision to the Supreme Court, the justices reversed in a one-paragraph decision and returned the case the case to the 9th Circuit.

The other cases reviewed above, *McDaniel v. Brown*, *Patrick v. Smith*, and *U.S. v. Jernigan*, illustrate the 9th Circuit pattern of reversing trial courts decisions by reweighing the evidence and ignoring the jury verdict. Hopefully, the 9th Circuit may have gotten the message in its own case *of U.S. v. Nevis*. Here is the 9th Circuit's admission of its numerous errors in reviewing jury trials:

> "The Supreme Court's recent decision in *McDonnell v. Brown*, reversing a decision by [the 9th Circuit], highlights our [9th Circuit] error. In McDonnell v. Brown the defendant had been convicted of sexual assault of a child. On appeal, we concluded that the evidence was insufficient to establish defendant's guilt beyond a reasonable doubt. [*See, Brown v. Farewell*]. In so holding, we discounted the government's argument that the defendant had washed his clothes when he returned home in order to destroy physical evidence of the rape, stating that while the government's theory was plausibly consistent with him being the assailant," the defendant had provided an alternative reason for washing his clothes. The Supreme Court rejected this analysis, holding that 'had we reviewed the evidence [as required by the Supreme Court], we would have concluded that the evidence supports an inference that [defendant] washed the clothes immediately to clean blood from them, rather

than adopting an exculpatory explanation. The Supreme Court concluded that "the Court of Appeals analysis *failed to preserve the fact finder's role* as weigher of the evidence by reviewing all of the evidence . . . in the light most favorable to the prosecution.'

"Accordingly, to the extent [our previous cases and [their] progeny construed evidence in a manner favoring innocence rather than in a manner favoring the prosecution, and required reversal when such a construction was not 'any less likely than the incriminating explanation advanced by the government' those cases strayed from the test established in *Jackson v. Virginia*, and made 'plausible' the exculpatory constructions disapproved of in *McDonnell v. Brown*. We [the 9th Circuit] now overrule them."

This concession is a dramatic confirmation of the theory of this book. The 9th Circuit repeatedly ignores Supreme Court precedent, reweighs the evidence, and rules on review from a jury verdict that the defendant's testimony is equally "plausible" with that of the prosecution and therefore a guilty verdict cannot stand. This blatant usurpation of the jury's duties, ignoring the fact that the jury did not believe defendant's version of the facts and imposing the wrong legal test, has been the source of censurable injustice.

Carey (Warden) v. Musladin, 549 U.S. 70 (2006)
Reversing the 9th Circuit decision in *Musladin v. LaMarque (Warden)*, 427 F.3d 653 (9th Cir. 2005).
A jury convicted Musladin of murder. The California Court of Appeal affirmed the conviction and subsequently denied a petition for habeas corpus. Musladin applied for a writ of habeas corpus in federal court. The district court judge denied the writ, and Musladin appealed to the 9th Circuit.

During the original trial, several spectators wore buttons on their clothes depicting a photograph of the deceased victim. On appeal from the district court decision, the 9th Circuit panel incredulously concluded that spectators wearing buttons equated with shackling criminal defendants in the courtroom, a practice previously condemned by the Supreme Court. Citing that Supreme Court case as precedent, the panel reversed the conviction in an ambiguous and incoherent decision. The state sought review in the Supreme Court.

The Supreme Court reversed the 9th Circuit, reciting decisions of all the various federal Circuit Courts of Appeal in which those judges had relied extensively on their own prior appellate decisions resolving habeas corpus petitions filed within their own circuit jurisdiction. The Supreme Court in *Musladin* said appellate courts in their decisions can only invoke "clearly established federal law" (under the federal AntiTerrorism and Death Penalty Act; AEDPA; see, next case below) based on the 'holding' [main point] of cases as determined by the Supreme Court." The Supreme Court, emphasizing its ruling in the *Musladin* case noted, "[g]iven the lack of [rules] from this Court regarding the potentially prejudicial effect of spectators' courtroom conduct . . . it cannot be said that the state court "unreasonably applied clearly established federal law." And, it noted, "[judicial] determination of factual issues made by a State court shall be presumed to be correct."

To this comment by the Supreme Court, here is this petulant quotation in the *Musladin* case written by a 9th Circuit panel that holds the record for Supreme Court reversals: "In other words, federal courts must give effect to state courts incorrect applications of federal constitutional law . . . . Not a word from the 9th Circuit about its own "incorrect" applications of federal law reversed by the Supreme Court in record numbers.

When the Supreme Court returned the *Musladin* case to the 9th Circuit the panel affirmed the conviction and denied all other objections Musladin had alleged in his petition. *Carey v. Musladin* is a landmark decision prohibiting the 9th Circuit from deciding habeas corpus applications based on its own prior federal circuit court decisions. The Supreme Court mandates appellate courts to refer only to the [rulings] of Supreme Court decisions. Thus, a federal court in ruling on petitions for habeas corpus is required under AEDPA to review state court proceedings only pursuant to Supreme Court decisions. The 9th Circuit had frequently cited its own decisions in cases reviewing state court rulings. This practice is no longer allowed. The Supreme Court complained, "[T]his is a retrenchment from our former practice."

To illustrate the depth of opposition to Supreme Court rulings in the *Musladin* case, particularly on habeas corpus, one panel of 9th Circuit judges in the case *Irons v. Carey* decided to question the validity of Congressional restrictions on federal courts imposed by AEDPA. But prior to hearing the case, another 9th Circuit panel had written its decision upholding the right of Congress to impose AEDPA procedural limitations; *Crater v. Galaza*. The *Irons v. Carey* panel relegated the *Crater v. Galaza* decision in *Carey v. Musladin* to a footnote and reluctantly agreed its own case was governed by that decision. The full 9th Circuit court refused to rehear the *Irons* case, causing the original three-judge panel to complain again about the restrictions mandated by AEDPA.

But the *Irons v. Carey* panel clearly invited the petitioner seeking habeas corpus to petition for a rehearing by the full 9th court. The court denied the request, although one of the judges wrote an extensive dissent. In his dissent, the judge argued that federal courts of appeal should retain the power to reverse any state court judgment inconsistent with federal law. No one debates the general principle, but the underlying gratuitous presumption assumes the state court decision is wrong or, in the language of the Supreme Court: "unreasonable." Why is the 9th Circuit in any better position to determine whether a criminal conviction is "unreasonable" than a state court, particularly when the Supreme Court has repeatedly told the 9th Circuit its decisions are "wrong?"

Winzer v. Hall (Warden, 494 F.3d 1192 (9th Cir. 2007)
AEDPA requires federal courts to apply "clearly established federal law" in reviewing state court decisions in criminal cases, but this mandate rarely deters the 9th Circuit from ignoring it. This phrase can be as easily

finessed as the word "reasonable" in other contexts. In *Winzer v. Hall*, a California state court case had previously affirmed Winzer's conviction. The 9th Circuit panel, on habeas corpus appeal from the district court, reviewed a rule of evidence applied during trial, which, under some circumstances, allows a witness to testify to the statement of a third person who is "unavailable" for testimony (due to death, injury, or illness) but who had testified under oath in a previous hearing. The California court in *Winzer* ruled that the testimony of a witness at trial to the statements of an absent third person who had previously testified in the case did not violate the right of the defendant to confront the witness as required by the Confrontation Clause of the Sixth Amendment to the U.S. Constitution requiring all witnesses to appear in court and testify.

Writing in a habeas corpus hearing, the 9th Circuit in *Winzer* rejected the California Court of Appeal decision and held that the trial testimony of a witness to the statements of an absent witness did not qualify as an exception to the hearsay rule, intoning the ritual of applying "clearly established federal law under Supreme Court decisions." According to the judge dissenting in *Winzer* from the court granting a rehearing in the case, "[AEDPA] imposes a severe restriction on habeas petitioners' ability to secure federal relief from a state court determination that allegedly violates the Constitution." Apparently the state court decision that no violation of the Confrontation Clause of the Constitution occurred is irrelevant to the 9th Circuit.

Regardless of whether the 9th Circuit decision was correctly decided, the case illustrates the ability of that court to cite Supreme Court decisions as authority for the result it wants to achieve and ignores its application to the case.

Parle v. Runnel (Warden), 505 F.3d 922 (9th Cir. 2007). Reversed by the Supreme Court and rewritten.
Convicted of killing his wife, Parle appealed. The California Court of Appeals affirmed the conviction, albeit acknowledging the trial court

committed evidentiary errors but insufficient of themselves to affect the verdict.

Parle sought habeas corpus review in federal court, and the district court judge granted his petition. The State of California appealed to the 9th Circuit which actually reversed the district court judge and returned the case to that court. The same district court judge granted Parle's habeas corpus petition a second time, and again the state appealed. The 9th Circuit vacated the district court judge's ruling and returned the case again.

The district court judge again granted the petition. This time the 9th Circuit on appeal from that decision, affirmed the trial court, changed its mind and granted the petition. Citing AEDPA, the 9th Circuit panel examined "evidentiary errors" of the state court trial judge. The 9th Circuit panel noted that the state court allowed the prosecution to recall Parle's psychiatrist as a witness who had testified on the defendant's behalf at the trial. The 9th Circuit panel characterized this ruling as legal error.

Why is this error? When a witness (in this case, a doctor) testifies at trial, the defendant waives any privilege of confidentiality of communications between them . Apparently not in the 9th Circuit. Ignoring the routine law of every state, a party waives the privilege of a doctor not to disclose private conversations if called as a witness by a party to testify on the issues in trial. The evidence at trial established that the deceased wife of the defendant maintained a diary enumerating threats and violence committed by Parle. According to the trial court, evidence of a deceased witness or a party is admissible if the court concludes the statements were not prepared for litigation and otherwise trustworthy. (The Supreme Court has subsequently changed this rule, but it has no retroactive effect and inapplicable to Parle).

Other alleged erroneous evidentiary rulings included evidence of threats made by his wife; Parle's demeanor after the killing; his father's testimony. In other words, Parle admitted killing his wife (this defense is not an alibi or alleging responsibility of a third party; and the issue is whether he intended to kill his wife with malice, an element necessary for murder convictions.

The trial was unquestionably contentious, both sides dealt with two violent participants, and defense counsel argued to the jury that Parle killed his wife either in self defense or in the absence of malice. As the California Court of Appeal wrote, despite the erroneous evidentiary rulings, other evidence substantiated a jury verdict of first degree murder.

The 9th Circuit judges, with AEDPA requiring it to "defer" to state courts, needed an escape mechanism. They found it in the Fourteenth Amendment "Due Process" clause. The panel held that the evidentiary errors violated due process and warranted a reversal. The court found a way to reach the result it wanted.

Here is the language of the 9th Circuit in its decision: "Under traditional Due Process principles, cumulative evidentiary errors warrant habeas relief only where the errors have 'so infected the trial with unfairness as to make the resulting decision a denial of Due Process. Such infection occurs when the combined effect of the errors had a substantial and injurious effect or influence on the jury's verdict . . . To simplify, where the combined effect of individually harmful errors renders a criminal defense far less persuasive than it might [other wise] have been, the resulting conviction violates Due Process."

This verbiage is incoherent, subjective, and mindless. The decision not only lacks comprehension it completely ignores the jury. A jury does not sit in this kind of environment divorced from reality and incapable of finding facts based on the testimony of witnesses. The trial testimony was in conflict and, of course, the victim did not testify except indirectly through documents. Defense witnesses took the stand and testified in Parle's favor. Parle, in defense of himself, testified to his wife's threats. A doctor testified to the mental state of Parle, and another witness testified to Parle's demeanor after the death of his wife. The 9th Circuit panel was so engaged in academic hairsplitting and professorial theory that it lacked any understanding of the trial.

In other words, as the California Court of Appeal ruled, the total amount of evidence at trial was exposed to the jury and the jurors understood both sides. Jurors heard all the witnesses, examined all the evidence, and the judge correctly instructed the jurors on defense theories of malice and self defense. The jury unanimously voted against Parle. The 9th Circuit only read papers ('briefs" in legal parlance) and never heard a single witness. As has been said before by another judge, "that's why we have juries."

In an unrelated case, *Medina v. Hornung*, the 9th Circuit noted, "The overwhelming majority of trial errors are nonstructural (not fundamental) and do not trigger habeas relief unless the error resulted in substantial and injurious effect or influence in determining the jury's verdict." The court used this same language in Parle and it only confirmed the rule of Due Process" as abstract, subjective, incapable of objective proof, and invoked to justify any desired result.

The *Parle* decision is an example of federal court arrogance. The 9th Circuit reversed the district court judge who granted the petition for habeas corpus twice, but on the third appeal the appellate court granted habeas corpus. The delays, and the repeated review of a state court conviction it had originally affirmed, are inexcusable.

Neither former California Attorney General Brown nor his predecessor sought review in the Supreme Court.

Barajas v. Wise (Parole Agent), 481 F.3d 734 (9th Cir. 2007) [original decision]
2007 WL 3105756 (C.A.9); 2008 WL 865341 C.A.9) [subsequent decisions-not reported]
In 1998, defendant Barajas was convicted of conspiring to sell drugs based, in part, on the testimony of an informant who had testified in over one

hundred cases without objection by defense counsel. The informant testified her only role in this case consisted of "introducing" a third party to
Barajas who was ultimately convicted based on other evidence of a subsequent drug sale.

The California courts denied Barajas's motion to compel disclosure
of the name and address of the informant. The 9th Circuit on habeas
corpus, oblivious to the eight years Barajas took to file her habeas corpus
petition in federal court, ignored the excessive delay and commented indif-
ferently in one brief sentence: "After the conclusion of her state proceedings, Barajas filed her petition in federal court . . ." No mention of almost
a decade of delay.

The district court judge granted Barajas's motion to disclose, originally
denied by the state court, and the state appealed to the 9th Circuit asserting any disclosure would jeopardize the informant's life. Despite citing
AEDPA, the 9th Circuit panel agreed with the district judge, and ruled the
state court unreasonably denied Barajas the right to cross examine the witness as guaranteed by the Confrontation Clause of the U.S. Constitution.
After an extensive discussion of the facts, the 9th Circuit panel of judges
concluded the state court had "unreasonably" applied federal law and
granted the petition of habeas corpus. The 9th Circuit panel cited its own
prior case law, *Belmontes v. Brown*, to support its decision. (The Supreme
Court subsequently reversed that decision in *Ayers v. Belmontes*).

The state asked the court for a rehearing of the *Barajas* case, and in a
one page decision, the 9th Circuit panel incredulously said, without any
explanation, "We conclude that the prosecutor's reasons for non disclosure
were not conjectural and indeed were sufficient to justify withholding . . .
the informant's address." The court denied the petition for habeas corpus it
had originally granted. *Barajas* is a stark example of a court repudiating its
previous decision without citing any statutory or constitutional grounds,
rejecting its previous decision that the state had "unreasonably" applied
federal law, and then burying its decision unpublished.

District Attorney's Office for the Third Judicial District v. Osborne, 129
S.Ct. 2308 (2009) Reversing the 9th Circuit decision in *Osborne v. District
Attorney's Office for the Third Judicial District,* 521 F.3d 1118 (9th Cir.
2008).

Several years ago, an Alaska jury convicted Osborne and a co-defendant of
kidnapping, assault, and sexual assault of a young woman. In the course of
police investigation of the crimes, the officers found evidence subsequently
tested for DNA resulting in narrowing the identification of Osborne as one
of the culprits. During the trial, Osborne refused an offer to submit to a
more reliable DNA test available to all defendants at that time. The jury
ultimately convicted Osborne.

The Alaska court affirmed the conviction, but Osborne later sought
a court order seeking access to the results of the more sophisticated DNA
test. At an evidentiary hearing ordered by the Alaska court, the lawyer who
represented Osborne at the trial testified she believed he was guilty and did
not want to submit him to another more reliable DNA test. She intended
to rely on misidentification by the victim. Two Alaska Court of Appeals
denied the DNA request.

While serving his sentence, Osborne ultimately qualified for parole
and confessed to the crimes. At the parole hearing he repeated his confession. Based on the victim's identification at trial, the confessions, the DNA
test, and other corroborating evidence, the Alaska court denied Osborne's
request for access to current DNA testing as statutorily unavailable under
Alaska law. After release on parole from his convictions, Osborne was
arrested for another unrelated offense. The State of Alaska sought revocation of his parole.

Instead of filing habeas corpus to vacate his revocation of parole, and
without asserting "actual innocence," Osborne requested the district court
for access to currently available DNA testing of the evidence introduced at
trial by filing a federal statutory 42 U.S.C. § 1983 claim (allegation) for
"deprivation of any rights . . . secured by the Constitution," and alleging

a Fourteenth Amendment Due Process violation. The district court judge denied the request. On appeal, the 9th Circuit reversed and remanded (sent back) to the district court judge who subsequently agreed Osborne had a limited right to the test.

On Alaska's appeal from that ruling to the 9th Circuit, the court resolved neither the federal civil rights statutory claim nor the alleged due process violation. The three-judge panel unearthed *Brady v. Maryland*, an older Supreme Court case mandating prosecution disclosure of exculpatory or mitigating evidence to the defense. The 9th Circuit, citing no case applying the *Brady* rule to subsequent (post) trial procedures, nevertheless reversed the Alaska state court decision. Alaska sought review in the Supreme Court. Review was granted.

The Supreme Court reversed the 9th Circuit, summarily dismissing the *Brady v. Maryland* claim. Instead, the Court identified two grounds applicable to deny Osborne's request. First, Osborne essentially sought to reverse his state court conviction by obtaining access to a DNA test, but a federal court reviewing a state court conviction must proceed under the procedural rules of habeas corpus, precisely the kind of remedy Osborne should have sought. Instead he filed a civil rights claim (42 U.S.C. § 1983) and Due Process claim directly in federal court.

As noted earlier, federal courts reviewing state court convictions in habeas corpus proceedings must respect state court appellate rulings unless those courts violate "clearly established Supreme Court law" but none existed for the request Osborne sought- and the 9th Circuit knew about that rule. To finesse the rules of habeas corpus, and invoke 42 U.S.C. § 1983 and Due Process, the 9th Circuit needed a case decided by the Supreme Court for "clearly established law" and found the *Brady* case. Even defense counsel arguing in the Supreme Court agreed the *Brady* case inapplicable.

In addition, the Supreme Court has distinguished two categories of Due Process: procedural and substantive. Under the doctrine of Constitutional protection of "liberty interests" inherent in the Due Process Clause, federal courts will deny a remedy pursuant to a habeas corpus petition if the state provides an adequate procedural method for vindication of Constitutional rights. The Supreme Court examined Alaska law and cited several procedural mechanisms Osborne could have invoked to adequately protect his rights. As long as the state courts provide an adequate forum for resolution of that claim, and no procedural hurdles are unfair, the prisoner (or in this case a parolee) can attempt to vindicate his claim.

Substantive due process to protect "liberty interests," an amorphous doctrine at best, includes "principles of fundamental fairness rooted in the traditions and conscience of the American people as fundamental." In the Osborne case, no such history exists. Substantive due process constitutionalizes an issue and forecloses the American people or a legislature from amendment or revocation of a court decision. To confirm substantive due process in the context of the facts in Osborne, federal courts would be swamped in rule-making decisions not suitable to their role.

The Supreme Court conceded that Osborne could argue his "liberty interest" and identified several procedural avenues he could pursue to vindicate his alleged right to DNA access under Alaska law. The Supreme Court named forty-six state legislatures and the federal government who approve the right to post conviction DNA testing under certain conditions. The vast majority mandate a claim by an applicant of "actual innocence," of a crime, not just trial court error. Given the two confessions Osborne gave to the parole authorities, this is a significant hurdle.

Alaska is one of the few states that have not provided a comparable DNA statute. But as the Supreme Court points out, the Alaska courts do provide alternative remedies available to Osborne other than 42 U.S.C. § 1983 and the Due Process Clause.

The most important element in the Supreme Court's decision is refusal to allow a "free standing" substantive right under the Due Process Clause to compel a state to perform post trial DNA proceedings. The application of DNA testing is essentially an evidentiary issue best resolved in the laboratory of each state and its relevant law. The Supreme Court confirmed the right of individual states to legislate procedural conditions to avoid endless appeals in state and federal courts. In other words, the Supreme Court has acknowledged the role of state sovereignty in responding to the developing scientific world of DNA.

Justice Alito filed a succinct concurrence, noting, "Osborne denied submitting to a second DNA test during his trial in the Alaska courts. Once that strategic decision is made the defendant 'games the system' by asking for the test after conviction." This Justice understands criminal law and trial.

Waddington (Warden) v. Sarausad, 129 S.Ct. 823 (2009). Reversing the 9th Circuit in Sarausad v. Waddington, 479 F.3d 671 (9th Cir. 2007).

From the average juror's point of view, jury instructions read by the judge are one of the most important stages in the prosecution and defense of a trial. At the conclusion of the case, and after both sides have presented their evidence, the judge reads the rules that guide the jury in its deliberations. If the defendant is convicted, one of the grounds of appeal may allege that the judge read the wrong instructions or misread the instructions. Not all legally erroneous instructions require reversal on appeal, only those which mislead a jury or prejudice their deliberations. *Waddington v. Sarausad* is another example of 9th Circuit rulings reversed by the Supreme Court on an issue of an allegedly misleading jury instruction. The trial and appellate records reveal the 9th Circuit panel used this excuse and, in effect, reversed the conviction by retrying the case itself.

Sarausad belonged to a gang, and disputes arose between him and different gang members who alleged that Sarausad's members were "weak." Believing fist fights or shouting insults insufficient to establishing their toughness, Sarausad's gang members discussed retribution. Four members of the gang entered an automobile that Sarausad drove. As their car approached a school, one passenger in the car concealed his face with a bandanna and drew a handgun. Sarausad slowed the car and asked the passenger in the front seat if he was "ready." The passenger fired the gun, killing or wounding several people. Sarausad accelerated the vehicle and fled the scene. Other witnesses testified that Sarausad knew the other gang members would be armed, making a fistfight unlikely.

The prosecution charged Sarausad as an accomplice to the murder committed by the passenger. The prosecutor argued that the evidence established Sarausad had knowledge of the anticipated crime and aided and abetted (helped) the shooter as an accomplice. Under state law, a person who has knowledge of the crime and facilitates its commission is as guilty as the person who actually committed the crime. The jury convicted Sarausad of murder. The Washington state courts upheld the verdict on appeal by Sarausad and denied his petition for habeas corpus. Sarausad filed his petition for habeas corpus in federal court. The district court judge denied the petition, and Sarausad appealed to the 9th Circuit.

According to the 9th Circuit panel, only "weak" evidence established that Sarausad knew "the crime" was murder. Apparently ignoring the facts recited above, the court reversed Sarausad's conviction. The 9th Circuit panel argued that the jury instructions read by the trial judge misled the jurors by not informing them an accomplice must have knowledge of "the actual crime" committed (in this case, murder). Numerous 9th Circuit judges dissented from this decision but did not prevail when the court held a full hearing and upheld the earlier decision. The State of Washington sought review in the Supreme Court.

The Supreme Court dismissed the reasoning of the 9th Circuit in familiar tones of reproach. The Court said the 9th Circuit should not have dissected the prosecution closing argument, ignored the testimony of the witnesses, and misinterpreted the court instructions. The Supreme Court reminded the 9th Circuit of AEDPA, the federal statute limiting the role of federal courts in reviewing petitions for habeas corpus in state court convictions. Both the prosecutor and defense counsel argued to the jury the

element of "knowledge" of the crime at the trial and the court instructed
the jury it must find the defendant had "knowledge" of the murder to warrant his conviction.

The Supreme Court ruled that the state court judge had correctly read
the jury instruction on accomplice liability. The Supreme Court said: "To
the extent the [Ninth Circuit] Court of Appeals attempted to rewrite state
law by proposing [different language for the jury instruction] . . . it is not
the province of a federal habeas court to reexamine state court determinations on state court questions."

The Supreme Court reversed the 9th Circuit and returned the case for
"further proceedings not inconsistent with this opinion." The 9th Circuit
transferred the case to the district court judge without writing a decision. The
district court judge dismissed the habeas corpus petition sought by Saraausad.

Middleton (Warden) v. McNeil, 541 U.S. 433 (2004)
Reversing the 9th Circuit decision in *McNeil v. Middleton*, 344 F.3d 988
(9th Cir. 2003)
In a California state court, Sally McNeil was convicted of killing her husband. She appealed her conviction to the California Court of Appeal which
affirmed the judgment and subsequently denied her petition for habeas
corpus. McNeil filed a petition for habeas corpus in district court; denied.
On appeal from that decision the 9th Circuit granted the petition. The
State of California sought review in the Supreme Court. Granted.

The Supreme Court began its unanimous written decision in this case,
unsigned by an author but agreed to by the entire Court, as follows:

"Sally Marie McNeil killed her husband after an argument over his infidelity and spending habits. According to McNeil, she killed her husband
in self defense. At her trial, the judge correctly read four jury instructions
on self defense, but in one instruction failed to insert the word 'reasonable.'
The 9th Circuit found this error eliminated her 'imperfect defense claim,'
ignoring the other correct instructions. . . Said the Supreme Court: [This]
interpretation . . . would require such a rare combination of extremely

refined lawyerly parsing of an instruction to the jury, and extremely gull-ible acceptance of a *result that makes no conceivable sense.*"

After the Supreme Court reversed the 9th Circuit, it returned the case to that court. Upon receiving the case, the 9th Circuit conceded the Supreme Court had excoriated its three -judge panel for "lawyerly parsing." The same 9th Circuit panel affirmed the conviction in a 2-1 decision, but one panel-ist continued to engage in the kind of analysis repudiated by the Supreme Court. The Supreme Court denied the prisoner any further review.

3. Sentencing

Lockyer v. Andrade, 538 U.S. 63 (2003).

Reversing the 9th Circuit decision in *Andrade v. Attorney General of California*, 270 F.3d 743 (9th Cir. 2001)

California voters, angered and frustrated with the escalating crime level and disgusted with the inability of its state legislature to respond, enacted (by the Initiative process) its "Three Strikes Law" increasing punishment for repeat offenders. Though the law was admittedly strict, and on occa-sion arguably unsuitable, the California courts upheld its provisions; but the 9th Circuit subsequently invalidated the state statute.

The Supreme Court reversed the 9th Circuit decision in Lockyer v. Andrade. The Court wrote: "The Ninth Circuit made an initial error in its 'unreasonable application [of the law] analysis' . . . [and] '"fails to give proper deference to state courts . . . It is not enough that a federal habeas court, in its 'independent review' of the legal question, is left with a 'firm conviction' that the state court was 'erroneous' We have held precisely the opposite."

Mayle (Warden) v. Brown, 538 U.S. 901 (2003)

Reversing the 9th Circuit decision in *Brown v. Mayle*, 283 F.3d 1019 (9th Cir. 2003).

The 9th Circuit wrote another decision vacating the "Three Strikes" law also subsequently reversed by the Supreme Court in *Mayle v. Brown.* On return of the Supreme Court decision to the 9th Circuit, the court conceded its error and buried its decision unpublished.

Gill v. Ayers (Warden), 342 F.3d 911 (9th Cir. 2003)

In 1997, twenty-three years after the jury found him guilty of assault with a deadly weapon, Gill filed a habeas corpus petition seeking an order allowing him to testify that one of the three "strikes" (a prior conviction of assault with a deadly weapon) under the Three Strikes statute could not be counted in his subsequently increased sentence for an unrelated crime because he had not been personally armed with a deadly weapon as required by the statute. California courts denied his petition, and Gill sought habeas corpus in federal court. The district court judge denied his petition, and Gill appealed.

In *Gill v. Ayers* a 2-1 majority of 9th Circuit panel judges reversed the district court ruling. In his petition Gill wrote he wanted to testify that he did not use a deadly weapon. Of course the prosecution could not rebut this assertion after the extensive lapse of time. Citing two irrelevant Supreme Court cases, the 9th Circuit panel held that the defendant could testify. The dissenting judge in *Gill* notes the prosecution submitted the original probation report to the court in which Gill admitted he used a weapon in his prior conviction. Gill never disputed this admission made twenty three years earlier.

The California Attorney General (Lockyer) did not seek review in the Supreme Court in *Gill v. Ayers*. Incredibly, the 9th Circuit panel invited the Attorney General to discuss settlement of the case-which he refused to do. Attorney General Lockyer did not appeal a clearly erroneous decision. Apparently some arrangement was made, but it does not appear in the record.

On the same day as the decision in *Gill v. Ayers*, the Supreme Court reversed another 9th Circuit decision and upheld the constitutionality of the "Strikes" Law, confirming the decision of the California Supreme Court.

All these decisions by the 9th Circuit reducing sentences imposed by the trial judge had invalidated California voter approval of the Three Strikes Law and ignored California courts' confirmation of the sentences. By invalidating the Three Strikes Law the 9th Circuit not only overruled the California Supreme Court but defied the millions of people who had voted for the Three Strikes Initiative. Fortunately, the Supreme Court reversed the 9th Circuit and, incidentally, wrote another chastisement in its decision.

Ornoski (Warden) v. Reyes, 399 F.3d 964 (9th Cir. 2005)
The record in this case speaks for itself. The state appellate court affirmed Reyes' conviction for perjury, two prior convictions for armed robbery, and a juvenile conviction for burglary. The trial court sentenced Reyes under the "Three Strikes" rule to twenty-six years in prison, and California courts affirmed the sentence. On habeas corpus in federal court, Reyes alleged the disproportionate sentence violated the Eighth Amendment prohibiting cruel and unusual punishment and was Constitutionally invalid. The Supreme Court had already ruled, denying each of these contentions. In an unpublished decision, *Reyes v. Woodford,* a 2-1 majority of the 9th Circuit three- judge panel denied the Reyes petition in 2003.

Two years later, one of the judges in the majority changed his mind and voted to grant the petition. This dissenting judge in the original decision wrote the new decision and sent the case back to the district court to develop the record as to whether armed robbery was a "crime of violence." At no time did Reyes raise this issue on appeal. The federal rule requires a petitioner to develop this record initially in state court, but Reyes never did.

As expressed by the judge who originally dissented in the original decision, this case is inexplicable. One of the three judges who had denied the original habeas petition changed his mind without explanation and rewrote the decision. All the reasons for granting the petition are facetious. Is "armed robbery" not a "crime of violence?"

Regrettably, the California Attorney General (Lockyer} never publicized this "flip flop. More disturbing is the failure of the Supreme Court to review the case, and no further record of the ultimate disposition of the case is cited.

Briceno v. Scribner (Warden), 555 F.3d 1069 (9th Cir. 2009)
Christmas Day, 2000, Briceno and another defendant, both of whom were gang members, robbed four different individuals. The evidence at trial was overwhelming. A police officer who specialized in gang enforcement testified at the trial, explaining the pattern of the robberies and that this crime was gang related. The jury found Briceno guilty of multiple robberies and street terrorism.

The California Supreme Court affirmed the conviction and the enhanced sentence for gang related crimes. The district court judge agreed with the California Supreme Court and denied Briceno's petition for habeas corpus. Briceno appealed the decision to the 9th Circuit.

Federal courts do not sit to review interpretation of state statutes in habeas corpus proceedings, and the statute violated by Briceno imposed an increased sentence for felonies committed by gang members. This rule apparently did not apply to the 9th Circuit panel of judges, who reinterpreted the statute and held the evidence insufficient to support the gang enhancement. Here is the language of the dissenting judge in *Briceno*:

> "The majority disregards the clear holding of the California appellate courts that a criminal act intentionally committed with another known gang member demonstrates specific intent to assist in criminal conduct by gang members. This decision sustains the state court's finding of sufficient evidence to support the gang enhancement in Briceno's case. The majority's disregard of the [California] Court of Appeal's decision is unwarranted because there is no convincing evidence suggesting that the Supreme Court would decide the question differently. The California Supreme Court had

already placed its stamp of approval on the state Court of Appeal's conclusion in this case based on the evidence, and, regardless of the statutory interpretation, Briceno's crimes warrant the sentencing enhancement . . . [The] Court of Appeal was not unreasonable in finding that a rational trier of fact applying state law could find the sentencing enhancement was proven beyond a reasonable doubt."

The record does not show the then California Attorney General (Jerry Brown) took any action to review this case.

4. Sex Offenses

Additional cases (and trials) involving sexual molestation, brutality, and the exploitation and death of women and children can be found in Chapter 5, "The Death Penalty," and Chapter 6, "The Lawyers." The vast majority of states have enacted strict punishment and regulation for commission of these crimes. This Section describes the attacks on this legislation by the 9th Circuit.

Gonzales v. Duncan (Warden), 551 F.3d 875 (9th Cir. 2008)

Gonzales was convicted in state court of failing to update his annual address as a registered sex offender, as required by state law. Because of his prior record of felony convictions of serious crimes, this latest conviction qualified him for sentencing under California's Three Strikes Rule. The trial court sentenced him to twenty-eight years in prison. Here is his record as reported in the California Court of Appeal decision in *People v. Gonzalez*:

"Gonzales was convicted in 1988 of possession for sale of a controlled substance. Also in 1988 he was convicted of felony joyriding. Less than two months after he was paroled in 1989, he was arrested and later convicted of attempted rape and committing a lewd act on a child under the age of 14. He was paroled in 1992 and less than a year later, was arrested and convicted of robbery.

Once paroled, he committed at least three violations, including battery and spousal abuse, for which he returned to prison in 1997, 1998 and 1999. "

Gonzales' failure to annually update his sex offender registration, the offense for which he was convicted here, occurred after his birthday in February 2001, less than one year following his discharge from parole. The probation report for the sex offender violation identifies three aggravating and no mitigating factors: (1) Gonzalez has engaged in a pattern of violent conduct which indicates a serious danger to society; (2) his prior convictions as an adult . . . . are numerous or of increasing seriousness; and (3) his prior performance on probation or parole was unsatisfactory. Based on this evidence, the trial court acted well within its discretion by finding Gonzalez could not be deemed outside the [Three Strikes] scheme's spirit, in whole or in part.

Gonzalez also asserts his sentence violates the Constitutional prohibition against cruel and unusual punishment but provides no Eighth Amendment analysis and contends the analysis is the same under both state and federal law. We would not reach a different result under the federal Constitution . . . '[T]he principles developed by our court [regarding cruel or unusual punishment] are similar to those developed by the United States Supreme Court . . . and] the federal high court's reminder that appellate courts, 'of course, should grant substantial deference to the broad authority that legislatures necessarily possess in determining the types and limits of punishments for crimes."

After the losing the appeal of his conviction, denial of his habeas corpus petitions in state court, and denial of a petition for habeas corpus in the district court, Gonzales appealed to the 9th Circuit contending his punishment violated the Eighth Amendment to the U.S. Constitution prohibiting cruel and unusual punishment. According to the 9th Circuit, failure to annually register his change of address is a "regulatory process of *minimal importance* and bears no relationship to Gonzales' previous extensive criminal history."

Ignoring this deplorable record of criminal behavior as relevant, the 9th Circuit panel granted the petition for habeas corpus despite the absence of any objection to the sentence in the trial court, and the issue resolved against him in the California Court of Appeal. This case is another example of federal arrogance and an indifference to public safety. The 9th Circuit panel shows no deference to the state court as required under AEDPA and simply injects its own opinion. As noted above, the Supreme Court has reversed the 9th Circuit for its two previous opinions invalidating the "Three Strikes Law."

California Attorney General Brown took no action to review this case in the Supreme Court.

Smith v. Doe, 538 U.S. 84 (2003)
Reversing the 9th Circuit decision in *Smith v. Doe,* 259 F.3d 979 (9th Cir. 2003)
On the same day the Supreme Court reversed the 9th Circuit in the Three Strikes case (*Lockyer v. Andrade*), the justices reversed another 9th Circuit case from an Alaska state court: *Smith v. Doe.* The Alaska legislature had enacted a statute requiring convicted sex offenders to register with a local police department and notify the department of any change of address. Two plaintiffs, identified in court as Does, filed a petition seeking to void the Alaska statute on grounds they were not subject to its provisions because the registration and notice requirements were punitive and violated a Constitutional provision prohibiting enforcement of legislation for crimes committed prior to enactment of the new law. Petition denied by the state court.

The district court also denied the petition. The Does appealed to the 9th Circuit. In its decision, the 9th Circuit panel cited AEDPA but held federal habeas corpus review of state court decisions should be reviewed [anew]. The State of Alaska sought review of the 9th Circuit decision in the Supreme Court and said this: "We disagree with this approach [of the Ninth Circuit] . . . and the only question that matters . . . [is] whether a state court decision is contrary to, or involved an unreasonable application of, clearly established [Supreme Court] law." In effect, the 9th Circuit had relied on the wrong law.

Although the case is a procedural one, i.e., determining whether the statute applied to the Does, the Supreme Court decision essentially upheld the law against a challenge to its validity and enforcement. The 9th Circuit worried that the statute would make the Does *completely unemployable* (emphasis in the original) because "employers will not want to risk loss of business when the public learns that they have hired sex offenders." The Supreme Court responded, "This is conjecture." As to the balance of the 9th Circuit decision, the Supreme Court said: "Neither argument [against enforcing the statute] is persuasive."

In summary, that the 9th Circuit disallowed enforcement of a sex offender registration statute enacted in every state of the union despite evidence the "risk of recidivism is frightening," according to the U.S. Department of Justice: "When convicted sex offenders reenter society, they are much more likely than any other type of offender to be rearrested for a new rape or sexual assault [citing Department of Justice statistics]. The 9th Circuit decision would also have eviscerated the California statute (known as Megan's Law).

When the Supreme Court returned this case to the 9th Circuit, the two Does argued that the statute violated the substantive Fourteenth Amendment Due Process "rights to life, liberty and property." Because the 9th Circuit in its original decision had stricken the statute on other grounds, this allegation had never been addressed. This case is another illustration of the duplicity of the 9th Circuit in not deciding all issues in one decision. By doing this, when the Supreme Court reverses a 9th

Circuit decision and returns the case to that court, the judicial panel can again decide to invoke habeas corpus on previously undecided grounds. This practice is routine in death penalty cases, and increases costs, wastes judicial resources and undermines finality of cases.

When the Supreme Court did return the case, the 9th Circuit panel did exactly that. The 9th Circuit panel denied the Due Process contention but only reluctantly, and peevishly, by writing this:

> "The [Supreme] Court has described the 'fundamental' rights protected by substantive due process as 'those personal activities and decisions that this Court has identified as so deeply rooted in our history and traditions, or so fundamental to our concept of constitutionally ordered liberty, that they are protected by the Fourteenth Amendment.' We [the Ninth Circuit] *are forced to conclude* that persons who have been convicted of serious sex offenses do not have a fundamental right to be free from registration and notification requirements set forth in the Alaska statute. While fundamental liberty interests require that any state infringement of these rights be 'narrowly tailored to serve a compelling state interest,' state actions that implicate anything less than a fundamental right require only that the government demonstrate a 'reasonable relation to a legitimate state interest."
>
> "As the [Supreme] Court has already determined in *Smith v. Doe*, the statute's provisions serve a legitimate non-punitive purpose of public safety, which is advanced by alerting the public to the risk of sex offenders in their community.' Moreover, the [Supreme] Court held the broad categories of offenses differentiated in the Act and the corresponding length of the reporting requirement, are reasonably related to the danger of recidivism, and this is consistent with the regulatory objective. Thus, although the Does possess liberty interests that are indeed important, Smith v. Doe precludes our

granting them relief . . . Because we do not believe that [Supreme Court cases] permit us to reach any other result in this case, we conclude that the Alaska law does not violate the Does' rights to substantive due process."

This petulant language speaks for itself and confirms the ideological bent of the 9th Circuit.

B. The Federal Cases

In this section the focus is on trials in federal court, but criminal procedure is roughly similar to state court. Several of the cases selected differ in content from state cases but nonetheless represent the policy of the 9th Circuit. These cases are heard on "direct appeal" from district courts as distinct from habeas corpus cases heard collaterally from previous convictions in state courts.

After the judge informs an arrestee of the charges, and considers bail (or custody), defense counsel can file a variety of motions challenging the charges alleged by the prosecution. For example, contending the arrest and search were invalid under the Fourth Amendment; the confession was the product of noncompliance with a judicially invented rule to advise him of his right to counsel and to decline answering questions; demanding personnel records of the arresting officers; or requesting disclosure of any evidence in police or prosecution custody favorable to a defense or warranting a reduction in sentence.

The district court judge hearing on these issues will determine whether the challenged evidence is admissible prior to selection of the jury. If the judge concludes a violation of federal law has occurred, the penalty is exclusion of some or all the incriminating evidence. Of course, that decision is subject to appeal to the 9th Circuit under certain circumstances.

As in state cases, arrestees are entitled to release from custody without any type of security for subsequent appearances in court if they can establish a commitment to return for further proceedings (release on one's "own recognizance") and abide by certain restrictions imposed by the court. In the alternative, the arrestee must post "bail" (security or cash) to assure his reappearance. In the vast majority of cases, arrestees are unable exercise either option and must remain in jail until the next scheduled hearing. Needless to say, prosecution and defense counsel engage in arguments to the court arguing over the necessity of either bail or release on certain conditions.

1. Pre trial Release from Custody and Bail

In determining whether to "set bail" the court must consider a number of factors: the gravity of the crime, the longevity of an arrestee's life in the community, drug and alcohol history, prior arrests and convictions, probation or parole status. Various "bail bond" offices near the courthouse commit to assuring future appearances of the arrestee who must post a bond. Failure of the arrestee to appear in court forfeits the bond and the court issues a "bench" warrant for arrest of the fugitive. To recapture the party who does not return to court on a scheduled date, the bail bond company may employ "bounty hunters," although law enforcement agencies re arrest fugitives in most cases.

U.S. v. Scott, 450 F.3d 863 (9th Cir. 2006)

As noted above, after an arrest occurs a Nevada statute required anyone released from custody on their "own recognizance" (O.R.) to sign a form agreeing to comply with certain conditions. Under the statute in drug-related cases, the accused defendants agrees to submit to random testing enforced by police searches of their house for drugs at any time and without a warrant. Scott was arrested for drug possession and signed the "consent to search" form permitted by the statute to secure his release from custody. Later, officers went to Scott's house, administered a drug test that registered positive, and a search revealed a shotgun.

The federal grand jury indicted Scott for unlawful possession of a firearm by a felon. Scott subsequently filed a motion to suppress the weapon as evidence at trial on the grounds the officers lacked neither "probable cause" to search nor possessed a search warrant to search his house. The trial judge in district court denied his motion, but on appeal of this ruling to the 9th Circuit a majority panel disagreed and suppressed the shotgun from admissibility in evidence.

In the full court (en banc) review of this decision the 9th Circuit judges argued that pretrial release of a person charged with a crime is distinct from restrictions imposed on probationers and parolees who have been convicted of a crime. Citing one of its own previous decisions prohibiting searches of individuals on probation, a case subsequently reversed by the Supreme Court, the 9th Circuit panel required an "individualized" governmental reason for requiring pretrial release of arrestees in custody to submit to search and seizure of their person and property.

The dissenting judges in U.S. v. Scott wrote: "The majority's ground-breaking opinion misconceives the reality of pretrial release and the applicable constitutional principles, and substantially undermines and seriously burdens pretrial release proceedings in the nine states covered by our Circuit. I cannot endorse their flawed approach . . . we regrettably succumb to a dangerous, disruptive and poorly conceived sea change foisted upon all the states and federal district courts encompassed by Ninth Circuit [jurisdiction]. Allowing the panel majority decision to stand distinguishes our circuit's pretrial release procedures from every other circuit in a manner detrimental to both prosecutors and defendants alike."

The dissent is not alone. The California Supreme Court specifically approved warrantless searches in conjunction with pretrial release. Scott is another example of naïveté inflicted on the people by the 9th Circuit majority. Apparently indifferent to the vast number of crimes committed by narcotic users, and ignoring the discovery of a shotgun in Scott's house, the court suppressed the evidence. No better example of abuse of the Fourth Amendment exclusionary rule is illustrated than by this case, as discussed in Chapter 7 on Search and Seizure.

Had this case been filed in a Nevada state court the result would have been different. The Supreme Court had previously removed federal habeas corpus jurisdiction from state court decisions on search and seizure in cases where the defendant alleges invalidity of an arrest and search; *Stone v. Powell*. The 9th Circuit cannot invalidate the arrest and search *per se* in state court, but it achieved the goal of suppressing evidence indirectly when the government filed the *Scott* case in federal court.

The U.S. government took no action to seek review in the Supreme Court. The record also does not disclose the reasons for prosecutors filing the case in federal court instead of state court.

U.S. v. Twine, 344 F.3d 987 (9th Cir. 2003)
Rehearing denied, 362 F.3d 1163 (9th Cir. 2004)
Here are the facts in this case as summarized in U.S. v. Twine: Twine was arrested in possession of a firearm and had been previously convicted of a felony. Under federal law, at least two factors are considered in setting bail: the "dangerousness" of the crime, and whether the crime alleged is a crime of "violence" as defined by the relevant federal statute. The district court held the statute sufficiently clear to conclude Twine "dangerous" and possession of a firearm an "act of violence."

On appeal from that decision, is Twine entitled to bail? What justification is there for a felon to carry a firearm given the high rate of recidivism among state and federal prisoners? According to the 9th Circuit, the scenario in *Twine* was neither "dangerous" nor does the act of possessing a firearm qualify as a "crime of violence." What do people (and felons) do with guns? But in the 9th Circuit, without any citation of previous decisions or authority to support its decision, Twine could not be considered "dangerous" under the statute and should be released on bail. This interpretation of the federal statute for a felon in possession of a firearm is inconceivable.

As frequently noted in other chapters, the 9th Circuit is oblivious to public safety in this case and in others. The average person confronted with the set of facts described above would not hesitate to disallow bail. Yet no other judge in the 9th Circuit disagreed with the decision of the three-judge panel when the court denied a petition for rehearing.

2. Pleas of Guilty

Federal crimes are often serious felonies and carry lengthy sentences. As a result, when a defendant pleads guilty to a crime in federal court, (or in state courts), the judge explains significant legal protections to confirm the plea is entered knowingly and voluntarily. Anyone accused of a crime is advised of the Sixth Amendment right to a jury trial; to confront witnesses; and the Fifth Amendment right not to incriminate themselves.. The U.S. Attorney representing the federal government often consults with counsel for defendants and they frequently work out "plea bargains." The prosecution will recommend a sentence in exchange for a defendant's plea of guilty, and both sides thereby avoid a jury trial. The defendant agrees to enter a plea, but with an understanding that the judge is not necessarily committed to abide by the terms. Defendants who do not enter a plea risk a jury trial, and, if the jurors find them him guilty, the court will frequently sentence more severely than the terms of the plea bargain.

U.S. v. Ruiz, 536 U.S. 622 (2002)
Reversing the 9th Circuit decision in *U.S. v Ruiz,* 241 F.3d 1157 (9th Cir. 2002)
The majority of criminal cases in state and federal courts are resolved by pleas of guilty. As noted above, prior to pleading "guilty" the defendants in most cases are required to sign an agreement waiving their Constitutional rights. Although the prosecution must disclose evidence in its possession

favorable to the defendant, or in mitigation of the sentence prior to trial, the plea agreement also requires the defendant to waive (surrender) an appeal to any evidence that might contradict the prosecution witnesses.

The defendant Ruiz ultimately pled guilty to unlawful drug possession, refusing to accept the government's offer to recommend reducing the penalty (the plea bargain) but later he was disappointed with the sentence imposed by the court. The district court denied her request to withdraw the plea. Ruiz appealed to the 9th Circuit, contending the requirement in the plea bargain to waive the right to obtain evidence favorable to her violated her Constitutional right to due process and could not be enforced.

The 9th Circuit agreed and reversed the district court judge ruling. The U.S. government sought review in the Supreme Court, contending mandatory disclosure of evidence to a defendant applies only to trials, not entry of pleas. The Justices granted the request. Not only did the Supreme Court reverse the 9th Circuit, it characterized the unprecedented decision as dangerous, irresponsible, and exposing government agents to retaliation and death. The Court wrote:

> "The Ninth Circuit's rule risks premature disclosure of Government witness information, which . . . could disrupt ongoing investigations and expose prospective witnesses to serious harm . . . We have found no legal authority embodied either in the [Supreme] Court's prior cases or in cases from other [circuit courts] that provides significant support for the Ninth Circuit's decision.
>
> Consequently, the Ninth Circuit's requirement could force the Government to abandon its general practice to a defendant pleading guilty to any information that would reveal the identities of cooperating informants, undercover investigators or other prospective witnesses. We cannot say that the Constitution's Due Process Clause requirement demands so radical a change in the

criminal justice process to achieve so comparatively small constitutional benefit."

The Supreme Court language could not be more explicit. The 9th
Circuit decision was not only unsupported by any case law, it exposed
men and women to serious harm or death in retaliation for disclosure
of their identity. This decision was not only groundless and lacking any
semblance of "Due Process," the court endangered lives and undermined
public safety.

U.S. v. Benitez, 542 U.S. 74 (2004)
Reversing the 9th Circuit decision in *U.S. v. Benitez,* 310 F.3d 1221 (9th
Cir. 2002).
In this case the prosecutor warned Benitez in court that if he pled guilty
the judge might not necessarily impose a particular sentence. The judge
failed to orally inform Benitez he could not withdraw his plea if the
district court judge did not accept the prosecution recommendations.
Nevertheless, Benitez did sign a written plea agreement specifically
informing him of the "conditional" plea. After entering his plea of guilty,
Benitez sought to set it aside six months later, but during a court hearing
he stated "at no time have I decided to go to any trial." The district court
judge denied a motion to withdraw the plea and Benitez appealed to the
9th Circuit.

The 9th Circuit reversed on the grounds a court rule required the trial
judge to admonish the defendant of the conditional plea. Accordingly, the
failure to do so warranted reversal of the judgment on grounds substantial
rights were affected and the failure to warn was clearly erroneous. The federal government sought review in the Supreme Court. Reversed.

The Supreme Court wrote in *Benitez*: ". . . but "the standard [used
by the 9th Circuit Court of Appeals] does not allow consideration of any
record evidence tending to show that any misunderstanding was inconsequential to the defendant's decision . . . [R]elevant evidence that the

Court of Appeals thus passed over . . . included [defendant's] statement that he 'did not intend to go to trial' and that his counsel confirmed that fact. Other matters [escaping] notice under the 9th Circuit's test are the overall strength of the Government's case and any possible defenses that appear from the record." The Supreme Court unanimously reversed the 9th Circuit.

When the Supreme Court returned the case to the 9th Circuit, here is its response upon receiving the Supreme Court order: "Pursuant to the Supreme Court's decision in this case . . now AFFIRM [capitalization in the original] the conviction. Our decision does not affect Benetiz's right to file a petition for habeas corpus."

What right does a court have to suggest this kind of gratuitous information? The only claim Benitez filed was to challenge his plea.. The Supreme Court denied his absurd request and told the 9th Circuit of its error. Habeas corpus would only allege the same factual scenario. No trial had been held, and the only allegation on appeal challenged the plea. This kind of conduct unquestionably confirms the 9th Circuit attempts to sidestep the Supreme Court and impose an unnecessary case load on the courts and a financial burden on the taxpayer. After reading the Supreme Court decision, one of the 9th Circuit judges conceded that two of its other cases previously decided were, in effect, overruled by the Supreme Court reversal.

3. Federal Trials and Investigation

U.S. v. Ressam, 553 U.S. 572 (2008)

Reversing the 9th Circuit decision in *U.S. v. Ressam,* 474 F.3d 597 (9th Cir. 2007)

In attempting to enter the United States from Canada in his vehicle, Ahmed Ressam gave false information of his identity to a border inspector. At a secondary Customs location, agents discovered explosives in the trunk of his car intended for use in a terrorist attack in California. After his arrest, the U.S. Attorney General charged Ressam with violating a federal statute by "making a false statement to customs officials and carrying explosives during the commission of a felony." Convicted of both crimes in district court, Ressam appealed to the 9th Circuit.

The 9th Circuit panel majority of judges (2-1) interpreted the statutory language "during the commission of a felony" to require a "relationship" between the underlying felony (in this case giving false information to the Customs officer) and the act of carrying explosives. Finding none, the court reversed the conviction on that charge. Not only did the 9th Circuit panel ignore decisions of two other Circuit Courts of Appeal on the same issue, the court also relied on one of its own prior cases as precedent despite the fact that case was decided prior to Congressional amendment of the statute.

Because of the three-judge panel split decision, the entire 9th Circuit panel of judges (full court) reheard the case. Despite the obvious need to correct the original panel decision, a majority of the court declined a rehearing over the objection of six judges. Here is an excerpt from the dissenting judge, minus a chilling description of the evidence of potential death to untold numbers of California citizens if Ressam had succeeded in his plans. "I dissent from the denial of rehearing en banc (full court) because we have not only usurped the congressional function, but have also created a split of authority with every other United States Court of Appeals that has addressed this question."

The Supreme Court granted review of the case. In a brief 8-1 decision the Court rejected 9th Circuit reasoning and was peremptorily dismissive of the decision. "There is no need to consult dictionary definitions of the word 'during' in order to arrive at the conclusion that [Ressam] engaged in the precise conduct described [in the statute]. The term 'during' denotes a temporal link; that is surely the most natural reading of the word as used in the statute. Because [Ressam's] carrying of the explosives was contemporaneous with his violation of the statute (false information to customs agent), he carried them 'during' that violation." The statutory language was so obviously unambiguous that two of the Justices concurred in a single sentence, impliedly reversing the 9th Circuit decision without the necessity of even writing an opinion.

The Supreme Court reversed the 9th Circuit decision and returned the Ressam case to that court. Here is the edited language of the 9th Circuit upon receiving the case from the Supreme Court: "The mandate [order] of the United States Supreme Court having issued on Ahmed Ressam's appeal from his conviction for carrying an explosive during the commission of a felony is issued." Not a word was included about the Supreme Court "reversing" the 9th Circuit.

On the same day the Supreme Court reversed the 9th Circuit in *U.S. v. Ressam*, the Justices also reversed *U.S. v. Rodriguez*. Although the Supreme Court decision in *Rodriguez* is a technical review of sentencing under federal law, the government argued that the defendant's five-year sentence imposed by the district court should have been ten years. The 9th Circuit, opting for leniency, affirmed the five-year sentence for the defendant who was previously convicted of three prior felonies before being arrested and convicted of possession of a firearm.

The U.S. Attorney sought review in the Supreme Court. In granting review of the Rodriguez case, the Supreme Court noted this in reversing the 9th Circuit: "The Ninth Circuit's holding that the maximum term was five years contorts [the statute's] plain terms." The Justices used similar language in *Ressam* when it held that the 9th Circuit ignored the simple term "during."

The *Ressam* case was returned to the district court judge who sentenced Ressam disproportionately low under federal sentencing guidelines. The government appealed to the 9th Circuit again, arguing the leniency of the sentence. This time the 9th Circuit panel agreed and returned the case to the district court judge for resentencing.

Ashcroft v. Al-Kidd, 131 S.Ct. 2074 (2011)

Reversing the 9th Circuit decision in *Al-Kidd v. Ashcroft,* 580 F.3d 949 (2010); Rehearing of the case by the 9th Circuit denied in 598 F.3d 1129 (9th Cir. 2010)

The philosophic split among 9th Circuit judges is dramatically displayed in this case. Immediately after 9-11, when the horrific and unprovoked attack of fanatic Muslims killed approximately three thousand innocent American citizens, the unprepared federal government began a series of defensive measures to foreclose another attack and simultaneously secure the country. The United States was not prepared to surrender in 2001 any more than in 1941 when it undertook to defend itself against a similar Japanese attack at Pearl Harbor.

Attorney General John Ashcroft and the Bush administration (of President George W. Bush) developed a series of actions in a desperate attempt to defend the United States against a repetition of such attacks. In a democracy, limitations on the governmental role do not allow the options utilized by some countries' governments to initiate any number of courses of action without accounting for their responsibility. In the United States, the federal government is limited by Constitutional mandate. In a time of crisis, the demands on the government are extraordinary, and officials constrained by law in some cases cannot unilaterally invoke effective measures.

The Attorney General announced he would use every possible legal measure to secure the safety of the American people. He invoked the "Material Witness" Act, a federal statute permitting the Attorney General to detain individuals for future testimony at trial. Abdullah Al-Kidd, a Muslim, was detained. Eventually he was released and never charged with a crime, but he filed a lawsuit alleging the Attorney General personally responsible for his detention. Al-Kidd alleged he had been unlawfully searched and seized in violation of the Fourth Amendment.

Ordinarily, lawsuits filed against government employees in their official capacity allege misconduct in the course of fulfilling their duties. The law recognizes the danger of frivolous lawsuits and, in exchange, federal officials are entitled to personal immunity (not subject to lawsuits) from civil liability. If sued, government officials may file a motion to dismiss the case on grounds of immunity, and they did so in this case. The district court judge granted the government motion and dismissed the case after a hearing.

Al-Kidd appealed to the 9th Circuit, and the judicial panel said, in effect, "No immunity in this case" and allowed the case to go to trial over the objection of the U.S. Government. In effect, the 9th Circuit ruled that Al-Kidd could sue former Attorney General Ashcroft for money damages based on the alleged violation of the Material Witness Act. That interpretation may or may not be legally correct but the Attorney General certainly should not be personally liable for invoking a federal statute under times of extreme distress.

The dissenting 9th Circuit judges n the case skewered the majority reasoning, but an insufficient number of their colleagues agreed to change the decision. In the context of another case, the Seventh Circuit Court of Appeals (another federal appellate court) wrote that the Constitution is not a "suicide pact." Neither is the Material Witness Act. Apparently the 9th Circuit disagreed. How many lawyers will agree to serve as Attorney General if every government decision is subject to litigation alleging personal liability?

The Supreme Court unanimously reversed the 9th Circuit in a cursory decision criticizing the court for using the wrong legal test. The only legal issue in the case involved the reasonableness of a search that led to Al-Kid's arrest. In this case the FBI agents obtained a warrant from a judge containing enough information to warrant Al-Kidd's detention as a material witness. A judicial order to detain a person ought to be enough to immunize the Attorney General. The Supreme Court agreed and reversed the 9th Circuit.

U.S. v. Begay, 567 F.3d 540 (9th Cir. 2009)

A three-judge panel reversed the conviction of Begay in district court. On rehearing, the full panel reversed the district court judge and affirmed the conviction; 591 F.3d 1180 (9th Cir. 2010.).

The overwhelming majority of criminal cases are tried in state court, and appeals are conducted in state appellate courts, but some crimes committed on federal property are prosecuted under federal criminal law. *Begay* involved a crime committed on an Indian reservation, subjecting the culprits to federal law. Two cars met in a preconceived location evidenced by their respective flashing of headlights at each other. Begay exited his car and spoke to the driver of the other car. Returning to his car, he removed a rifle from the rear seat and walked back to the occupants of the other car. Without saying a word, he fired the rifle thirteen times at the driver, killing him instantly. The passengers died several days later.

Convicted by the jury of murder in district court, Begay appealed. The crime of murder in the first degree requires evidence of a state of mind that includes "premeditation, that is, contemplating and deliberating the act of killing, and a malicious state of mind. Otherwise, in the absence of malice or premeditation the crime is manslaughter, and the difference in sentencing in the event of a conviction is substantially different.

On appeal to the 9th Circuit from the conviction in district court, and indifferent to the jury verdict, the three-judge panel found no "premeditation." What other state of mind could have existed? Begay did not act in self defense, and did not act "in the heat of passion" (manslaughter). Regardless of what was said between the parties, no conduct of the victims provoked him. He spoke to the occupants of another car, walked over to his car containing a rifle, walked back to the victims' car, and shot them. He obviously had enough time to contemplate his act and possessed the means of carrying it out.

The 9th Circuit panel reversed the conviction. Assuming no evidence of "premeditation," most judges would vacate the first degree murder conviction and enter a conviction for second degree murder or manslaughter. Not in the 9th Circuit. According to the 9th Circuit panel, in order to vacate a conviction and impose a different crime, the Attorney General must present that argument to the court, and the trial judge can resentence the defendant. Since the Attorney General did not raise that issue, said the 9th Circuit panel, both convictions are set aside. This "reasoning" speaks for itself.

Undoubtedly the U.S. Attorney thought the evidence sufficient for murder, and to ask for a lesser sentence as an alternative was irrelevant. As a result of the 9th Circuit panel decision, the conviction for murder was set aside and Begay was convicted of neither one. The full panel of the 9th Circuit granted a rehearing in this case and reversed the original panel decision. The language of reversal consisted of nothing more than writing the obvious result that the evidence warranted a conviction for murder.

U.S. v. Miguel, 338 F.3d 995 (9th Cir. 2003); 425 F.3d 1237 (9th Cir. 2005)

After several young Asian men spent the night drinking and engaging in debauchery, they decided to rob the occupants of a cabin located at a nearby U.S. Army Recreation Center. During their attempt to break into the cabin, the occupants awoke, yelled at them, and threatened to call the police. One of the group fired a rifle, killing one of the occupants. The group fled. Police subsequently arrested all the participants, including Miguel, a minor, and the U.S. Attorney indicted him for murder on federal property.

Under federal law, officials who arrest a minor held in custody must transfer the arrestee to a juvenile facility (Transfer Act). During the police transfer of Miguel from a juvenile facility to adult custody, he admitted his presence at the scene and told federal agents he accidentally fired the rifle that killed the victim. The prosecution, to avoid severing (separating) the trial of all the young defendants, did not introduce the statement at trial. At trial, two other members of the group identified Miguel as the shooter.

The only physical evidence at the scene was a shell casing discharged from the weapon at the time of the shooting. Miguel did not testify. The jury convicted Miguel and another defendant of felony murder killing in the course of perpetrating a felony (in this case, a burglary). Defense counsel focused on the location of the shell casing and its proximity to the location of Miguel compared to one of the group who testified against Miguel at trial. The defense lawyer contended this witness was closer to the shell casing at the time the rifle was fired and was more likely the shooter. The district court judge, aware of the pretrial ruling not allowing the confession of Miguel, ruled there was no evidence the witness was the shooter, and refused to allow defense counsel to make that argument.

Convicted of murder in district court, Miguel appealed to the 9th Circuit. Despite his confession, the 9th Circuit agreed with defense counsel that the witness who testified against Miguel stood closer to the shell casing and could have been the shooter despite the obvious pandemonium at the scene. And the panel majority also ruled that the district court judge should not have considered the Miguel confession as a factor in disallowing the defense argument.

The Transfer Act assumes the truth of statements made by an arrestee during transfer of custody (in this case, Miguel's admissions) and admissible in evidence. Case law supports the statutory mandate, and the trial court correctly considered Miguel's statement in not allowing it in evidence because of evidence rules. The 9th Circuit panel majority ignores the statute, allows defense counsel to prevent admission of Miguel's confession, and to simultaneously argue that another witness was responsible for the shooting. Defense counsel raised the same argument on appeal as at trial that someone other than Miguel shot the victim only because of the location of the shell casing. The jury rejected this conjecture.

What the 9th Circuit panel majority does not do is concur with the jury verdict. Miguel admitted firing the weapon to federal agents, but defense counsel knew that if Miguel testified at trial the prosecution could rebut any defense argument by introducing the confession in evidence otherwise prohibited by the pretrial agreement. Miguel did not testify despite the evidence.

In effect, the appellate court reweighed the evidence, ignored the fact that the jury believed the witnesses, and accepted defense counsel's argument describing the location of the shell casing as a factor. There was no defense evidence except an isolated shell casing found subsequent to the shooting precipitated by a group of debauched men. The 9th Circuit reversed the case and returned it to the district court for retrial. Quoting the words of a dissenting judge reviewing the evidence in the case, he criticized the majority for retrying the case. As has been noted before in the text, he said: "that's what juries are for."

What are the chances of a retrial and conviction after this passage of time? *Miguel* is a deplorable decision and exemplifies another injustice committed by the 9th Circuit. Inexplicably this unjust decision was denied a hearing in the Supreme Court. There is no record of any retrial.

U.S. v. Hinkson, 526 F.3d 1262 (9th Cir. 2008)
Reversed on rehearing: *U. S. v. Hinkson*, 585 F.3d 1247 (9th Cir. 2009)
Some of the judges on the 9th Circuit act as though their role is a "super trial court," re-reweighing the evidence, speculating on the potential of a different outcome at the trial, and ignoring similar cases previously decided by other courts. Only an insatiable quest for error, unburdened by the inability of the Supreme Court to review 9th Circuit innumerable mistakes, enables these judges to repeatedly ignore juries.

Here are the dissenting judge's opening remarks commenting on the 2-1 judge 9th Circuit panel majority opinion reversing the conviction in *U.S. v. Hinkson*. "In granting a new trial, the majority has assumed the role of super trial court rather than a reviewing court. The bottom line is that nowhere does the majority give any deference to the district court's detailed findings. Instead, in an effort to reconstruct the trial from the bottom up and in hindsight, the majority goes to great length to marshal the evidence, vigorously arguing the facts and the inferences from those facts, and forgetting . . . we cannot simply substitute our judgment for the district court."

What manipulation of the evidence is the dissenting judge referencing? In an unrelated prior trial, defendant Hinkson unambiguously hated an investigator and a prosecutor who had previously conducted an investigation into his business relationships. Hinkson repeatedly urged a man named Joe Swisher to murder these two people as well as the district court judge who presided at the trial. Eventually Swisher reported these threats to the government.

As a witness at the trial, Swisher testified to the threats and to his relationship with Hinkson, which unfortunately ended an unpleasant note. On the witness stand, Swisher wore a small lapel pin on his suit replicating a military Purple Heart medal as evidence of his military experience and honors in the Korean War. Later in the trial, evidence disclosed Swisher had exaggerated his service record and he was impeached by the defense on this point.

The issue of late disclosure of Swisher's false military records at trial led to an investigation by the defense and an extensive discussion with the district court judge. No one questioned Swisher's military record in general, but the misrepresentations regarding his Korean War decorations were the subject of considerable disagreement among the parties. The prosecution conceded Swisher's distortion of his military record, but the defense made only a tepid argument to the jury in its attempt to impeach him. The prosecutor warned defense counsel that any attempt at impeachment would meet with a significant rebuttal of incriminating evidence against Hinkson.

The evidence established that Swisher owned numerous weapons and, coupled with his Korean War experience, qualified him as a candidate of murder for hire. Although Swisher lied about his military record, Hinkson nevertheless believed his expertise in firearms. The prosecutor called numerous other witnesses at trial, and other evidence corroborated Swisher's testimony. The jury convicted Hinkson. After the trial court judge denied a motion for new trial, Hinkson appealed. The 9th Circuit panel majority reversed and ordered a new trial based on evidence "newly discovered" by the defense after the trial confirming Swisher's misstatement of his combat record.

The panel majority consumed endless pages citing the testimony and arguments of counsel during the trial. The result of this review is incomprehensible. The panel majority focused exclusively on the Purple Heart pin and the fabrication of military records. As the dissenting judge points out, wrongfully wearing a lapel pin replicating a Purple Heart medal hardly disqualifies a witness. Falsifying a personnel record is inexcusable, but a trial does not hinge on collateral damage. The principal evidence at trial was Swisher's detailed testimony of threats corroborated by other witnesses. The false recitation of military history, believed by Hinkson, convinced him that Swisher and his war experience in Korea qualified him as an assassin.

At a subsequent court hearing, one witness testified Swisher was obviously attempting to receive additional governmental benefits, and falsified his military records long before Hinkson solicited him for murder. The trial judge had initiated an extensive examination of the military records and, aware of their falsity, denied the motion for a new trial on grounds this extraneous evidence was irrelevant as to Hinkson's state of mind. The prosecution never asked Swisher any questions about his Purple Heart or other medals he was awarded (wrongfully), and focused on the Hinkson threats.

The decision granting Hinkson a new trial is another example of appellate judges inexperienced in jury trials who heard no testimony, observed no witness demeanor, and ignored the decision of the trial judge that no error occurred. As the dissenting judge wrote, the majority acted "as super trial judges" - an all too familiar pattern of 9th Circuit judges.

Unsurprisingly, the full 9th Circuit reheard the case, rewrote the decision in accord with the district court record, affirmed the conviction, and reversed the three-judge panel. The Supreme Court denied review of this decision.

U.S. v. Gonzales, 533 F.3d 1057 (9th Cir. 2008)
When police officers are on trial for allegedly committing violations of federal law, the 9th Circuit ignores inconsistent testimony, downplays legal errors, and dismisses testimony of the officer.
In *U.S. v. Gonzalez* the defendant, a Los Angeles County deputy sheriff, was charged with violations of 18 U.S.C. 242 (inflicting personal injury) on three women. One woman (CeceliaTirado) testified she had been stopped while driving her car in the early morning of July (or August) 2002 by a man dressed as a policeman and carrying a gun. According to the witness, he had driven her around the area and subsequently raped her. The witness testified she had made no report of this incident until six months later when she responded to a police survey of police performance in her area, and identified a City of Southgate police officer as the culprit. Investigators determined the area she described was patrolled by the Los Angeles, County Sheriff. Shown a preselected photo lineup, she identified Gabriel Gonzales. Apparently no formal (in person) lineup was ever conducted.

Witness Kussy Guzman testified she had been stopped in her car late at night in the "last days" of 2002, searched by an officer who touched her hips, waist and breasts, then let her go. She made no report.

Witness Pamela Fields, a prostitute, testified that while walking in the center divider of Long Beach Boulevard late at night in January 2003 she was stopped by an officer who asked her to get into his car. She subsequently engaged in oral sex with him, and the officer let her go. She made no report to police. Later that night, Fields testified she "flagged down" other officers when she encountered them after she "escaped" (quote from the 9th Circuit decision) from the officer who stopped her. These officers testified they observed her in the company of her husband, who was then under a restraining order not to be in her company.

Fields described the circumstances of her encounter to the officers who encountered her walking with her husband, and testified to the license number of the car driven by the officer who stopped her.. An investigating officer subsequently determined the license belonged to a day shift officer of the Sheriff's Department, but the license number sequence was wrong. Fields nevertheless identified Gonzales from photographs.

Another witness, Shirley Munoz, on parole, identified Gonzales as an officer who also had stopped her late at night, touched her hips, waist, and breasts and let her go. She made no report.

Witness Chavez, not alleged by the prosecution as a victim, was also driving late at night and had been stopped by an officer who made her partially undress; put his hands on her breasts and released her. She had made no report to police.

Eventually the investigation focused on Deputy Sheriff Gonzales. The FBI subsequently searched the defendant's on-board computer and the names of Guzman, Munoz, and Chavez "turned up." Gonzales was arrested, indicted, and convicted. He appealed.

The 9th Circuit panel began by conceding that the district court judge committed errors in ruling on the evidence. The court had allowed a police officer to testify to repeat the statement that witness Tirado gave him during the investigation, despite her earlier testimony on the same subject in court through a Spanish interpreter. Under the Federal Rules of Evidence, this repetition translating the same testimony of a witness constitutes inadmissible hearsay by the police officer "vouching," in effect, for a witness's testimony including her identification. The 9th Circuit panel wrote: A jury would "very probably [have] believed that she could remember her assailant" despite the fact she never reported the alleged rape and her identification occurred by viewing photographs of suspects shown to her six months later.

A nurse testified she had examined the witness who told her that Fields had orally copulated an officer. According to the 9th Circuit panel, this qualified as an exception to the hearsay rule under the Federal Rules as a statement made "for the purpose of medical diagnosis or treatment." The court said: "True, she was collecting evidence, but that a forensic function did not obliterate her role as a nurse." But nurses neither diagnose nor treat.

Field's story was also retold in court by an officer who had questioned her after she told them she had "escaped." But they also saw her in the company of her husband in violation of a restraining order. This testimony of her "escape" also qualifies as inadmissible hearsay. "No," said the 9th Circuit panel, this testimony was admissible to rebut her cross examination when she admitted filing a lawsuit against the County, the Sheriff, and Deputy Gonzales. The officers contradicted her testimony that she "flagged them down," and testified they had initiated the contact with Fields due to their awareness of an outstanding restraining order against her husband.

Two of the other witnesses, Chavez and Munoz, neither of whom were named by the prosecution in any charges against Gonzales, testified an officer had stopped them while they were driving their cars, fondled them and let them go. Curiously, the prosecution did not charge Deputy Gonzales with crimes against either Chavez or Munoz, the two women who testified on the issue of "identity" of the suspect (Gonzales), yet they experienced conduct against themselves equivalent to the conduct the prosecution alleged against Tirado, Fields, and Guzman.

In its written decision the 9th Circuit panel wrote: "We have taken note of the minor discrepancies . . . in the witness's accounts." Those "minor discrepancies" would have justified a reversal of the conviction if Gonzales were not a law enforcement officer. The only confirmation of the identity of Gonzales as the culprit was a fingerprint of Fields, a prostitute, found on the defendant's patrol car. This evidence proves she might have been in or near his car as a prostitute. The prosecution introduced no evidence she was injured.

An impartial observer could agree with the 9th Circuit panel - and the jury - although the decision on appeal recites no submission of defense evidence. But the prosecution case consisted of five witnesses, none of whom initially reported misconduct except Fields, and her testimony was contradicted by police witnesses. Tirado identified the defendant as a City of Southgate police officer, never reported the rape, and the court agreed the retelling of her testimony was erroneous. Fields, a prostitute, testified she performed oral sex on the officer, and the fingerprint only confirms she was in or near the car. An officer retold her story in the company of her husband, ostensibly to rebut her testimony that she had filed a lawsuit against the County. Guzman was on parole and was never raped or performed oral sex. Chavez never reported misconduct.

Compare this case with the "baby shaking" case of *Smith v. Patrick* discussed earlier. In that case, the 9th Circuit panel weighed the evidence, accepted the defense version of the evidence, and reversed the conviction. In the *McDonnell v. Brown* case discussed earlier, (the four brothers case), the court repeated the same analysis of defense evidence as in *Gonzales* and agreed with the defense of misidentification. In other words, with an admittedly erroneous admission of evidence in Deputy Gonzales's case, the absence of a report by any of the women alleging misconduct, and a prostitute and a parolee as witnesses, a court could arguably reverse the conviction. Instead, the panel supported the idea that a jury could have "reasonably believed" the women could identify the defendant six months after they were raped, corroborated by testimony from a prostitute and a parolee. Unfortunately the 9th Circuit ignored that perception in cases like *U.S. v. Miguel.*

4. Sentencing

Sentencing in federal cases is similar to state courts except guidelines are different. This Section should be compared with the subsection on sentencing in State Courts in General (this Chapter).

U.S. v. Horvath, 522 F.3d 904 (9th Cir. 2008)

Aside from the issues in a trial, the most controversial component of a criminal case is sentencing. In the vast majority of criminal cases the judge sentences the defendant in a courtroom empty of spectators and occupied only by the judge, the lawyer for the defendant(s), the prosecutor, and court staff. But in highly controversial cases, the press and spectators pack the courtroom, reporters scribble notes, and the TV cameras wait outside. In those cases, whatever the sentence, some proportion of the population rejoices that "justice" has been done while others rail against "injustice." Occasionally, riots or sporadic unlawful activity occur. In most of these controversial cases, the issue is "race." These crowds did not hear the witnesses, did not see the evidence, did not understand judicial rulings, and failed to hear the argument of counsel. The crowd made up their minds before trial without knowing the facts presented in the courtroom.

In any event, sentencing is controversial, but state and federal courts provide the trial lawyers and the defendant with a report prepared by the probation department summarizing the defendant's criminal, mental, and social record to assist the judge in imposing sentence. The probation officer interviews the defendant, if possible, collects information from various interested parties, unearths prior arrests and convictions, and files the report with the judge.

The judge, having heard the evidence at trial and read the report can evaluate the appropriate sentence if the jury convicts. If the defendant pleads guilty, the judge has heard no evidence at all, relies entirely on the probation report. Defense counsel asks for some measure of leniency, arguing any mitigating factors in the report, and the prosecutor often asks for a longer sentence. If the defendant has pled "guilty" the prosecutor may recommend a sentence but the judge is not necessarily bound by it. In California, under its "Three Strikes Law" the judge is mandated to impose a severe sentence if previous convictions of the defendant are proven.

Sentencing is contingent on the personal evaluation made by the judge, and numerous studies disclose divergent sentencing practices among the judiciary. Nothing will change the humanity of the judge, whether sympathetic or not, but state legislatures or Congress can, with some limitations, mandate imposition of sentence terms. The trial judge in a district court sentences often within certain advisory guidelines the Supreme Court has ruled are discretionary, permitting judges to sentence accordingly. Initially, congressional legislation intended the federal guidelines to limit discretion and minimize disparate sentences. Some judges objected to confining their sentencing authority, but the congressional objective was undoubtedly well intentioned. Under the current Supreme Court ruling the guidelines are clearly discretionary and disparate sentences are permissible.

The 9th Circuit judges have reviewed innumerable sentencing decisions of district court judges. Although all cases are essentially fact specific, we can notice how individual trial and appellate judges review sentencing in a general sense when each reads a record differently. The trial judge obtains an indisputably better assessment of the defendant than a court of appeal judge who only reads a cold record.

For example, in *U.S. v. Horvath*, the defendant pled guilty to a federal crime punishing a defendant who lied to a probation officer. A probation officer had interviewed Horvath previously for a crime but he and his father had lied about his military service. During sentencing for the original crime, Horvath's counsel had offered this "mitigating" evidence to reduce the sentence. Investigation led to a determination of the falsity of this mitigating evidence and subsequently the government indicted Horvath for lying to the probation officer.

The details of the court decision are irrelevant, but a 9th Circuit panel inexplicably interpreted the statute inapplicable to a person who lies to a probation officer. The dissent of several judges decried this incredulous decision as irreconcilable with the relevant statute. In reply to the dissent, one of the judges engaged in a judicial screed criticizing the dissenters.

The full court declined to rehear the case, and the U.S. Attorney did not seek review in the Supreme Court.

CHAPTER 5

THE DEATH PENALTY

Introduction

The cases in this Chapter and the Chapter on "The Lawyers" are closely tied together. The chapters overlap because the subject matter is similar, but the cases are selected to demonstrate Supreme Court criticism of the rationale used by the 9th Circuit reversing death penalty cases. Accordingly, some of the cases cited in each chapter are interwoven.

In a sterile downtown Los Angeles courtroom, other "victims" of a murder came forward at a sentencing hearing to confront the man convicted of killing their friends or family members. Not "eyewitnesses" to the commission of any crimes but people with lives shattered by the despicable man who sat before them. Eyeing the killer, one woman said "You should go to hell." Another, "I hate you." The real victims of the crime were dead, but their survivors' lives lay in shambles. None of these survivors suggested abolishing the death penalty. Neither did the jury who voted for capital punishment, nor the judge who sentenced the defendant. No chanting pickets demanding abolition of the death penalty marched outside the courthouse.

In Connecticut, a local church congregation had repeatedly demanded the abolition of the death penalty but became abruptly silent when three of its active members were murdered. Suddenly aware of the difference in safely when criticizing the death penalty from afar, they reeled when they learned "one of our own members," incontrovertibly guilty, was convicted of murder and subject to the death penalty. The previous emotional letters written to the editor abhorring the death penalty vanished, lobbying of their legislators ended, and picketing and marching disappeared. As one parishioner said, "What do you say to their survivors?"

Unfortunately, the voices of retribution will diminish and fade. Time does not march in death penalty cases. It trudges, it slogs, wending its weary way through the courts. Twenty years routinely pass between sentence and completion of seemingly endless appeals. In almost every term of the Supreme Court the Justices reviewed trials conducted decades after conviction and sentence of the defendant.

Defying persistent vocal and written criticism of the death penalty, California voters have endorsed capital punishment for commission of first degree murder committed under statutorily defined "special circumstances." Despite citizen support for the law, the 9th Circuit has imposed procedural barriers interminably delaying imposition of the sentence by invoking the federal law of habeas corpus, a doctrine previously discussed, that allows federal courts to review alleged violations of the federal Constitution occurring in state court trials. In all these cases state appellate courts have previously confirmed the conviction and sentence. Abuses of the writ of habeas corpus by the 9th Circuit have resulted in virtual extinction of the death penalty in California and other western states. No other court has contributed more to this inequitable and deplorable consequence.

To some degree, delay in capital cases is understandable. Lengthy trials, innumerable transcripts of mind-numbing testimony, stacks of legal papers and court hearings all contribute to the process of judicial review. Although the Supreme Court has limited imposition of the death penalty to some extent, its decisions have neither challenged the right of states to invoke capital punishment for murder nor sought to directly negate the Eighth Amendment to the Constitutional prohibition against cruel and unusual punishment. The California Supreme Court, statutorily mandated to review every death sentence, has affirmed the vast majority of verdicts of conviction and sentence in California. But the 9th Circuit, when reviewing state court decisions in California and other western states, has repeatedly set these convictions or sentences aside.

Although the Supreme Court has consistently reversed the 9th Circuit, the Justices frequently return the case to the 9th Circuit for "further proceedings consistent with [our] decision]." This order often requires the 9th Circuit to write another decision or transfer the case to the district court for another hearing. Decades pass during this endless process.

Death penalty opponents cite the danger of executing an innocent person- an understandable and legitimate concern. But in all California state court cases reversed by the 9th Circuit during the Supreme Court terms of 2006-2014 every prisoner alleged procedural errors in the course of the trial, and none asserted actual innocence of committing a crime(s).

Reversing convictions for crimes committed ages ago mocks the finality of litigation as echoed in the words of a California appellate court: "[D]elays between commission of the crime and punishment are the direct result of attempts to create perfect due process for those receiving the death penalty. Of course, when the time lag between crime and punishment is more than a quarter of a century, all deterrent effect of the punishment is lost. The truth of the matter is that opponents of the death penalty have won." Unquestionably, this pessimistic assessment rings true in one sense. Yet state court juries nationwide continue to unanimously vote imposition of the death penalty.

Maybe the quotation above is correct, but jurors are ignoring this judicial quote. In 2007 a New York jury voted the death penalty for the murder of a police detective. In 2008 a Los Angeles jury voted the death penalty for the murder of a deputy sheriff and, several weeks later, jurors voted similarly for the serial killer of eleven women. In 2009 the jury voted the death penalty imposed on an arsonist who had set hillside fires causing the death of five firemen. In 2010 the jury convicted and voted the death penalty for a man who had brutally slain four women.

In that particular case, the 9th Circuit had previously reversed the defendant's conviction for a single count of murder. In the retrial the prosecution charged him with four murders, and the jury voted the death penalty again. Jurors who listen to the harrowing testimony in a murder case and vote the death penalty are speaking for the public. Jurors continued to vote the death penalty in 2011, 2012, 2013, and 2014.

Critics of the death penalty abound in the United States. Several polls have allegedly established waning interest in capital punishment, and the Supreme Court has written decisions requiring increased scrutiny of courts that impose the sentence. Yet juries in the western states under federal jurisdiction of the 9th Circuit repeatedly vote the death penalty despite public dissent or judicial obstacles.

The reason for the disconnection between critics of the death penalty and jurors is easily explained. Jurors listen to gruesome, horrific, and chilling tales of premeditated murder committed by those defendants who either previously killed others or led unremittingly violent lives. Jurors considering evidence of overwhelming guilt committed by indifferent and remorseless killers experience little hesitation in voting the death penalty.

The size of California alone accounts for the singular number of murders in this state. Under California law, every death penalty conviction and sentence is automatically reviewed by the California Supreme Court. By any measure this court has repeatedly, although not exclusively, upheld verdicts and sentences in death penalty cases. These California court judges, as well as those of other western states, can only bristle at decisions of the 9th Circuit subsequently reversing an often unanimous state supreme court.

Several years ago, the Supreme Court began to review court state court convictions on grounds the lawyer representing the defendant at trial did not properly prepare for trial, sentencing, or appeal. Although the Justices cautioned federal circuit courts not to "second-guess" defense lawyers in state court trials or impose judicial hindsight of tactical decisions by counsel, the 9th Circuit has repeatedly reversed convictions or sentences on the ground of "ineffective assistance of counsel"(summarized in the next chapter on "The Lawyers)."

The death penalty stirs the passions of those who argue the "evolving values" of society condemn execution of anyone convicted of murder regardless of the brutality or horrific facts of a crime. Critics cite federal and state laws authorizing capital punishment as an exception to the jurisprudence of other countries, and demand rescission of any death sentence imposed by an American court. The argument is essentially a moral objection—not a legal one—to executing anyone regardless of the circumstances. Supporters of this perspective include the European Court of Human Rights, the Supreme Court of Zimbabwe, and the Supreme Court of India.

Here is the response of Supreme Court Justice Thomas to the argument that a prisoner languishing in prison for decades should not be executed:

> "In 1981, the petitioner in this case was convicted and sentenced to death for three brutal murders he committed in the course of a robbery. He spent the next 29 years challenging his conviction and sentence in state and federal judicial proceedings and in a petition for executive clemency. His challenges were unsuccessful. He now contends that the very proceedings he used to contest his sentence should prohibit the State from carrying it out, because executing him after the "lengthy and inhumane delay" occasioned by his appeals would violate the Eighth Amendment's prohibition on "cruel and unusual" punishment.
>
> I [am] unaware of any constitutional support for [this] argument…There is simply no authority in the American constitutional tradition or in this Court's precedent for the proposition that a defendant can avail himself of the panoply of appellate and collateral procedures and then complain when his execution is delayed."

Proponents of the death penalty often speak in terms of retribution for the killing of an innocent person caused by a venal and unrepentant murderer. An irretrievable loss decimates a family, and the crime of murder angers a public revolted by the inexcusable death of the victim. Men and women in law enforcement, repeatedly exposed to the ravages of crime, universally support capital punishment.

As noted earlier, federal interference with state court judgments has not gone unnoticed by Congress. Frustrated by federal court intervention in state court implementation of the death penalty and simultaneous erosion of "finality" in the state court justice system, Congress enacted the Antiterrorism and Effective Death Penalty Act (AEDPA) in 1996. This statute prevents federal courts from setting aside state court convictions and sentences unless those decisions violate "clearly established Supreme Court law" or the state court has "unreasonably" applied correct law to the facts.

AEDPA has not deterred the 9th Circuit in setting aside death penalty cases, and the Supreme Court has conceded the term "unreasonable" is no doubt difficult to define. But the Justices added: "Suffice to say, however, that a state-court factual determination is not unreasonable merely because the federal court would have reached a different conclusion in the first instance. While [t]he term 'unreasonable' is no doubt difficult to define, it is a common term in the legal world and, accordingly, federal judges are familiar with its meaning. We note[d] that even if reasonable minds reviewing the record might disagree about the [state court] finding in question, on [federal court] review that does not suffice to supersede the [state] trial court's determination."

In this Chapter and in Chapter 6 on Lawyers, all of the cases summarized involve crimes of inexcusable brutality and depravity. In Chapter 6 the 9th Circuit repeatedly finds lawyers derelict in presenting a defense, either to the crime or to the death sentence, on the ground of "ineffective assistance of counsel" in their role. These 9th Circuit judges, with only a few exceptions, have never tried a criminal case or presided in a criminal trial. The reasons for emasculating the death penalty are simplistic, naive, unreasonable, and ensue only because of personal opposition to the death penalty. The 9th Circuit has allowed only a handful of executions in a decade of vacating state supreme court decisions, and in one case the Supreme Court had ordered the 9th Circuit not to intervene in the future.

In a case of unmitigated brutality, here is the language of the 9th Circuit Chief Judge dissenting in *Pinholster v. Ayers* and excoriating the majority for setting aside a *1984* death penalty case affirmed in state court:

> "The majority [of a Ninth Circuit court] reaches the contrary conclusion [of deferring to state court decisions] through a series of mistakes that have, unfortunately, *become far too common in our circuit*. First, the majority relies on evidence never presented to the state courts . . . Second, the majority applies retrospectively [in the past] a standard for counsel's performance that bears no relationship to that prevailing in California at the time of Pinholster's trial in 1984.Third, and perhaps worst of all, the majority accords no deference to the California Supreme Court's superior expertise in determining what constitutes competent representation among the members of its bar and the likely consequences (or lack thereof) of any deficient performance.
>
> Few state court judgments can withstand even one such error . . . But in combination they are deadly. I had hoped that our [full court] would sweep away these mistakes and bring our case law into conformity with AEDPA. Instead, the majority repeats and magnifies the errors in these prior cases so that they will be very difficult, probably impossible, for us to correct. This perpetuates a habeas regime where few death sentences are safe from federal judges who know ever so much better than those ignorant state judges and lawyers how capital trials ought to be conducted. Because I don't believe we are the ultimate font of wisdom on such atters, I must dissent. The majority's methodology has become an *unstoppable engine for setting aside death sentences* [emphasis added].

The Supreme Court agreed with this dissent and reversed the 9th Circuit decision in *Cullen v. Pinholster*. This 1984 conviction upheld by the Supreme Court in 2011 chastised the 9th Circuit for allowing Pinholster, despite the statutory limitations of AEDPA, to present evidence in a district court hearing that he had never presented in the state court at any stage of the proceedings. The Supreme Court quoted the dissenting 9th Circuit judge who called that practice "sandbagging."

To demonstrate the decisions of judges who repeatedly reverse convictions and death penalty sentences previously confirmed by state courts, several cases are excerpted from Supreme Court decisions reflecting its frustration and impatience with the 9th Circuit.

Brown (Warden) v. Payton, 544 U.S. 133 (2005)
Reversing the 9th Circuit decision in *Payton v. Brown*, 346 F.3d 1204 (9th Cir. 2003).
In 1980, Payton raped a woman and subsequently stabbed her to death with a butcher knife. He then entered the room where another woman was sleeping with her child. In stabbing this woman and attempting to stab the child, his knife broke and he began searching an adjoining room seeking another knife. When discovered by third parties, Payton dropped a knife he had found and fled the room. At trial, the prosecution introduced evidence that Payton had previously stabbed another woman; committed a prior rape; had been convicted of a drug-related felony. One witness testified to highly graphic conversations with Payton about his distaste for women. The jury convicted Payton and voted the death penalty.

After the California Supreme Court affirmed Payton's conviction and sentence on appeal, he began a series of hearings alleging an erroneous jury instruction. Ultimately the 9th Circuit reversed the death penalty sentence in 2002; *Payton v. Woodford* [Warden]. To justify the reversal, the 9th Circuit had engaged in an incomprehensible rhetorical exercise analyzing the language of a jury instruction read to the jury by the state court judge.

The State of California asked the Supreme Court to review this 9th Circuit decision. The Supreme Court reversed the 9th Circuit, saying: "Jurors do not sit in solitary isolation booths parsing [jury] instructions for subtle shades of meaning in the same way lawyers might. Differences among them in interpreting instructions include a common sense understanding of the instruction in the light of all that has taken place at trial and likely to prevail over technical hairsplitting."

The Supreme Court returned the case to the 9th Circuit, and that court again reversed the trial court invoking a different argument. Defense counsel had introduced evidence at the penalty phase of the trial recounting Payton's religious conversion while in prison. According to the 9th Circuit, the trial court had not included a jury instruction for jurors to specifically consider this evidence as a mitigating factor to deciding the appropriate penalty.

The State of California sought review of this decision, and the Supreme Court reversed the 9th Circuit again. The Supreme Court wrote: "The determination of the California Supreme Court that the text of the jury instruction directing jurors to consider '[a]ny other circumstance which extenuates [reduces] the gravity of the crime even though it is not a legal excuse for the crime allowed the jury to consider . . . mitigating evidence of defendant's religious conversion, was not contrary to or an unreasonable application of precedent of the United States Supreme Court, and the California Supreme Court reasonably applied precedent of the United States Supreme Court.

Yarborough (Warden) v. Gentry, 540 U.S. 1 (2003)
Reversing the 9th Circuit decision in *Gentry v. Roe,* 320 F.3d 891 (9th Cir. 2002).
On the same day the 9th Circuit reversed *Payton* for the first time, the Supreme Court reversed that court in another death penalty case; *Yarborough (Warden) v. Gentry.* The 9th Circuit had criticized the trial

lawyer as "ineffective assistance of counsel," based upon its review of his closing argument at the trial. The Supreme Court, in reversing the 9th Circuit, gave the appellate judges an extensive lecture on trial advocacy, writing that the "Ninth Circuit's conclusion not only that [defense counsel's] performance was deficient, but that any disagreement with that conclusion would be objectively unreasonable gives too little deference to the state courts that have primary responsibility for supervising defense counsel in state criminal trials." On return of the case by the Supreme Court, the chastened 9th Circuit said nothing about its reversal.

Schriro (Warden) v. Smith (Robert), 546 U.S. 6 (2005)
Reversing the 9th Circuit decision in 241 F.3d 1191 (9th Cir. 2001).
Smith was convicted of murder and sentenced to death in an Arizona state court in 1982. He began filing innumerable habeas corpus petitions in federal courts, including one granted by the 9th Circuit but later reversed by the Supreme Court in 1996

As a consequence of a subsequent Supreme Court decision in an unrelated case six years later (*Atkins v. Virginia*), prohibiting execution of mentally retarded state court prisoners, Smith petitioned for another writ of habeas corpus on this same ground. Although the district court judge denied the writ, the 9th Circuit on appeal reversed that decision and ordered the state of Arizona to provide the defendant with a jury trial on the mental incapacity issue discussed by the Supreme Court in the Atkins v. Virginia case. The State of Arizona sought review in the Supreme Court.

The Supreme Court, in its one-page unanimous opinion in *Schriro v. Smith* rendered twenty-five years after Smith's conviction, wrote: "The Ninth Circuit erred in commanding the Arizona court to conduct a jury trial . . . in *Atkins v. Virginia* we stated in clear terms that 'we leave to the States the task of developing appropriate ways to enforce constitutional restrictions upon [their] execution of sentences . . . Arizona had not even had a chance to apply its chosen . . . procedures when the Ninth Circuit preemptively imposed the jury trial condition . . . Because the Court of Appeals exceeded its limited authority the judgment below [in the 9th Circuit] is vacated."

In the *Schriro v. Smith decision* the Supreme Court reversed the 9th Circuit without considering any written argument from Smith's lawyer, required no oral argument, and, in a unanimous opinion, reproached the appellate court. Despite reversing any of the federal Courts of Appeal, the Supreme Court ordinarily writes in restrained judicial rhetoric and explains its rationale in a written decision. Rarely does the Supreme Court summarily reverse an appellate court without even ordering the parties to brief (summarize and orally argue) the issues.

Brown (Warden) v. Sanders, 546 U.S. 212 (2006)
Reversing the 9th Circuit decision in 373 F.3d 1054 (9th Cir. 2004)
The Supreme Court began its 2006-2007 term by reversing the 9th Circuit in a death penalty case originally affirmed on appeal by the California Supreme Court. Sanders began filing a series of petitions for habeas corpus in state court. All petitions were denied at every state court level, and subsequently denied in federal district court. On appeal from the district court, the 9th Circuit granted Sanders's federal petition for habeas corpus based upon its conclusion that the trial court had erroneously instructed the jury. The State of California sought review of that decision in the Supreme Court.

In a seven-to-two decision, the Supreme Court reversed the 9th Circuit and returned the case after extensively reviewing technical rules of sentencing criminal defendants. In its decision, the Court wrote tersely: "Because the jury's consideration gave rise to no Constitutional violation, the Court of Appeals erred in ordering [habeas corpus] relief." The Court order: "Reversed and remanded [to the 9th Circuit] for further proceedings consistent with this opinion.

Undeterred, on return of the case the 9th Circuit wrote an unpublished decision dated March 16, 2006 concluding that Sanders was entitled to another hearing on his claim of "ineffective assistance of counsel." The trial record unambiguously establishes that Sanders had repeatedly ordered his counsel not to introduce mitigating evidence during sentencing, yet the 9th Circuit panel ordered an evidentiary hearing. The court said counsel had a duty to investigate regardless of contrary directions from the client. At the hearing, Sanders presented "mitigating evidence," enough for the 9th Circuit to find counsel at trial was "ineffective" for not introducing this evidence although instructed by his client to do nothing.

This case is another example of the 9th Circuit tactic of not deciding all issues on the first habeas corpus petition filed by an inmate. Initially, Sanders frivolously challenged a jury instruction, but the court said nothing about the role of counsel. After being reversed by the Supreme Court on the jury instruction, and the case returned to the 9th Circuit, it found another ground for reversal.

No further action has been reported for this *1981* conviction. California Attorney General Jerry Brown filed no further request for review by the Supreme Court.

Schriro (Warden) v. Landrigan, 550 U.S. 465 (2007)
Reversing the 9th Circuit decision in 441 F.3d 638 (9th Cir 2006)
On May 14, 2007, one year and two months after the 9th Circuit issued its second decision ordering an evidentiary hearing for Sanders, the Supreme Court reversed another 9th Circuit case on similar facts. Landrigan was convicted of murder in 1982, stabbed another inmate in 1986 and was convicted of assault and battery, escaped from prison and murdered a second person. Convicted of this murder by a jury, he also specifically refused to offer any evidence to mitigate his sentence despite questioning by the trial court on the reason for his refusal to present evidence. The trial court imposed the death penalty.

On appeal of the sentence, the Arizona Supreme Court affirmed the conviction and sentence, as did the district court on habeas corpus. Landrigan appealed that decision to the 9th Circuit, which reversed the sentence, contending the lawyer for Landrigan had failed to present mitigating evidence despite the demands of his client not to do so. The 9th Circuit ruled, in effect, that counsel should have sought mitigating evidence regardless of the client's instructions. The Supreme Court repudiated this rationale and stated the trial record "conclusively dispels that interpretation." This characterization of the 9th Circuit decision is charitable at best, written by the Supreme Court in a brief and summary decision reciting the futility of a "frivolous" and "meritless" claim on appeal. The Court quoted these two words written earlier by the Arizona Supreme Court when it originally confirmed Landrigan's conviction and sentence on appeal. In addition, this decision confirms the 9th Circuit erroneous ruling.

The 9th Circuit subsequently acknowledged its reversal by the Supreme Court (*Landrigan v. Schriro*), and having been obviously chastised, wrote this cryptic remark: "[W]e vacate our [previous] decision . . . [W]e again adopt the three-judge panel holding in *Landrigan v. Stewart*, with respect to additional sentencing issues raised on appeal." A 1982 conviction finally ended, but the language of the court ambiguous as to whether the original sentencing was still viable;

Ayers (Warden) v. Belmontes, 549 U.S. 7 (2006)
Reversing the 9th Circuit decisions in 414 F.3d 1094 (9th Cir. 2004); 608 F.3d 1117 (9th Cir. 2010).
In 1981, Belmontes, armed with a steel dumbbell, entered a home to burglarize the contents. He unexpectedly encountered a young woman and killed her by repeatedly striking her on the head with the dumbbell. The jury convicted Belmontes and voted the death penalty. The state appellate court affirmed the conviction as did the federal district court on habeas corpus.

Belmontes began a series of appeals and filing writs of habeas corpus. The court records reveal endless hearings and rehearings until the 9th Circuit eventually reversed his conviction. The Supreme Court reversed the 9th Circuit and returned the case to that court, ordering the appellate court to reconsider its decision. On return of the case from the Supreme Court, the 9th Circuit again reversed the conviction on exactly the same grounds as the Supreme Court had reversed its previous decision. The 9th Circuit panel seized on a jury instruction that allowed the jurors to consider evidence mitigating imposition of the death penalty, but argued that the instruction misled the jurors.

The state sought review again in the Supreme Court and the Justices reversed the 9th Circuit again. The Supreme Court wrote: "The Court of Appeals erred by adopting a narrow, and, we conclude, an unrealistic interpretation of [the jury instruction] . . . the Court of Appeals' analysis is flawed." During the course of their decision, the Supreme Court chided the 9th Circuit for ignoring its previous decisions. In fact, the Supreme Court had previously reversed the 9th Circuit twice before in other cases challenging the identical jury instruction used in *Belmontes.*

The 9th Circuit decision reversing the *Belmontes* case had not been unanimous among all its judges. Here is what the dissenting judges said: "Twenty-one years after Belmontes' trial and fifteen years after the California Supreme Court ruling [affirming the conviction], the [Ninth Circuit] panel's decision reverses Belmontes' sentence [for mis instructing the jury] . . . This conclusion defies the record and clear Supreme Court precedent . . . The [Ninth Circuit] panel's decision undermines the 'strong policy against retrial after the first trial where the claimed error amounts to no more than speculation . . . The panel reaches its conclusion despite the California Supreme Court's unanimous conclusion that 'no legitimate basis for believing that the trial court misled Belmontes' jury instruction about its sentencing responsibilities.'"

To summarize the history of this case: the California Supreme Court affirmed the conviction on appeal; denied all subsequent petitions for habeas corpus; the district court denied the petition seeking a writ of habeas corpus; and the 9th Circuit granted the writ and was reversed by the Supreme Court twice based upon a jury instruction previously approved by the Justices in an unrelated case. Belmontes was convicted in 1988. The Supreme Court affirmed his conviction in 2006. As one of the dissenting judges in *Belmontes* points out, "the majority opinion citing its own case precedent subsequently reversed, contradicts every precedent previously cited by the Supreme Court." The Supreme Court returned the case to the 9th Circuit for "further proceedings not inconsistent with this opinion."

But the case was not over. On return to the 9th Circuit, Belmontes argued this time that his counsel rendered "ineffective assistance," never having raised this argument before although the majority of the original three-judge panel insists he did raise it in the state court. A two-to-one majority of judges again issued habeas corpus on the usual excuse that counsel had not prepared effectively for sentencing. In an exceedingly lengthy and rambling opinion, the judge authoring the decision again displayed his unambiguous objection to the death penalty on any ground possible. The dissent skewers the majority reasoning.

The full 9th Circuit panel denied a petition to rehear the case. Eight judges dissented, and the author of the *Belmontes* opinion, concurring with himself in denying a rehearing, wrote a pathetic self serving defense of his earlier opinion. He denied that the 9th Circuit had set aside the death sentence for the third time. Apparently he counts differently from anyone else.

Citizens of California should be outraged at this obstruction of justice. Belmontes's appeal of his conviction was denied in the California Supreme Court, and his habeas petitions were denied in state court. Although reversed by the Supreme Court twice, the 9th Circuit reversed the penalty phase of the trial again in an inexcusable defiance of the law. The State of California sought review in the Supreme Court (on March 30, 2009) and the Supreme Court reversed the 9th Circuit again in *Wong v. Belmontes*.

As noted above, Belmontes repeatedly smashed the victim's skull with a dumbbell in the course of burglarizing her home. In setting aside the death penalty a second time, the 9th Circuit wrote that the crime did not involve the victim's "needless suffering." The Supreme Court disagreed, noting,

"We agree with *the state court's* characterization of the murder ('an intentional murder of extraordinary brutality') . . . and [we] simply cannot comprehend [that conclusion] by the Ninth Circuit. The jury saw autopsy photographs showing [the victim's] mangled head, her skull crushed by 15 to 20 blows from a steel dumbbell bar the jury found to have been wielded by Belmontes.

"[The victim's] corpse showed numerous defensive bruises and contusions on [her] hands, arms, and feet, which plainly evidenced a desperate struggle for life at [Belmontes's] hands. Belmontes left [her] to die, but officers found her still fighting for her life before ultimately succumbing to the injuries caused by the blows from Belmontes. The jury also heard that this savage murder was committed solely to prevent interference with a burglary that netted Belmontes $100 he used to buy beer and drugs for the night. [The victim] 'suffered', and it was clearly 'needless.'"

"The evidence of Belmontes' guilt at trial was indisputable and he never alleged factual innocence. In an attempt to submit mitigation evidence at the penalty hearing, defense counsel paraded nine witnesses before the jury. They testified to Belmontes' tumultuous childhood, his religious conversion in prison, and his current good relationship with friends and family. Counsel carefully limited their testimony to avoid the potential for rebuttal by prosecution evidence of Belmontes' prior murder-to which he had confessed to parole authorities and other witnesses. At trial, his defense counsel succeeded in convincing the judge to deny admission of this evidence during the prosecution case in chief. Nevertheless, the judge told defense counsel the prior crime would be admissible as rebuttal in the penalty phase if the defendant attempted to establish mitigation of the sentence by offering his character as a nonviolent person."

The Supreme Court confirmed the strategy of defense counsel in avoiding prosecution rebuttal evidence of the prior murder. But, more critically, the Justices also noted that in the original 2003 decision by the 9th Circuit the court had actually confirmed the "substantial nature" of the mitigating evidence Belmontes presented. In response to that assessment the Supreme Court wrote: "On [return] from [our] Court the Court of Appeals in addressing Belmontes' ineffective assistance [of counsel] for the first time-changed its view of this evidence. Instead of finding [defense counsel's] mitigation case 'substantial,' as it previously had the 9th Circuit this time around labeled it 'cursory.'"

The Supreme Court continued:

"Compare also [the original 9th Circuit decision in Belmontes, labeling the mitigation evidence [defense counsel] presented 'substantial' with the [second decision in Belmontes], labeling the same evidence 'insubstantial.' More evidence, the Court of Appeals now concluded, would have made a difference; in particular, more evidence to humanize' Belmontes, as that court put it, no fewer than 11 times in its opinion...The Court [of Appeals] determined that the failure to put on this evidence prejudiced Belmontes.

In the Court of Appeals' view, Belmontes should have presented more 'humanizing evidence' about Belmontes' difficult childhood and highlighted his positive attributes. But as [we] recounted above and recognized by the state courts and, originally, this very [Ninth Circuit] panel, [defense counsel] did put on substantial mitigation evidence, much of it targeting the same "humanizing' theme the Ninth Circuit highlighted (e.g., effect of death of a ten-month-old sister; difficult childhood; family member's addictions; family strife and abuse; strong character as a child; close relationship with siblings; relationship with grandparents; participation in community religious events.)

In its 'reconsidered 'decision,' the 9th Circuit also criticized defense counsel for not presenting expert witnesses. To this the Supreme Court responded "But the body of mitigating evidence the 9th Circuit would have required [defense counsel] to present was neither complex nor technical. It required only that the jury make logical connections of the kind a layperson is well equipped to make. The jury simply did not need expert testimony to understand the 'humanizing' evidence; it could use its common sense or own sense of mercy."

The Supreme Court ended its decision with this reproach: "It is hard to imagine expert testimony and additional facts about Belmontes' difficult childhood outweighing the facts of [the victim's] murder. It becomes even harder to envision such a result when the evidence that Belmontes had committed another murder, the most powerful imaginable aggravating evidence,' as Judge Levi put it . . . but the notion that the result could have been different if only [defense counsel] had put on more than the nine witnesses he did, or called expert witnesses to bolster his case, is fanciful."

The Supreme Court strains to contain its indignation, but the language clearly reflects not only an impatience with the 9th Circuit but demonstrates evidence of outright contradiction of language - to characterize it mildly. The Supreme Court returned the case to the 9th Circuit, and the panel finally relented with this language: "We have reviewed the briefs filed by the parties following the Supreme Court's issuance of its opinion . . . in *Wong v. Belmontes*. In light of that opinion we are compelled to affirm the district court's order denying the writ of habeas corpus."

In a case decided two months later after this reproach, *Cullen v. Pinholster*, the 9th Circuit again vacated a death penalty verdict oblivious to the Supreme Court decision in *Belmontes*. The Supreme Court reversed the 9th Circuit in this case as well.

Uttecht (Warden) v. Brown, (Cal) 551 U.S. 1 (2007)

Reversing the 9th Circuit decision in 451 F.3d 946 (9th Cir. 2006).

Here is the 9th Circuit description of the defendant in this case: "Cal Brown is not a nice man. In May 1991, he carjacked [the victim] and drove her to a motel . . . Brown robbed, raped and tortured her while holding her hostage for two days. He bound and gagged her, penetrated her with a foreign object, whipped her and shocked her with an electrical cord. Eventually, Brown put [the victim] in the trunk of her car, slit her throat, stabbed her and left her to bleed in a parking lot." The decision then recites similar horrendous conduct perpetrated on another woman. According to the 9th Circuit, Brown is "not a nice man."

In death penalty cases, as discussed earlier in general, the prosecution and defense are both entitled to delve into potential jurors' opinions on the death penalty. Unsurprisingly, both sides disagree on whether a juror's answers to questions disqualify that person from sitting on a jury. The Supreme Court decisions on this issue are fact intensive, and the court reviews the questions asked and answers given to ensure a jury neither death oriented nor death opposed. In all criminal cases, the prosecutor and defense counsel can excuse jurors without explanation based on a statutory right permitted under California law as long as the decision is not based on grounds of ethnicity or gender.

Although the California Supreme Court had previously affirmed Brown's conviction and sentence, a 9th Circuit panel of judges ruling on his petition for habeas corpus, previously denied by a district court judge, concluded that the prosecutor had improperly excused a trial juror. When defense counsel objected at trial to the prosecutor excusing a juror, the trial court held a hearing and denied the objection. Despite a concession by the 9th Circuit panel that the trial judge occupied a position superior to that of an appellate court in determining whether a juror is properly excused, it reversed the conviction. The Supreme Court granted review.

In *Uttecht v. Brown*, on June 5, 2007, the Supreme Court reversed the 9th Circuit, and wrote one of its best decisions in explaining the role of trial courts. When prosecution and defense counsel disagree on whether a party is legally entitled to excuse a prospective juror, the trial court must hold a hearing outside the presence of the jury and make a decision. The Supreme Court had unequivocally explained in a previous case: "The trial court bases its judgment [in excusing a juror] in part on the juror's demeanor, a judgment owed deference by [appellate] courts. The trial court is in a superior position to assess demeanor, a factor critical in assessing the attitude and qualifications of potential jurors." The 9th Circuit judges recited this formula in their *Uttecht v. Brown* decision and then ignored it.

The Supreme Court also cited the federal statute governing appellate review of state court convictions pursuant to petitions by a convicted defendant seeking habeas corpus. "The Anti Terrorism Effective Death Penalty Act (AEDPA) requirements provide additional and binding directions to accord deference [to state courts], creating an independent and high standard to be met before a federal court sets[aside] state court rulings." And the conclusion: "By not according the required deference [in *Brown*] here, the 9th Circuit failed to respect the limited role of federal habeas relief in this area." No need to read between these lines. The 9th Circuit is put on notice. Reversed and returned to the 9th Circuit.

Brown v. Uttecht, 530 F.3d 1031 (9th Cir. 2008)
On return of the case to the 9th Circuit from the Supreme Court in *Uttecht v. Brown*, 551 US1 (2007). The reversal of the 9th Circuit decision by the Supreme Court in *Uttecht v. Brown* did not terminate the case.

After its reversal and return of the case in a post conviction hearing held by the district court, defense counsel in the original trial described his herculean efforts to avoid the jury from voting the death penalty, including retention of a "mitigation specialist," an investigator, a social worker, three lawyers, and a clinical psychologist. Counsel explained his trial strategy to the district court in detail and presented a formidable case. That court denied the petition, and an appeal to the 9th Circuit followed. Two of the three 9th Circuit judges concurred and affirmed the denial of habeas corpus. Despite the overwhelming evidence presented in support of defense counsel's strategy, and in spite of the reproach issued by the Supreme Court in the original case reversing the 9th Circuit, one judge dissented. (The same judge who has never affirmed any death penalty case).

Part of the reason for the errors of several 9th Circuit judges in reviewing state court convictions is their absence of prior trial experience. Reviewing a cold record of the trial, unaware of the chemistry of a criminal trial, unfamiliar with trial strategy, and ignoring their role as appellate judges, these 9th Circuit judges repeatedly reverse cases to the dismay of state court judges, prosecutors, and witnesses who must be located to relive the emotional expense of a second trial. In cases of defendants convicted a quarter century ago, this delay almost guarantees interring the death penalty.

The Supreme Court denied Brown's petition for review (*Uttecht v. Brown*).

Clark v. Brown (Warden), 450 F.3d 898 (9th Cir. 2006)

Under established Supreme Court law, erroneous state court rulings on jury instructions are not subject to federal appellate review unless "[it] so affected the entire trial that the resulting conviction violates due process; *Lewis v. Jeffers*. In 2006, under the rubric of "Due Process," the 9th Circuit reversed Clark's *1982* conviction. In his trial alleging a vicious premeditated murder by arson, Clark testified he committed the crime and described the facts in detail. Guilt was never an issue and the jury sentenced him to death.

In *Clark v. Brown* the prosecution had charged Clark with rape, murder of multiple victims, and arson. The rape (of Clark's former wife) occurred on the evening of November 19, 1981. When Clark told her his mother was very ill, she admitted him to her apartment. He then forced her to submit to sexual intercourse. The other offenses were committed on January 6, 1982, when Clark, after throwing gasoline into a home occupied by a man, a woman, and their infant daughter, ignited the gasoline vapors with high-way flares. The male victim, who suffered second and third degree burns over 90 percent of his body, died on January 14, 1982. His wife was so seriously burned that she was hospitalized for ten months, lost her fingers and nose, and suffered additional permanent injuries. The child was rescued unharmed by a heroic neighbor.

The jury convicted Clark. On automatic appeal from the conviction, the California Supreme Court reviewed an earlier case it had authored that sought to draw a distinction between a jury instruction on murder in the course of committing certain felonies (felony murder), and a felony murder "special circumstances" jury instruction rendering the defendant potentially death eligible; *People v. Green*. In *Green* the trial court had failed to distinguish these instructions for the jury. According to the California Supreme Court in Green, the "special circumstances" referred to in these instructions are not established "if the arson was merely 'incidental' to the commission of the crime." Whether this semantic distinction registered with the jury is questionable in light of the evidence.

The California Supreme Court acknowledged the confusing language of the jury instruction in the previous *Green* case, revised its interpretation, and held that the overwhelming evidence nevertheless established defendant's guilt and sentence of death regardless of any instructional error. The 9th Circuit seized on this admission as an impermissibly retroactive change in the law violating the Due Process Clause of the Fourteenth Amendment. Engaging in a rhetorical and semantic distinction of a jury instruction only a linguist could understand, the author of the 9th Circuit decision concluded with this remark: "This new interpretation and its retroactive application were unexpected and indefensible." Regrettably, this sophistry eluded the Supreme Court, and on November 6, 2006 the Justices denied a hearing for a crime that occurred in 1986.

*Williams v. Woodford.*384 F.3d 567 (9th Cir. 2004)

In 1981, a jury convicted Williams of four counts of murder and armed robbery, and the court sentenced him to death. The California Supreme Court reviewed his case on appeal and affirmed the conviction after conducting an evidentiary hearing in response to Williams's petition for habeas corpus. Upon denial of that request, Williams sought review in district court, but the court denied the petition. Surprisingly, the 9th Circuit panel confirmed the denial on appeal.

The defendant's request for a rehearing by the entire 9th Circuit was also denied but not without a group of dissenting judges who complained the composition of the jury lacked any black jurors. What transpired was a dissertation on social science methodology and the familiar complaints about injustice. Of course none of the judges attended the trial and, as frequently observed by the Supreme Court, the trial judge is the best judge of impermissible rejection of jurors. Interestingly, the complaint about the composition of the jury arose neither on appeal to the California Supreme Court, nor in the district court, but only on appeal to the 9th Circuit.

The facts of this case are horrendous. The defendant, a gang member, shot a convenience store clerk in cold blood during a robbery. Several weeks later he killed two motel operators. The prosecution produced numerous witnesses, and police found a shotgun in defendant's possession that matched the bullets removed from the dead victims. After denying Williams' petition for habeas corpus, the panel of 9th Circuit judges could not help soliciting consideration for him: "We note, however, that the federal courts are not the only forum for relief, and that Williams may file a petition for clemency with the Governor of California . . . We are aware of Williams' Nobel Peace Prize nomination for his laudable efforts opposing gang violence from his prison cell, notably his line of children's books and his creation of the Internet Project for Street Peace."

This solicitude for a gang member who intentionally killed four innocent people is deplorable. In denying a panel rehearing of this decision, and despite the overwhelming evidence of Williams' guilt, several 9th Circuit judges argued for reversal of the conviction.

Despite affirmance of the conviction, the State of California sought review in the Supreme Court. The defendant had contended he was "factually innocent." The State replied that the 9th Circuit judges had required only a low threshold of evidence in order to establish "factual innocence" offered by an inmate. The State argued this allegation contradicted Supreme Court law and all other federal circuit court judges who require an extraordinarily high threshold to establish this defense. The State urged the Supreme Court to review the Williams case solely on its evidentiary ruling prospectively jeopardizing untold numbers of convictions. Regrettably, the Supreme Court denied the request. "Finality" of litigation in the 9th Circuit is an illusion.

Smith (Joe) v. Arizona, 128 S.Ct. 466 (2007)
Republished in 552 U.S. 985 (2007) denying review of the 9th Circuit 2-1 decision granting habeas corpus for resentencing the defendant. The excerpt here includes the dissenting language of the judge in *Smith v. Stewart*, 189 F.3d 1004 (1999).

On October 15, 2007 the Supreme Court denied a hearing to Joe Smith who had been sentenced to death in 1976. A state court jury had convicted Smith, who was on probation for rape at the time of the murders, based on evidence of a brutal and senseless killing. Police found the nude bodies of two women in a ditch with dirt in their taped-shut mouths, causing asphyxiation. Both women were bound at their wrists and ankles, stab wounds in their pubic region, vaginal tears caused by penetration, and needles inserted in their breasts. The jury found Smith guilty and sentenced him to death.

After the Arizona Supreme Court affirmed his conviction on appeal, Smith filed a petition for a hearing subsequently denied in state court. He sought habeas corpus in the district court but the court denied his petition.

Smith appealed to the 9th Circuit, and the 2-1 panel majority held Smith's counsel rendered "ineffective assistance" under the rule of a Supreme Court case *Smith v. Stewart* [Warden]. Here is the language of the judge who dissented from the 9th Circuit decision: "If we take off our legal lenses for a moment and step back to look at this record and what Smith did to his unfortunate victims, the decision to return this case for re-sentencing almost takes one's breath away, if, indeed it is not too incongruous to say that anything touching a process as slow as that which exists in this country can ever be called breathtaking…With all due respect, legal lenses should not be blinders."

The 9th Circuit three-judge panel sent the case back to state court, and Arizona retried Smith. Again the jury voted the death penalty, and the Arizona Supreme Court affirmed the conviction and sentence. Smith sought a hearing directly in the Supreme Court, but his petition was denied. Convicted in 1976 and sentenced in October 2007. The Supreme Court published the dissent of one of the Justices who wondered whether a convicted murderer imprisoned thirty years earlier might have suffered "cruel and inhuman punishment." Presumably the families of the victims do not share this view. Unsurprisingly, none of the other Justices shared this absurd comment by a colleague worrying about a convict who delayed his execution by repeated appeals in state and federal court.

Of course this case is not over, though no further action has been reported. Smith can file a petition for habeas corpus in federal court.

Hedgpeth (Warden) v. Pulido, 129 S.Ct. 530 (2007)
Reversing a 9th Circuit decision in *Hedgpeth v. Pulido,* 487 F.3d 669 (2007).
The 9th Circuit reversed a state court trial conviction of guilt (that had been affirmed on appeal by the California Supreme Court) on the specious ground that a typographical error in the jury instructions misled the jury despite overwhelming evidence Pulido was guilty and in light of the jury verdict rejecting his testimony at the trial. The Supreme Court reversed

the 9th Circuit decision in *Hedgpeth v. Pulido* on grounds the 9th Circuit used the wrong legal test in its decision. After return of the death penalty case to the 9th Circuit for reconsideration under the correct test, the 9th Circuit ordered the legal issue sent to the district court in March 2009; (*Pulido v. Chrones*).

Three months later the 9th Circuit panel granted reconsideration of its decision, vacated that order, and instructed the parties to brief the legal issue under the correct legal test; *Pulido v. Chrones.* The court gave no explanation for its decision. Three months later it vacated that order and ordered the parties to submit additional briefing; eventually the 9th Circuit affirmed the conviction in 2010; *Pulido v. Chrones.*

The Supreme Court reversal of the original 9th Circuit decision in *Pulido* is not surprising. The lawyer representing Pulido in the Supreme Court conceded the 9th Circuit used the wrong legal test. Moreover, the Supreme Court in Pulido overruled another case previously decided by the 9th Circuit; *Gibson v. Ortiz.*

Summerlin v. Schriro (Warden), 427 F.3d 623 (9th Cir. 2005)
The 9th Circuit, in reversing a previous decision of the Arizona Supreme Court affirming Summerlin's conviction and death penalty sentence (*Schriro v. Summerlin*), held that earlier Supreme Court cases should be applied retroactively to anyone who filed a habeas corpus petition in federal court. That interpretation, if applicable, would have reversed Summerlin's death penalty case. The Supreme Court in *Schriro v. Summerlin* reviewed the 9th Circuit opinion and reversed: "The Ninth Circuit's conclusion [of the earlier Supreme Court decisions] is particularly remarkable in the face of the Arizona Supreme Court's previous conclusion to the contrary;" Schriro v. Summerlin. The Supreme Court reversed the 9th Circuit and returned the case to that court for further proceedings, whereupon a panel of judges found Summerlin's counsel rendered "ineffective assistance" and ordered a rehearing of the sentence. The State of Arizona sought review

of this decision, but the Supreme Court denied its petition. Cases subsequently decided by the Supreme Court in its 2011–2012 term would not have reached that decision.

At the hearing on resentencing, the state withdrew its request seeking the death penalty.

Cooper v. Brown (Warden), 510 F.3d 870 (9th Cir. 2007)
The aversion to death sentences evidenced by some of the 9th Circuit judges who regularly refuse to enforce it is on display in *Cooper v. Brown.* In a rare 9th Circuit case affirming the death penalty that began with a *1983* trial, and after multiple appeals and hearings in state and federal court, the opening line written by a 9th Circuit judge dissenting to the decision apparently intends to frighten the reader: He wrote: "The State of California may be about to execute an innocent man [Cooper]." What follows is the judge's retrial of the case, a reweighing of the evidence, indifference to the facts found by the jury, and oblivious to innumerable findings of other judges who heard the case. The dissenting judge abandoned his role as a member of a Court of Appeal by retrying the case, arguing with the evidence, disagreeing with the jury, and disregarding the trial judge and all the other courts that had heard the case.

The majority of judges of the 9th Circuit affirmed the conviction and sentence, to their credit, by rebutting the obvious attempt by the dissenting judge to manipulate and ignore the evidence. Indeed, this rebuttal is a rare occasion in which a 9th Circuit panel affirms a sentence, but a welcome rejoinder to an irresponsible dissenting opinion.

Harrison v. Gillespie, 596 F.3d. 551 (9th Cir. 2010)
The original opinion was written by three-judge panel. In an amended opinion on rehearing by the full court, the judges reversed the three judge panel (discussed below) and affirmed the trial court district judge: *Harrison v. Gillespie,* 640 F.3d 888 (9th Cir. 2011).

As noted earlier, 9th Circuit judges repeatedly seek to reverse trial courts on grounds of alleged improper exclusion of jurors, prosecutorial misconduct, evidentiary errors committed by the trial court, insufficiency of the evidence, faulty jury instructions or "ineffective assistance of counsel." The nadir of their opinions is a Nevada state court decision in *Harrison v. Gillespie.* The jury in the original trial found the defendant guilty of murder but could not agree on the appropriate sentence of life without the possibility of parole or death. The jury foreman had informed the judge that the jury was at impasse and could not reach a verdict. The judge declared a mistrial and discharged the jury without polling (asking questions) jurors for their agreement or disagreement with the jury foreman.

The 9th Circuit majority panel on appeal from the district court held that the State of Nevada could not retry the defendant on the penalty phase citing grounds of double jeopardy (the state cannot try the defendant twice for the same crime). The dissenting judge noted the majority had not cited a single case supporting its decision. Polling a jury whose foreman has declared the jurors are at "impasse" and unable to reach a verdict, is discretionary with the judge, although undoubtedly good trial practice, but failure to do so certainly does not warrant reversal on grounds of double jeopardy. The dissenting judge wrote,

> "The foreperson's answers to the judge's questions about the vote of the jurors were categorical, unequivocal, uncontradicted, and consistent with the jury's failure to return a written verdict. Conspicuously missing from the majority opinion is a single federal case, or indeed any case, establishing a constitutional right to a partial verdict when it comes to sentencing, and certainly not when a jury is required to "weigh" intangible factors and ultimately determine a just punishment as a matter of discretion. The verdict in a penalty phase trial is the [essence] of the jury's weighing and balancing the evidence, and its moral judgment. It is the jury's final decision that counts, not its thoughts in progress. Whether or not

the state judge could have engaged in more detailed questioning, the federal constitution simply does not require an inquiry into the status of unfinished deliberations in a profoundly discretionary matter such as this before declaring a mistrial."

In fact, the Supreme Court decided a similar case approximately two months after the decision in *Harrison v. Gillespie*. In *Renico (Warden) v. Lett* the trial court judge declared a mistrial after the jury foreman reported the jury was at impasse. Unlike the *Harrison* decision, the Supreme Court wrote:

> "We have expressly declined to require the 'mechanical application' of any 'rigid formula' when trial judges decide whether jury deadlock warrants a mistrial. We have also explicitly held that a trial judge declaring a mistrial is not required to make explicit findings of 'manifest necessity' nor to 'articulate on the record' all the factors which informed the deliberate exercise of his discretion. And we have never required a trial judge, before declaring a mistrial based on jury deadlock, to force the jury to deliberate for a minimum period of time, to question the jurors individually, to consult with (or obtain the consent of) either the prosecutor or defense counsel, to issue supplemental jury instructions, or to consider any other means of breaking the impasse."

The Court added, in particular for the benefit of the 9th Circuit, "[b]ecause AEDPA authorizes federal courts to grant relief only when state courts act unreasonably, it follows that '[t]he more general the rule at issue, and thus the greater the potential for reasoned disagreement among 'fair-minded judges, the more leeway [state] courts have in reaching outcomes in case-by-case determinations."

The Supreme Court continued: "AEDPA prevents defendants-and federal courts-from using federal habeas corpus review as a vehicle to second-guess the reasonable decisions of state courts. Whether or not the Michigan

Supreme Court's opinion reinstating Letts' conviction in this case was correct, it was clearly not unreasonable." Without repeating the additional language of the dissent in *Harrison v. Gillespie* or *Renico v. Lett*, the 9th Circuit reheard this case and reversed the three-judge panel indefensible decision described above.

These death penalty cases, and those described in the chapter on Lawyers, can be summed up by the words of Supreme Court Justice Scalia in Allen v. Lawhorn: "With distressing frequency, especially in capital cases . . . federal judges refuse to be governed by Congress' command that state criminal judgments must not be reversed by federal courts unless they are 'contrary to, or involve an unreasonable application of, clearly established Federal law, as determined by the Supreme Court of the United States . . . This Court invites 'continued lawlessness' when it permits a patently improper interference with state justice as that which occurred in this case to stand."

CHAPTER 6

THE LAWYERS

On March 11, 2010, a 9th Circuit panel of three judges reversed the death penalty sentence in *Stanley v. Schriro* on grounds the lawyer for defendant Stanley was "ineffective" in preparing and presenting evidence in the penalty phase of the trial. The court returned the case to the district court judge for a hearing on this issue. Because the attorney who represented Stanley is deceased, any hearing was futile, and the 9th Circuit had stymied another death penalty.

The following quotation from the dissenting judge in the *Stanley* case confirms the theme of the entire text of Chapter 5 on the death penalty and the cases discussed in this Chapter: "The delay (Stanley was convicted in 1986) matters here because the only issue is what may seem to be an *unspoken rule in our circuit that anyone sentenced to death had ineffective assistance of counsel* (emphasis added) during the sentencing phase of his trial or at least needs an evidentiary hearing decades after sentencing to find out." This quotation is the most succinct and accurate description of many of the 9th Circuit judges.

The most difficult decision in criminal law for defense counsel in capital cases can run the entire gamut of options: whether to plead the client guilty to the charge of murder contingent on the prosecution not asking for the death penalty; to assure selection of a jury not predisposed to vote the death penalty; to attempt to reduce the defendant's degree of culpability from murder to a lesser offense (manslaughter) at trial; to rely on alibi witnesses; to decide whether to let the defendant testify; to submit all legally relevant jury instructions; to weigh the best method of arguing the defense to the jury; and to prepare for the penalty phase in the event of an adverse jury verdict of "guilty."

Other issues exist, but paramount in these cases is preparing evidence to rebut the statutory "special circumstances" a prosecutor must establish in order to render the defendant eligible for the death penalty. If the jury finds the defendant guilty of the crime(s) alleged, the prosecutor will submit evidence of "aggravating" circumstances warranting imposition of the death penalty. Examples include prior convictions; escape from jail or prison; arrests, probation, or parole status; and testimony from other witnesses. Counsel for the defendant submits evidence of "mitigating" circumstances in an attempt to convince the jury to extend leniency based on youth; drug history; mental imbalance; and/or other factors. In almost all cases each side presents testimony from psychiatrists who obviously differ in their opinions on mental standards.

For a variety of reasons, defense counsel may submit only minimal evidence during the trial yet argue at the penalty phase that the prosecution evidence does not warrant execution. In some cases the defendant refuses to cooperate or participate with counsel; in others the brutality and horrific circumstances are unlikely to dissuade the jury regardless of any "mitigating" circumstances. In any event, whether the defendant wants such evidence submitted or not, and despite the hopeless nature of the case, the 9th Circuit insists that defense counsel scour family history, research drug and alcohol addiction records, test prior mental deficiency, and solicit psychiatric testimony.

Several years ago the Supreme Court became concerned about the level of representation afforded defendants convicted of murder and sentenced to death. In 1984, with no precedent to guide the Court, and once again imposing its decision on state courts under the Sixth Amendment right to counsel guaranteed by the U.S. Constitution, the Justices concluded that an accused is entitled to "effective counsel." In *Strickland v. Washington*, the Supreme Court ruled that professional legal errors committed by counsel during trial or sentencing must establish that counsel represented the defendant deficiently, and the representation was prejudicial to the defense, that is, a "reasonable probability that *but for* those errors the result of the trial would be different."

The Supreme Court specifically rejected a rule that the defendant had to prove it "more likely than not" that the outcome would have been altered [by ineffective representation]. The Supreme Court characterized a two-part test in *Strickland* as: (1) whether "counsel's representation fell below an objective standard of reasonableness," and (2) "whether the deficient performance caused prejudice to the defendant on trial." Introducing the concept of "reasonableness" in the *Strickland* case opens the door for the 9th Circuit to "second guess" counsel despite an admonition from the Supreme Court not to do so.

The Supreme Court in *Strickland* recognized the perennial application of hindsight and condemned it several years later: "There is a natural tendency to speculate on whether a different trial strategy might have been more successful. We adopted the rule of contemporary assessment of counsel's conduct because a more rigid requirement could only dampen the ardor and impair the independence of defense counsel, discourage acceptance of assigned cases, and undermine the trust between attorney and client. Unreliability or unfairness [of a trial] does not result if the ineffective counsel does not deprive the defendant of any substantive or procedural right to which the law entitles him."

The Supreme Court added, "[Judicial] scrutiny of counsel's performance must be highly deferential, and a fair assessment of attorney performance requires that every effort be made to eliminate the distorting effects of hindsight. The defendant must overcome the presumption that, under the circumstances, the challenged action might be considered sound trial strategy." The 9th Circuit easily evades this rationale as evidenced in the cases excerpted below.

The Supreme Court and other federal Circuit Courts of Appeal have struggled to apply the *Strickland* test. The rule, understandably amorphous, conceptual, and fact-specific, encourages any state prisoner to file habeas corpus in federal court if unsuccessful in state court on the grounds of "ineffective assistance of counsel." The Supreme Court has recognized this concern: "The essence of an ineffective assistance claim is that counsel's unprofessional errors so upset the adversarial balance between defense and prosecution that the trial was rendered unfair and the verdict rendered suspect;" Nix v. Whiteside.

This explanation is equally vague. As the following cases demonstrate, the 9th Circuit has reversed almost every case in the last decade on grounds of "ineffective assistance of counsel." Because the test for "ineffective assistance of counsel" is so vague, fact driven, and susceptible to verbal manipulation, the Supreme Court has been unable to fashion an infallible test. That goal is impossible to achieve, and the 9th Circuit judges know it as recited from the quotation cited above.

A case from the Sixth Circuit Court of Appeals (another federal appellate court) reversing a death penalty case on grounds of "ineffective assistance of counsel" is another example of an exasperated Supreme Court; Bobby v. Van Hook. According to the Supreme Court, defense counsel is not mandated to undertake massive duplicative searches of the defendant's social history. Every case is different factually, and a broad rule of whether defense counsel tried a case "effectively" cannot serve as a "bright line." But this comment is not universally true in the 9th Circuit where every death penalty case reversed is frequently the result of "ineffective assistance of counsel."

Woodford (Warden) v. Visciotti, 537 U.S.19 (2002)
Reversing the 9th Circuit decision in *Visciotti v. Woodford,* 288 F.3d 1097 (9th Cir. 2002).
In its *Woodford v. Visciotti* decision the Supreme Court unanimously wrote a harsh criticism of the 9th Circuit for its decision concluding that counsel

had been of "ineffective assistance." The Supreme Court wrote, "The Ninth Circuit interpreted the state supreme court [decision], which had affirmed the conviction and penalty of Visciotti, as ". . . "requiring [his lawyer] to prove, by a preponderance of the evidence, that the result of the sentencing proceedings would have been different. That is in our view a mischaracterization of the state court opinion, which applied the proper standard for evaluating prejudice."

According to the 9th Circuit, the state supreme court decision had failed to use the word "probable," as distinct from "reasonably probable," in a jury instruction. The Supreme Court noted, "The Ninth Circuit Court of Appeals made no effort to reconcile the state court decision using the term "probable" with its use elsewhere nor did not even acknowledge, much less discuss, the California Supreme Court's proper framing of the question of whether the error undermines confidence in the outcome . . ."

The Supreme Court continued its discussion of the *Strickland* test as applied by the 9th Circuit with this observation: "Ultimately [the Ninth Circuit court] substituted it own judgment for that of the state court in contravention of the Anti Terrorism and Effective Death Penalty Act [AEDPA]." This observation is repeatedly noted by the Supreme Court in other 9th Circuit decisions.

In the *Visciotti* case, the Supreme Court reminded appellate courts that the *Strickland* test is reviewed congruent with the language of AEDPA: whether the state court decision constituted an "unreasonable application of federal law clearly established by the Supreme Court." And if the state court application of federal law is challenged on appeal, it must not only be erroneous but "objectively unreasonable." Judicial determination of facts made by a state court is presumed correct and must be overcome by clear and convincing evidence. The AEDPA statute provides: "In a proceeding instituted by an application for a writ of habeas corpus by a person in custody pursuant to the judgment of a State court, a determination of a factual issue made by a State court shall be presumed to be correct. The applicant shall have the burden of rebutting the presumption of correctness by clear and convincing evidence."

In one of its subsequent cases the Supreme Court unanimously issued a stinging rebuke of a 9th Circuit opinion that had chastised defense counsel for a weak closing argument. The Justices gave the 9th Circuit several lessons in alternative trial strategies that a lawyer can invoke in crafting a closing argument, and a court should acknowledge this fact. Unsurprisingly so, since few of the 9th Circuit judges served as trial lawyers and never addressed a jury.

The Supreme Court returned the *Visciotti* case to the 9th Circuit. The 9th Circuit ordered the case to the district court judge for further hearing without admitting it had been reversed; (*Visciotti v. Brown*). This order was issued on May 9, 2005.

Yarborough (Warden) v. Gentry, 540 U.S. 1 (2003)
Reversing the 9th Circuit decision in *Gentry v. Roe,* 320 F.3d 891 (9th Cir. 2002).
Approximately one year after the *Visciotti* decision, the Supreme Court lectured the 9th Circuit again on reviewing the performance of the trial lawyer representing a defendant (*Gentry v. Roe*). The jury had voted the death penalty, and the California Supreme Court had affirmed the conviction and sentence. The 9th Circuit had skewered the defense lawyer's closing argument and substituted its own version of the proper way to address the jury. Several 9th Circuit judges dissented from the decision.

In reviewing the trial record, the 9th Circuit majority of judges could find no fault with the prosecutor improperly excusing a juror on gender or ethnic grounds; or that the prosecutor committed misconduct; or the trial judge committed any legal error; or that the jury instructions were flawed. Bereft of any evidence to reverse the conviction, the majority of judges focused on defense counsel's closing argument to the jury, and found it, "ineffective." The State sought review in the Supreme Court, where the Justices promptly and unanimously reversed the 9th Circuit.

The judges of the 9th Circuit who had dissented from the majority decision setting aside the death penalty and who had found Gentry's lawyers "ineffective" noted:

> "This case is part of a developing body of circuit law substituting our judgment on defense tactics and presentation of evidence for the judgment of defense counsel and state courts. More often this occurs in death penalty cases, but the trend is seeping beyond them to more routine cases . . . The last thing criminal defendants and the public need is a 'Ninth Circuit form book' of approved argument and strategies, yet that is what we're giving them. We're telling [lawyers] in great detail how to investigate their cases and forcing them down rabbit tracks that divert their time from better application; or that they have to produce psychiatric arguments . . . Now they apparently have to make, and refrain from making arguments . . . regardless of what they think will most likely persuade the jury to consider seriously whether there is a reasonable doubt.
>
> "This growing body of law is a very bad idea. We ought to have more respect for the dedicated lawyers who defend criminal cases, and respect the judgments and instincts they apply in light of much greater knowledge of their clients and cases than we have. And we ought to have more respect for the considered judgments of our equally learned counterparts on the state courts. Our legal duty and the controlling Supreme Court decisions demand this deference. So does the wise administration of justice."
>
> When criminal defense lawyers shape and present their cases, they ought to be thinking about the jury. They shouldn't be reading their office form book of approved and disapproved defense techniques. They should be paying attention to the jury, not looking over their shoulders at us."

Again the Supreme Court reversed the decision, reminding the 9th Circuit of the federal statute (AEDPA) and *Strickland v. Washington* requiring deference to the state court which had affirmed the conviction, as had the district court on habeas corpus. The Supreme Court noted that "a defense attorney's summation [to the jury] is highly deferential, and doubly deferential when it is conducted through the lens of habeas corpus [in federal court]."

The Supreme Court referenced several commentaries by experienced lawyers recommending techniques to influence juries in closing argument. The majority panel of 9th Circuit judges, presumably never having tried a criminal case, were unaware of trial practice. All nine Supreme Court Justices reversed the 9th Circuit in a unanimous decision. One other case, *Belmontes v. Woodford*, which the 9th Circuit had relied on heavily in its *Yarborough* decision, was reversed by the Supreme Court in *Wong v. Belmontes*, discussed earlier in Chapter 5. Here is the language of the 9th Circuit upon receiving reversal of its *Yarborough* case from the Supreme Court: "Based upon the Supreme Court's decision in this case the judgment of the district court is affirmed, and the mandate [order] shall issue forthwith." Not a word about "reversal."

Knowles(Warden) v. Mirzayance, 129 S.Ct. 1411 (2009)
Reversing the 9th Circuit decision in *Knowles v. Mirzayance,* 175 Fed. Appx. 142 (9th Cir. 2006), unpublished.
In many state courts the defendant can enter a plea of "not guilty or "not guilty by reason of insanity." These pleas are tried to a jury separately.

After the jury convicted Mirzayance of first degree murder, his experienced defense counsel elected to withdraw the previously entered "not guilty plea by reason of insanity," intuiting that jurors who had unanimously found the evidence at trial established Mirzayance had a specific intent to kill the victim, with premeditation and malice (elements of first degree murder), were unlikely to find the defendant insane. In addition, defense counsel could not secure testimony from the parents of Mirzayance because they had not appeared at the trial and declined to testify in the event of an insanity hearing. Under these circumstances, any hope of a favorable jury verdict was futile, and counsel and client withdrew the plea.

On automatic appeal, the California Supreme Court affirmed the conviction. The district court judge also confirmed the conviction on habeas corpus, and Mirzayance appealed to the 9th Circuit. In a 2-1 panel decision the two-judge majority reversed the district court (and, in effect, the state court) on grounds of "ineffective assistance of counsel." *Mirzayance* is another example of inexperienced appellate court judges "second guessing" a lawyer's tactical decision to withdraw the plea of "not guilty by reason of insanity." And here is the "explanation" the court majority wrote:

> "In fact, insanity and premeditation are not mutually exclusive. To establish insanity under California law, the defendant must prove he was incapable of knowing or understanding the nature and quality of his or her act and of distinguishing right from wrong at the time of the commission of the offence . . . Incapacity to know the nature and quality of one's act and to distinguish right from wrong is not incompatible with capacity to premeditate and deliberate, which does not necessarily require knowledge or understanding of the nature of the act premeditated or deliberated."

No juror would possibly understand, let alone apply, this academic hairsplitting or "lawyerly parsing" of jury instructions condemned by the Supreme Court in the *Payton* case previously described in Chapter 5.

The 9th Circuit panel majority of judges had initially returned this case to the district court judge to hold a hearing on Mirzayance's challenges to his conviction on grounds of "ineffective assistance of counsel." After four days of testimony, the district court judge made findings of fact, ignored by the majority of the 9th Circuit panel, that counsel had diligently represented his client. The two-judge 9th Circuit majority also did not bother to cite the need for applying the *Strickland* test, as noted in the dissenting opinion.

Another case of "substituted judicial judgment." The dissenting judge, citing the evidence as determined by the district court judge, skillfully shredded the majority decision and dismissed any reason to criticize the lawyer who defended Mirzayance. The State of California sought review of the decision in the Supreme Court.

Incidentally, not one word about the nature of the crime appeared in the 9th Circuit decision buried in an unpublished format (never officially reported). Nevertheless, the Supreme Court summarily reversed the 9th Circuit decision and ordered that court to rehear the case under established Supreme Court law; Knowles v. Mirzayance).

On return of the case to the 9th Circuit, the judges reheard this case and essentially parroted their original decision of reversal. The Supreme Court granted review on June 27, 2008. On March 25, 2009 the Court unanimously reversed the 9th Circuit in dismissive language and returned the case again to that court with instructions to deny Mirzayance's petition. The Supreme Court in Mirzayance told the 9th Circuit it had applied the wrong rule in evaluating the doctrine of "ineffective assistance of counsel;" criticized the court for not deferring to the state court decision affirming the conviction; ignoring the factual findings issued by the magistrate judge; and derided the notion "the law requires counsel to investigate every conceivable line of mitigation evidence"

This case is another example of 9th Circuit intent to avoid the application of the Anti Terrorism and Death Penalty Act (AEDPA, requiring federal courts to defer to state courts in the absence of an "unreasonable" state court ruling. The reason for the 9th Circuit's avoidance of AEDPA is obvious: to prevent imposition of the death penalty.

Arave (Warden) v. Hoffman, 552 U.S. 117 (2008)
Reversing the 9th Circuit decisions in *Hoffman v. Arave*, 481 F.3d 686 (9th Cir. 2007) and 518 F.3d 656 (9th Cir. 2008).
In 1989 an Idaho state court jury convicted Maxwell Hoffman of murder, and the judge imposed the death penalty. The Idaho Supreme Court affirmed the judgment. Hoffman filed two petitions seeking habeas corpus

review in district court and the judge denied both. Hoffman filed a petition for habeas corpus in the 9th Circuit. The court issued two decisions, one setting aside the death penalty in the state of Idaho. In a third decision, the 9th Circuit panel set aside the sentence on grounds Hoffman had received ineffective assistance of counsel during the sentencing hearing, but not on the plea bargain (agreement to plead guilty) he had rejected prior to trial.

In *Hoffman v. Arave*, the 9th Circuit reviewed the proceedings in the plea agreement in state court. The prosecution had offered to accept a plea of guilty to murder and not seek the death penalty or, alternatively, the defendant could go to trial and risk the jury verdict. Hoffman could afford to go to trial, knowing the 9th Circuit had previously ruled the Idaho death penalty statute unconstitutional. Counsel for Hoffman knew his options. The 9th Circuit would likely reverse the Idaho court in the event of a conviction and consequent death penalty sentence; or the judge could impose a lesser sentence; or the jury would be unable to reach a verdict. Defense counsel understandably agreed to try the case. The jury in the Idaho state court found the Hoffman guilty and the judge imposed the death sentence despite the 9th Circuit ruling. Both sides ultimately sought review in the 9th Circuit.

On March 6, 2007, the 9th Circuit set aside the sentencing and the plea agreement offered by the prosecution on grounds of "ineffective assistance of counsel." The court ordered the State of Idaho to either release Hoffman or offer him the agreement to plead guilty and avoid the death penalty consistent with the other terms originally offered by the prosecution. Despite Hoffman's original decision to reject the plea agreement, knowing the Idaho court could not impose the death penalty, the 9th Circuit never discussed its rationale. Instead, the court substituted its own version of defense trial strategy, despite its previous decision setting aside the Idaho death penalty, and concluded the defendant should have accepted the plea bargain and not gone to trial.

Several 9th Circuit judges angrily dissented: "The [majority] decision has effectively written out of the law the requirement that prejudice (to Hoffman) be pleaded and proved to meet the test of ineffective assistance of counsel (citing the Supreme Court decision in *Strickland v. Washington*). Further, they commented, "in what may be a new high in self-effacing candor, the majority of the panel holds that it is ineffective assistance of counsel to rely on 9th Circuit precedent [striking down the Idaho death penalty] with respect to federal constitutional law applicable in states located in this Circuit."

The State and Hoffman both sought review of the 9th Circuit decision in the Supreme Court, and the Justices agreed to review the case. Hoffman subsequently abandoned his ineffective counsel claim allegedly occurring at plea bargaining and sought only resentencing originally offered by the prosecutor, rejected by Hoffman, and ordered by the 9th Circuit. The State of Idaho agreed to dismiss its request for review of the 9th Circuit decision, having earlier abandoned its claim of sentencing error in the district court in light of earlier 9th Circuit opinions holding the Idaho death penalty law unenforceable; *Arave v. Hoffman*.

The proceedings in the Supreme Court are curious. Hoffman, in moving to withdraw his claim that counsel was ineffective during plea bargaining, stated he "no longer seeks or desires the relief ordered by the Court of Appeals with respect to the plea offer," and asks the Supreme Court to return his case to the district court for resentencing. By that request, and the State of Idaho having abandoned its appeal of sentencing error, no issue remained in the Supreme Court. The Court stated, "[W]e vacate the judgment of the Court of Appeals to the extent that it addresses [Hoffman's] claim," but that decision says nothing about the 9th Circuit order commanding the Idaho court to resentence Hoffman. This decision saved the 9th Circuit from another reversal on grounds of ineffective counsel when the prosecution offered not to seek the death penalty during plea bargaining.

Convicted in 1989, having averted the death penalty three times by the
9th Circuit, Hoffman now may proceed in state court. With his appeal of
"ineffective assistance of counsel" abandoned, the only plea on record is one
of "not guilty." The State of Idaho and counsel for Hoffman have probably
agreed to a change of plea to "guilty." The 9th Circuit, having invalidated
the Idaho death penalty in an earlier decision, leaves the prosecution only
the option to recommend sentence in compliance with its original offer.

In its *Strickland v. Washington* case the Supreme Court warned appellate courts against interposing their personal views of defense strategy
rather than decisions made by counsel: "[W]e will not second-guess tactical decisions made by counsel." Hoffman having been convicted in 1989,
and despite a Supreme Court decision instructing appellate courts to avoid
second-guessing counsel, escaped the death penalty after eighteen years
after his original conviction.

Schriro (Warden) v. Landrigan, 550 U.S. 465 (2007)
Reversing the 9th Circuit decision in *Schriro v. Landrigan,* 441 F.3d 648
(9th Cir. 2006). Note: This case was reviewed in Chapter 5 on another
issue (death penalty).
In this case the Supreme Court again criticized the 9th Circuit's erroneous
reasoning in "second- guessing" defense counsel, and reversed that court's
decision. When the Supreme Court returned the case to the 9th Circuit, that
court did not acknowledge the reversal but used this language: "In light of
the Supreme Court mandate we vacate our [full court] decision." [*Landrigan
v. Schriro*]. On the same day, the 9th Circuit reversed another case, *Lambright
v. Schriro,* on the same grounds of "ineffective assistance of counsel."

Lambright v. Schriro (Warden), 490 F.3d 1103 (9th Cir. 2007), amended
July 2, 2007
The facts in this case are, unsurprisingly, horrendous. After telling a friend
"he would like to kill somebody just to see if he could do it," Lambright

picked up a woman hitchhiker, stabbed her, and crushed her skull with a rock. Lambright admitted complicity in the murder, but denied he personally killed the woman, and implicated a third party. In legal parlance, it makes no difference whether someone murders another person or is an accomplice. Lambright never contended his innocence.

In 1982 the jury convicted Lambright. The state court judge sentenced him to death for first degree murder, kidnapping, and sexual assault. The Arizona Supreme Court affirmed his conviction on appeal and denied all his subsequent habeas corpus petitions in state court. In 1999 a 9th Circuit panel reversed Lambright's case on procedural grounds but was itself subsequently reversed by other members of the same court. Upon return of the case by the full court to the original three-judge panel, it ordered the district court to hold an evidentiary hearing to determine whether counsel for Lambright received "ineffective assistance of counsel."

The district court judge held a hearing, ruled that Lambright was not a credible witness, resolved the disagreement between mental health experts of prosecution and defense in favor of the State of Arizona, and upheld the death penalty sentence. The district court judge made numerous findings of fact, summarized the evidence, reviewed defense counsel's performance as the trial lawyer, and concluded none of the evidence presented at the hearing established a reason to label counsel as "ineffective" even if he did not thoroughly investigate every avenue of mitigation evidence. Lambright appealed to the 9th Circuit.

A three-judge panel of the 9th Circuit cited a Supreme Court decision mandating defense counsel in capital cases to present mitigating evidence in the form of tests for IQ or mental impairment, regardless of the brutality of the crime. After all, said the panel, "[we] should "treat each defendant in a capital case with that degree of respect due to the 'uniqueness' of the individual." Obviously the defendant failed to treat the victim with the same degree of respect.

Lambright submitted no evidence of a low IQ, and nothing in the record supported his intellectual deficit. But, said the panel, a history of drug abuse could mentally impair a person to a degree equivalent to a low IQ, and counsel should have introduced Lambright's drug history as evidence potentially mitigating imposition of the death penalty. Despite Lambright's drug history, none of the evidence at the district court hearing warranted a finding that he was under the influence of drugs when he murdered the victim.

The 9th Circuit panel, ignoring the district court judge findings, concluded that the state court sentencing judge was wrong; the district court had invoked the wrong legal test, and the Arizona Supreme Court was wrong on appeal and on state habeas corpus. The panel undertook an indescribably lengthy and prolix condemnation of the defense lawyer. What followed was a complete misapplication of the law by the panel in its decision. The 9th Circuit subsequently issued an amended decision in Lambright on a Friday, July 3, 2007 - one day prior to a national holiday thereby avoiding publicity. Accordingly, the decision received little press coverage despite the fact the case it had centered around a grisly and horrifying murder. "Innocence" was never in doubt.

The 9th Circuit panel engaged in writing a litany of factors the defense lawyer should have investigated. Continually citing its own prior decisions to implement this task, the court ruminated that counsel must investigate mental health records, interview family members, and obtain psychiatric records and testimony, medical and physical health records, drug history, and evidence of child abuse (the probation report and the report of a mental health expert appointed by the court had been submitted to the sentencing judge who had already documented this evidence). In conclusion, said the panel again, counsel should present evidence to "humanize the defendant."

According to the 9th Circuit panel, the sentencing judge was unaware of the frequent family moves preventing Lambright from "developing stable social relations as a young child." And the sentencing judge was unaware "of the poverty that Lambright experienced while growing up." The 9th Circuit panel discussed evidence of post traumatic stress syndrome introduced at the hearing in the district court. The district court judge had found that Lambright's testimony on this issue was "less than credible." Despite that finding, said the 9th Circuit panel, the district court judge failed to address other possible mental illness, using this language: "Expert testimony presented at the evidentiary hearing also 'suggested' Lambright may suffer from a personality disorder . . . This diagnosis . . . could have had a mitigating effect under Arizona law]."

A judge concurring in the decision could not help but link Lambright to his service in the Vietnam War even though the district court judge found no credible evidence of Lambright's testimony on post traumatic stress syndrome attributable to his brief military service in Vietnam. But, said one of the 9th Circuit judges, many unrelated mental health problems emerged after Lambright returned home. The sentencing judge, the Arizona Supreme Court, and the district court judge didn't think so.

In reversing the district court judge and requiring another evidentiary hearing, the 9th Circuit cited two Supreme Court cases mandating counsel to introduce evidence of "mitigation" to avoid the death penalty. Other than those two cases, the panel cited only previous cases the 9th Circuit had decided-all reversing the death penalty on grounds of "ineffective assistance of counsel."

In *Lambright*, despite its unnecessarily repetitive decision, the panel reviewed only three elements of mitigating evidence: drug abuse, childhood abuse, and mental health. The sentencing judge was aware of Lambright's drug abuse history recited in the probation report but regarded this factor as irrelevant in this case. Prosecution and defense mental health experts disagreed on whether Lambright had suffered post traumatic stress syndrome but the trial judge validated the prosecution doctor's testimony compared to the doctors who testified for the defense. The sentencing judge had read the probation report documenting all these factors, and the court had disbelieved the defendant at the evidentiary hearing. The panel criticized the absence of family members whom counsel had previously interviewed but who presumably were unavailable or had refused to testify. In summary, there was not the slightest possibility the judge would have imposed a different sentence.

Convicted in 1982, and repeatedly filing writs of habeas corpus denied by the Supreme Court, Lambright still remains confined. There is no evidence he did not commit willful murder and no evidence of mental disorder worth consideration. Childhood poverty and drug abuse do not excuse the inexcusable. The most disturbing element of this decision is its reliance on the *Summerlin* case, (previously discussed) a decision equally misguided. An appellate court is bound by the factual findings of the trial court and can only reverse for legal error prejudicing the rights of a defendant. In *Lambright*, the 9th Circuit judges merely substituted their opinion, as it did in other cases, disagreeing simultaneously with the trial judge, the Arizona Supreme Court on appeal, state habeas corpus, and the district court judge.

The Supreme Court denied a hearing to review the case (*Schriro v. Lambright*). The result of that decision required the district court judge to hold another evidentiary hearing. After its ruling denying further relief, Lambright appealed to the 9th Circuit panel of judges who reversed the district court judge again and sent the case back for another hearing. In 2010 the trial judge wrote an extensive decision denying further relief. The record is unclear, but the court held a hearing on the habeas corpus petition in February 2011 and continued it for additional briefing..

Moorman v. Schriro (Warden), 426 F.3d 1044 (9th Cir. 2005); 628 F.3d 1102 (2010)

Defendant Moorman, while on parole, strangled his elderly adoptive mother who had traveled to visit him, and dumped her dismembered body in a trash can. Police ultimately obtained evidence of Moorman's complicity and obtained a complete confession from him. The jury voted guilty after only two hours of deliberation and sentenced Moorman to death in 1985. The 9th Circuit reversed on grounds of "ineffective assistance of counsel" in October 2005. In its order, the 9th Circuit panel remanded the case to the district court judge for an evidentiary hearing on Moorman's claims. The Supreme Court denied review in January 2006.

On November 18, 2008, the district court judge wrote an opinion denying habeas corpus (Not Reported), and in 2010 the 9th Circuit affirmed the conviction. In other words, from 1985 to 2010 this case has been litigated in court. This case is included not so much to discuss the facts but to illustrate another example of delay attributable to the 9th Circuit. With one exception, every one of the cases in this chapter has subsequently been condemned by the Supreme Court based on the analysis of the 9th Circuit grounds of alleged ineffective assistance of counsel.

Earp v. Ornoski [Warden], 431 F.3d 1158 (9th Cir. 2005); 547 U.S.1159 (2006); 623 F.3d 1065 (2010). Review denied by the Supreme Court.
Earp was convicted of rape and murder of an eighteen-month-old child, and the jury sentenced him to death. The California Supreme Court affirmed Earp's conviction and death sentence in 1988 and subsequently denied his petition for habeas corpus. The district court judge denied his habeas corpus petition, and rejected Earp's allegations his counsel rendered "ineffective assistance."

On appeal from that decision, a 9th Circuit panel focused on whether counsel had conducted an extensive investigation of "mitigating" evidence admissible in the penalty phase of the trial. According to the panel, if prisoners make a "colorable claim" to "ineffective assistance of counsel," they are entitled to an evidentiary hearing. The 9th Circuit panel wrote, "Although counsel clearly has a duty to conduct a full and complete mitigation investigation, we find it difficult to know where a habeas [corpus] reviewing court may draw the line in deciding how far defense counsel must go in conducting the mitigation investigation of the penalty phase of a capital case."

In a word, this judicial concession can justify a preconceived result merely by arguing that counsel failed to investigate a host of sources such as prior criminal record, alcoholism or drug use, or family and academic records. Notably absent from this decision is any reference to the California state court decision affirming the conviction or the limits of federal jurisdiction recited in the Anti-Terrorism Effective Death Penalty Act (AEDPA).

Nevertheless, the 9th Circuit ordered an evidentiary hearing (not reported) and, regrettably, the Supreme Court denied a hearing on this 1988 conviction. The California Supreme Court had affirmed the conviction, and the district court judge agreed, noting the evidence of guilt was overwhelming. The 9th Circuit ignored both courts and the evidence, substituting its own judgment and again demonstrating its ignorance of criminal trials, its refusal to consider AEDPA, and revealing its obvious objection to the death penalty.

Daniels v. Woodford (Warden), 428 F.3d 1181 (9th Cir. 2005); Review denied by Supreme Court; 550 U.S. 968 (2007).
In its naïveté and abysmal lack of understanding of trial courts, the 9th Circuit in a 2005 decision concluded that in 1983 Daniels received "ineffective assistance of counsel" despite the California state court (in *People v. Daniels*) having affirmed his conviction.

Daniels had pled guilty to robbery, but was released on bail pending appeal. When he failed to appear at two hearings, the court issued a warrant for his arrest. Officers located Daniels and attempted to arrest him, but he removed a concealed weapon and killed both men. The testimony of an eyewitness, coupled with a confession from Daniels, was sufficient to find him guilty. The jury sentenced him to death. The California Supreme

Court affirmed the conviction and the district court judge denied his petition for habeas corpus. Daniels appealed to the 9th Circuit.

According to the 9th Circuit, the defense lawyer was Ineffective despite overwhelming evidence of Daniels's guilt and the failure of the defendant to testify at trial. Daniel's habeas corpus petition alleged he could not trust his court appointed lawyer; that his counsel had been conspiring with the district attorney; and his lawyer had not prepared for the penalty hearing. Incredibly, the 9th Circuit judges faulted the defense for not presenting a psychiatrist, ignoring the fact that Daniels had refused to speak with such a doctor. The 9th Circuit reversed and ordered an evidentiary hearing.

The district court judge held a hearing (this time with psychiatric testimony) and, unsurprisingly, doctors for the prosecution and defense disagreed with each other. The court denied the habeas corpus petition. On appeal, the 9th Circuit panel immediately reminded readers of its decision that AEDPA (enacted in 1996) did not apply because Daniels had been convicted twenty-four years earlier in 1983. But the Supreme Court had written: "The right to counsel does not guarantee a right to counsel with whom the accused has a 'meaningful attorney-client relationship;'" *Morris v. Sappy*. The 9th Circuit panel circumvented this rule, citing its own case decided in *Brown v. Craven*, and cited other cases involving conflict between counsel and defendant characterized by the court as "constructive conflict."

The 9th Circuit panel also cited other cases it had decided where in which a breakdown of communication allegedly denied defendant the right to "effective assistance of counsel." In other words, the defendant can assert any number of reasons why he distrusts his lawyer and these can result in a finding of "ineffective assistance of counsel." And this *bon mot* written by the court citing its *Brown v. Craven* case: "The trial court should have been sensitive to cultural and linguistic barriers to communication in considering a motion to substitute counsel. The court added this gratuitous insult: "[Daniel's] right to counsel had been mishandled by the trial judge from the beginning of the proceedings." A comment by a judge who had never tried a criminal case.

The panel cited the *Strickland* case, including its requirement that any claim of "ineffective assistance of counsel" must result in a judicial finding that "the trial cannot be relied on as having produced a just result." Two officers were murdered in the presence of an eyewitness whom Daniels forcibly compelled to assist him in his flight; ballistic evidence unequivocally established one officer's wounds came from his own gun; two other witnesses testified Daniels told them he had killed the officers; Daniels confessed to detectives after his arrest. Daniels did not testify and presented no witnesses. No lawyer could have prevented the conviction and sentence, and the outcome was never in doubt.

The 9th Circuit then delivered the *coup de grace*: Pretrial publicity had been so pervasive, that the trial court should have changed the location of the trial. The district attorney would now have to retry the murder of two police officers for a crime committed twenty-four years ago. Apparently Daniels never thought of this argument on the original appeal from his conviction.

The Supreme Court denied a hearing in this outrageous case.

Brown (Albert) v. Ornoski (Warden), 503 F.3d 1006 (9th Cir. 2007). Conviction affirmed in Supreme Court.
Ninth Circuit judges can deny a prisoner's attempt to secure a writ of habeas corpus from a federal court yet simultaneously undermine the death penalty.

On October 28, 1980, a police dog found the dead body of an eighteen-year-old female high school student lying face down and buried in dirt. Her body was nude below the waist and her bra was partially pulled out from under her blouse. A shoelace from one of her shoes was wrapped around her neck.

After the decedent's mother received several taunting telephone calls (some recorded) police focused on Brown. A search of Brown's house pursuant to a search warrant yielded items belonging to the decedent in Brown's house and in his work locker. At his trial, several witnesses positively incriminated Brown, and the prosecution introduced other corroborating evidence. Brown's alibi was that his mother had testified she had sent him to the store at the time the murder occurred.

At the trial in state court, the prosecution also introduced evidence that Brown had previously raped a fourteen-year-old girl. The jury convicted Brown of rape and murder of the eighteen-year-old girl within three hours of deliberation, including a vote for the death penalty, but the California Supreme Court reversed the conviction. The Supreme Court reversed the state court and reinstated the conviction and death sentence. Brown filed another appeal in state court, and the California Supreme Court reversed the trial judge again for having failed to make a proper trial record. The trial court subsequently completed the necessary record, and the state supreme court upheld the conviction.

Sixteen years after his conviction, and despite overwhelming evidence he killed the young student, Brown filed a petition for habeas corpus in district court alleging grounds of "ineffective assistance of counsel" at his sentencing. In an evidentiary hearing, the trial court denied the petition, and Brown appealed to the 9th Circuit. Surprisingly the panel affirmed the trial court and denied the petition. But in footnote 5 of its decision, the court panel said Brown could challenge the California protocol implementing the death penalty by filing a separate case without waiving his rights on habeas corpus. That a court should provide legal advice is incredible.

This case was originally tried in 1987, and Brown subsequently filed numerous habeas corpus petitions in state and federal court. The 9th Circuit actually affirmed the conviction in *Brown v. Ornoski*, and the Supreme Court denied review twenty-one years later. But the footnote gratuitously offered Brown another basis for court intervention.

Correll v. Ryan (Warden, 539 F.3d 938 (9th Cir. 2008)
As noted earlier, a Congress understandably frustrated with U.S. Circuit Courts of Appeal in general, and the 9th Circuit in particular, enacted the

Antiterrorism and Effective Death Penalty Act (AEDPA) in 1996 to restrict federal habeas corpus review of state court convictions. No case more dramatically illustrates the overwhelming need for this statute than the 9th Circuit decision in *Correll v. Ryan,* decided May 15, 2008. Because this case commenced prior to enactment of AEDPA in 1996, the 9th Circuit escaped the statutory restrictions and performed appellate review under the previous and more liberal law.

The facts of this case are horrendous but the reader would never know about the vicious murder of four victims by reading the author of the 9th Circuit majority decision. Writing perfunctorily and without any description of the facts, the author wrote that Correll was convicted of three counts of first degree murder, attempted first degree murder, four counts of kidnapping, armed robbery, and first degree burglary.

The dissenting judge in the case did explain the facts: Correll and a co-suspect entered the house of one of the victims, demanding money. Correll secured the victim and his girlfriend with duct tape, and when two other friends of the victim arrived, he secured and taped them also. After Correll and his companion raided the house for money and valuables, they forced three of the victims at gunpoint into a car and drove to a deserted area. Compelling them all to lie on the ground, Correll shot both victims in the head but one miraculously survived. He then helped his companion execute the other two victims. Police found the last victim in the house strangled to death.

The sole defense offered at trial was misidentification of Correll. The jury convicted Correll, and during the penalty phase the prosecution presented five "aggravating factors" which, under Arizona law, are conditions for imposing the death penalty. Counsel for Correll presented substantial "mitigating" evidence, attempting to paint his client as less culpable than the other killer. Counsel argued for mitigation on grounds Correll was under the influence of drugs and struggled with a troubled family history, but the judge sentenced Correll to death. The Arizona Supreme Court affirmed the conviction on appeal.

Correll filed habeas corpus proceedings in the state court alleging his counsel had been ineffectively assisting him the penalty phase of the trial by failing to present psychological evidence. After the state trial court held an evidentiary hearing, the judge denied the petition, commenting that "the Court specifically recalls the trial work of defense counsel was precise, careful and competent, and manifested strategic and tactical judgment of the same high quality."

Turning to the federal court, Correll filed a petition for habeas corpus. The district court denied the petition, but on appeal the 9th Circuit ordered an evidentiary hearing on grounds Correll had not received a full evidentiary hearing in state court. The 9th Circuit panel returned the case to the district court, where the judge held a nine-day evidentiary hearing and concluded counsel had been deficient in some areas but not to a degree insufficient to prejudice the petitioner. The court made specific findings of fact in a 109 page opinion. On appeal from this decision, the 9th Circuit majority of judges (having rejected the Arizona Supreme Court decision, the hearings in state court, and the district court judge) found counsel for Correll "ineffectively assisted." Their decision drew six angry dissenting opinions in the case from other 9th Circuit judges.

According to the majority of the court, counsel did not present mitigating evidence of brain damage incurred when Correll was seven years old, but the psychiatrist had testified Correll suffered no brain injury and was a fully functioning adult. The majority also criticized counsel's failure to present psychological evidence, although this strategy would have opened the door for the prosecution to offer damaging evidence of Correll's violent history. Correll had a previous conviction of armed robbery, and had been confined in a mental hospital for almost his entire adult life where he had repeatedly escaped, raped an attendant and engaged in disorderly conduct. He had never worked, had assaulted his sister, and spent his time injecting narcotics. This evidence did not suggest any "mitigation" evidence that would escape the death penalty as a sensible strategy.

The alternatives for defense counsel were either to introduce evidence of a lesser degree of culpability attributable to Correll, blame someone else, or submit other evidence casting doubt on the verdict. This strategy required counsel to either impute more responsibility to a co-suspect, offer evidence of intoxication at the time of the crime, or present other witnesses who would offer different character evidence. Casting doubt on the conviction, as distinct from attempts to dissuade the trier of fact from imposing the death penalty for reasons of mental instability, age, or lack of premeditation, is regarded as one effective alternative according to studies on this subject. But Correll had argued he was not responsible for the crimes, i.e., he was innocent. Forced by the jury verdict to disregard any alternative strategy, defense counsel confronted a mountain of rebuttal evidence in the prosecution file if he introduced mitigating evidence.

Defense counsel, confronted with devastating rebuttal evidence, and possessed of no favorable psychiatric evidence from testimony by doctors, lacked a resource to avoid the death penalty. More disturbing is the majority 9th Circuit decision disregarding the facts. According to the majority, counsel failed to explain mitigating evidence of drug use, brain damage, family history, or medical records. In fact, there is no evidence Correl was under the influence of drugs at the time of the murders, no evidence of brain damage, and counsel knew of no attempts by his family to offer mitigating evidence. The presentence report prepared by the probation department also provided additional damaging information to the trial judge.

The majority also contended that counsel did not seek testimony from a chaplain at prison. As the dissenting judge pointed out, the chaplain refused to testify and the court majority failed to mention that counsel interviewed thirty to forty witnesses, none of whom would have testified favorably. There was no expert testimony from psychiatrists.

The distortion of the facts in the majority decision identified by the dissenting judges is inexcusable, but not the first time the 9th Circuit had reweighed or ignored the evidence. The *Corell* case is another prime example of an appellate court reweighing the evidence and dismissing state and district court findings. Appellate courts were mandated to defer to factual findings supported by the evidence even prior to enactment of AEDPA. In 109 pages the district court judge had outlined its findings, essentially ignored by the 9th Circuit.

The majority in *Correll*, finding reasons not to impose the death penalty on grounds defense counsel was "ineffective," creates an insurmountable dilemma for lawyers in death penalty cases. If defense counsel had offered mitigation evidence, the prosecution could have introduced Correll's previous conviction for armed robbery, confinement and escape from a mental facility, rape, and molestation of his sister. If counsel does not submit mitigating evidence, the 9th Circuit criticizes him for not doing so. This is the classic "catch-22."

The Supreme Court test in the *Strickland* decision, discussed earlier, requires reversal on appeal only if assistance of counsel is ineffective to a point the defendant was prejudiced. This test is quintessentially fact specific and a court can always cite *Strickland* as justification for its decision - and then misapply it. But the judges on the 9th Circuit did not hear the evidence at trial, were not present at the trial or sentencing, and did not participate in the two evidentiary hearings. From a cold record and by misstating the evidence, the majority undermined the death penalty.

The Supreme Court has repeatedly cautioned Courts of Appeal from second-guessing trial counsel and their sentencing strategy at trial. The 9th Circuit majority in *Correll* had done just that in a case now almost a quarter century old. The 9th Circuit originally wrote the *Correll* decision in 2008.

The 9th Circuit dissenting judge explains:

> I respectfully dissent from the court's conclusion that Correll has met his "highly demanding and heavy burden of establishing actual prejudice" [citing Supreme Court decisions] in the pursuit of his claim of ineffective assistance of counsel during the penalty

phase of the trial. The majority ignores the mountain of precedent which provides that, in assessing prejudice, we must consider not only the likely benefits of the mitigating evidence counsel failed to present, but also its likely drawbacks. The majority also substitutes its independent analysis of the record for that of the district court [judge] and relies on its own view of the evidence rather than considering, as we must, the effect the evidence would have had on an Arizona sentencing judge twenty-two years ago. Because I do not believe that Correll has met his burden 'affirmatively [to] prove prejudice, I would affirm the judgment of the district court denying the petition for writ of habeas corpus."

In a subsequent hearing on resentencing, and without explanation, the State of Arizona withdrew its intention to seek the death penalty. Correll will now spend the rest of his life in prison. Once again 9th Circuit judges had stymied the death penalty by merely causing delay in a case unsupported by evidence and a violation of their duty as appellate court judges.

Harrington (Warden) v. Richter, 131 S.Ct. 770 (2011); Reversing the 9th Circuit decision in *Richter v. Harrington,* 578 F.3d 944 (9th Cir. 2009).
The state court had affirmed Richter's conviction on appeal from a jury verdict finding him guilty of murder and voting the death penalty. The district court denied Richter's petition for habeas corpus. Richter appealed to the 9th Circuit, and the three-judge panel affirmed that decision in *Hickman v. Richter.* The full 9th Circuit court reheard the case and reversed the trial court, granting the petition for habeas corpus. The Supreme Court reversed that decision in no uncertain terms.

Some judges on the 9th Circuit, uninformed of trial strategy in criminal cases, and ignoring the vast amount of prosecution evidence, continue to find some excuse for finding "ineffective assistance of counsel." In *Richter v. Hickman* the overwhelming evidence had established Richter's guilt, but the 9th Circuit on rehearing faulted defense counsel for not interviewing a "blood spatter" expert to examine evidence that had played almost no part in the case. The dissenting judges scathingly challenged the importance of this single piece of evidence (blood spatter) of no significant value in finding ineffective assistance of counsel.

Here is the opening paragraph of from the dissenting judges in the case reversed by the 9th Circuit majority of judges:

> "Years of consuming forensic science television shows have gone to our heads. We know the plot by heart: the hapless State has charged the wrong guy and our scientists-turned-sleuths will come up with the trial-changing evidence at the last minute. But *State v. Richter* isn't the pilot for *CSI: Sacramento* [California]. Real trials are rarely as gratifyingly formulaic as those seen on TV, and real defense attorneys can seldom boast the Holmesian [referring to Oliver Wendell Holmes] intuition imputed to them by savvy scriptwriters. In the real world, defense attorneys must often contend with an unsympathetic bench, financial and temporal pressures, and unexpected evidentiary developments. They must also sometimes decide between various unappealing defense strategies. When we ignore these gritty realities and do not adequately analyze the specific circumstances surrounding an attorney's performance, we inevitably fail to heed the Supreme Court's admonition about second-guessing trial counsel. The majority opinion is a model of the intrusive post-trial inquiry into attorney performance long rejected by the (Supreme) Court."

On appeal from the 9th Circuit majority decision granting the petition for habeas corpus, the Supreme Court used far harsher words in condemning the 9th Circuit judges for refusing to grant deference to state court findings previously affirming the conviction and sentence. Not only did the 9th Circuit fail to defer to the state court, said the Justices, but it employed the wrong legal test for reviewing a state court decision required by AEDPA.

Harrington v. Richter, an eight-to-one decision by the Supreme Court, rebuked the 9th Circuit in a verbal lashing that summed up years of its repeated defiance of AEDPA. The Richter case represents a line of 9th Circuit reversals on the same ground of "ineffective assistance of counsel" because it is the only legal device an appellate court can invoke in the absence of any errors in the trial. The 9th Circuit decision in *Richter* mocked the state court and the Supreme Court as it had done frequently in death penalty cases.

On return of the case to the court after reversal by the Supreme, the 9th Circuit upheld the conviction, but in an unsigned decision the court listed other issues originally undecided and not addressed by the Supreme Court.

People v. Alcala, (case remains in California Supreme Court awaiting mandatory appeal after conviction in Los Angeles Superior Court.
In 1979, Alcala was convicted of the brutal murder of a young woman. A forest service staff employee found the decomposed body of the girl, and subsequent examination revealed her severed hands and smashed skull. The evidence at trial was overwhelming against Alcala, and the jury returned a guilty verdict and voted the death penalty. Due to an erroneous trial court decision, the California Supreme Court reversed the conviction, and on retrial the jury again returned a guilty verdict and death sentence. The California Supreme Court affirmed the conviction.

Alcala filed habeas corpus in district court, and the judge granted the petition. The state appealed on this 1979 conviction, and the 9th Circuit agreed with the district court judge on the familiar "ineffective assistance of counsel," excuse, retrying the case in the appellate court without seeing the witnesses or hearing the evidence. This case was tried before AEDPA was enacted in 1996, allowing the 9th Circuit more latitude. The State did not seek review from the 9th Circuit opinion in the U.S. Supreme Court. Instead, the prosecutor filed four additional counts of murder and again sought the death penalty. Alcala sought court severance (separation) of the multiple counts of murder, each excruciatingly brutal. On June 18, 2008, the California Supreme Court filed its decision denying his request; *Alcala v. Supreme Court*. Alcala faced face multiple counts of murder instead of one.

On retrial in March, 2010, the jury convicted Alcala of four counts of murder and voted the death penalty. After his automatic appeal to the California Supreme Court, and assuming the court affirms the conviction and death sentence, the 9th Circuit will undoubtedly see this case again. But this time the court must review the verdict and sentence under the stricter standards of AEDPA, not the simplistic standards used in its original decision. Alcala, originally convicted in 1979, is still in the courts in 2014.

Premo v. Moore, 131 S.Ct. 733 (2011). Reversing the 9th Circuit decision in *Moore v. Czerniak* (Warden), 598 F.3d 1042 (2010); 534 F.3d 1128 (9th Cir. 2008) [original decision].
The original 9th Circuit decision reversing the district court judge was denied a rehearing by the 2-1 panel and a rehearing by the entire court; 574 F.3d 1092 (9th Cir. 2009). The Supreme Court granted review; Belleque, Supt. v. Moore, and reversed. Here are the words of the dissenting judge in the 9th Circuit decision:

"Randy Moore and others beat Kenneth Rogers until he bled, stripped him, bound him in duct tape, placed him in the trunk of a car, drove him to a remote location, and forced him to march up a hill at gunpoint. While marching Rogers through the woods, Moore shot Rogers-accidently he said-through the temple. Moore confessed the details of the crime to his older brother, Raymond, and his step-brother's girlfriend who had talked to police prior to Moore's arrest. Moore subsequently confessed to police, corroborating the evidence the police had already obtained."

These facts, taken verbatim from the dissenting judge's opinion in this case, were undisputed and provided by Moore himself. Before the prosecution sought Moore's indictment, defense counsel negotiated a plea bargain with the prosecutor who offered the lowest sentence available under Oregon law for murder. But according to the 9th Circuit panel majority (2-1), defense counsel should have made a motion to suppress Moore's confession. Had counsel done that, said the majority panel, he would have been in a better position to negotiate a plea other than the "harsh" sentence he received pursuant to the plea bargain. (The appropriate sentence for Moore, based on kidnapping and murder if the prosecution could prove its case at trial would be the death penalty).

The majority of 9th Circuit judges focused on failure of counsel to file a motion to suppress Moore's confession on grounds the police had failed to advise him of his right to counsel, failed to advise him of his right to remain silent in violation of the *Miranda* decision, and promised him leniency. Neither the Oregon courts reviewing the conviction, nor the district court reading Moore's petition for habeas corpus, agreed with the majority decision. Both state and federal courts had noted that prior to his confession to police, Moore had confessed to his brother and his stepbrother's girlfriend. In an evidentiary hearing held in state court, the brother repeated the essence of the confession with no indication he and the girlfriend would not testify for the prosecution. Nevertheless, for purposes of the appeal from the district court, the 9th Circuit majority and the dissenting judges in their 9th Circuit respective decisions assumed the confession to police inadmissible. The 9th Circuit majority of judges reversed on that ground.

Other than the multiple confessions, the evidence was overwhelming. A codefendant had led police to the location of the weapon used by Moore; police seized the car used in the kidnapping and found duct tape concealing the license plates; several other witnesses saw Moore leave a house with Rogers and other codefendants. Finally, the defense attorney in an evidentiary hearing held by the Oregon court had explained all the options available to Moore prior to his entering a plea.

The dissenting judge in the Moor case contended the majority judges again displayed a total misunderstanding of criminal law and procedure:

"The majority [decision] . . . reflect[s] an almost willful ignorance of the record evidence and the realities of criminal defense representation. In the first place, the prosecution had not indicted [charged] Moore, enabling him to plead without the necessity of an Information [formal charge of the crime] that would have alleged burglary, kidnapping, and felony murder. Secondly, a co-defendant refused to accept any plea bargain, went to trial, and the jury found him guilty; third, if counsel wanted to suppress the confession to police by filing a motion, the prosecution would have resisted and obviously withdrawn the plea agreement; fourth, a trial for felony murder and kidnapping is subject to the death penalty."

"Brushing aside AEDPA requiring federal court deference to state court decisions, the majority of the 9th Circuit panel faults counsel for not moving to suppress the confession, citing a Supreme Court case acknowledging the importance and devastating evidence of a confession; *Arizona v. Fulminante.* An obvious truism, except Moore never cited the case in his appeal, and in any event the evidence in *Fulminante* concerned a confession after trial, not prior to a plea agreement. The majority ignores the leading case on 'ineffective assistance of counsel' when a defendant pleads guilty, and the Supreme Court has reminded the 9th Circuit on more than one occasion, particularly when reviewing a state court conviction on habeas corpus, that second-guessing and ruminating about alternatives available to counsel is forbidden to an appellate court.

The Supreme Court test, ignored by the majority of 9th Circuit judges, to set aside a plea bargain on grounds of ineffective assistance of counsel dictates that : . . . the defendant must show that there is a reasonable possibility that, but for counsel's errors, he would not have pleaded guilty and would have insisted on going to trial. There is no evidence Moore wanted to go to trial in any state or federal court."

As the dissenting judge points out, because of this decision a defense lawyer must file any motion possible before a defendant enters a plea. The prosecution is unlikely to regard this tactic as an inducement to recommend a reduced sentence. The murder occurred in 1995, affirmed on appeal by Oregon courts and in a federal district court. On appeal of that decision to the 9th Circuit, the court heard argument in 2005 and filed its decision in 2008. Thirteen years passed between conviction and decision. The dissenting judge skewered the decision, contending the case should have been a candidate for a rehearing by the full court:

The language of his dissent:

"I cannot join anything the majority has written. For the reasons I have stated, I believe the majority to be wrong on the facts and the law, and I believe that it fails to accord the state court's decision the deference that AEDPA commands. At the end of the day, it is not clear what the majority has accomplished, for Moore or for anyone else. The majority grants Moore a writ of habeas corpus and orders the state either to permit Moore to withdraw his plea or to release him. Oregon will surely allow Moore to withdraw his plea and then prosecute him to the hilt. When it does, Oregon will be under no obligation to offer Moore any kind of a deal, and if it does decide to bargain, it has no obligation to offer Moore a plea bargain as attractive as what he got in this case. It may even decide to seek the death penalty. And even if Oregon were to offer a new plea deal, Moore's counsel must reject it until he has filed every conceivable pre-trial motion he can. After today's decision, no conscientious defense attorney should even consider accepting a plea deal no matter how good the bargain and no matter what other evidence the prosecutor has if there are potentially "meritorious" motions that can be filed.

"Oregon will try Moore and, given his confessions to family and friends, the available eyewitnesses, and other incontrovertible evidence, Moore will likely be found guilty of murder. For that, he is likely to receive a sentence well in excess of the bargain he negotiated. It is quite possible that Moore will be worse off for having prevailed here. Nor is it clear that anyone else after Moore will actually benefit from today's ruling. In fact, defendants whose counsel cannot negotiate plea agreements until after exhausting their pre-trial motions are likely to be worse off for the majority's effort."

Today's decision is not a liberty-enhancing decision. It will actually hamper defense counsel's ability to avoid trial and negotiate plea agreements. And our decision is so unnecessary. Moore is plainly guilty of felony murder, or worse. He took a fair deal from the prosecutor on the advice of competent counsel. Justice was served. There is no reason for us to up-end the orderly administration of justice in Oregon in this way."

Pirtle v. Morgan, 313 F.3d 1160 (9th Cir. 2002)
Without reciting all of the brutal facts in this case, suffice it to say Pirtle robbed employees in a restaurant and slashed several of their throats. The evidence overwhelmingly established his guilt, the jury convicted him, and he was sentenced to death. He appealed to the Washington Supreme Court without ever criticizing his lawyer. The Washington Supreme Court affirmed the conviction and death penalty.

The Washington state court sensibly disallows issues not presented on appeal to serve as grounds for subsequently granting a petition for habeas corpus after conviction. Pirtle filed a petition for habeas corpus in federal court. According to the 2-1 9th Circuit panel of judges, counsel for Pirtle neither offered evidence of "diminished capacity" (a plea equivalent of not guilty) nor a jury instruction on the issue, but did submit a jury instruction enabling the jury to find the defendant was intoxicated at the time of the murders. Counsel had presented evidence on that theory in the trial court.

As the dissenting judge on the 9th Circuit panel notes, the jury rejected intoxication as a defense and found the defendant guilty of first degree murder, a finding which requires evidence of premeditation. If the jury concluded the defendant was not intoxicated, as they did by finding premeditation, the diminished capacity instruction-which precludes premeditation-becomes irrelevant.

This case exemplifies the absurdity of two jurisdictions retrying the same case, and allowing federal courts to consider issues never raised on direct appeal in state court, aside from the absurdity of the 9th Circuit decision in itself.

Lewis v. Mayle, [Warden], 391 F.3d 989 (9th Cir. 2004)

Eight years after his conviction for murder, Lewis sought habeas corpus relief from the 9th Circuit after denial of his motion for a new trial by the state court judge. The California Court of Appeal had affirmed his conviction, and the district court judge had denied his petition for habeas corpus. Lewis alleged he had signed an invalid waiver of attorney "conflict of interest" form and additionally alleged the failure of counsel to effectively represent him at trial deprived him of his Sixth Amendment right to counsel.

A single witness testified he was present when Lewis shot and killed the victim. Undergoing cross-examination, the witness's credibility was questioned because of previous burglary convictions and evidence of personal enmity toward the victim. The California Court of Appeal noted that defense counsel for Lewis had conducted a withering cross examination of the witness but did not ask him about his recent drunk driving conviction and subsequent probationary status.

The defense attorney who represented Lewis at trial had previously served as counsel for the witness in his drunk driving prosecution. Counsel required Lewis to acknowledge the previous legal representation and agree, in writing, to waive the conflict of interest. Although the court advised Lewis to contact independent counsel prior to signing the waiver form, he never exercised this option. At a hearing held after the original trial, defense counsel testified he did not ask the witness about the drunk driving conviction because he thought it unnecessary. The witness had already been established as unreliable.

The 9th Circuit reviewed the signed waiver (also signed by the witness) and the only error the court could find was the defendant's failure to obtain independent counsel to review the waiver. The court said: "[T]here is no specific evidence that . . . defendant] understood any of the ramifications of his waiver." The 9th Circuit further concluded that the failure to cross-examine the witness on his drunk driving conviction and probationary status was ineffective and adversely affected the defendant's right to effective assistance of counsel.

Congress passed AEDPA to prevent exactly this kind of reasoning. Recitation of the facts at trial had alerted the trial judge to the potential conflict in legal representation, and he had discussed it briefly with Lewis (but not fully enough for the 9th Circuit). The record reveals the unsavory character of the principle witness, yet the jury had rendered a unanimous verdict.

For reasons not altogether clear, the same witness offered to pay counsel to defend Lewis. If the witness expected counsel to act ineffectively, he was surprised by his intensive cross-examination. The most obvious reason counsel failed to ask about the drunk driving conviction was the inadmissibility of misdemeanor convictions to impeach a witness under state law.

In its decision, the California Court of Appeal criticized the waiver also but did not rule on the issue, thereby enabling the 9th Circuit to review the waiver issue anew rather than deferentially as required by AEDPA. The 9th Circuit's panel efforts to reverse the conviction, despite affirmance by every other court reviewing the verdict that counsel failed to impeach the witness for a drunk driving conviction, defies understanding. California Attorney General (Lockyer) sought no review in the Supreme Court.

As noted above, the Supreme Court has repeatedly insisted the 9th Circuit defer to state courts as a matter of comity and federalism reflected in AEDPA. To illustrate the ability of the 9th Circuit to circumvent this statute and Supreme Court decisions, here is an excerpt from the judges' decision in *Lewis v. Mayle*: "[Under AEDPA] we still look to our own law for its persuasive authority in applying Supreme Court law. Our cases may be persuasive authority for purposes of determining whether a particular state court decision is an 'unreasonable application' of Supreme Court law."

In *Lewis v. Mayle* the 9th Circuit relied heavily on its own decision (*Belmontes v. Woodford*), a case reversed by the Supreme Court in *Wong v. Belmontes*. The 9th Circuit in *Lewis* v. *Mayle* reversed the trial judge who denied a motion for new trial, the California Court of Appeal, the California Supreme Court, and the federal district court judge. All had denied Lewis' motion.

Defense lawyers are often caught in a dilemma on trial strategy. Based on 9th Circuit opinions, if the court finds counsel rendered "ineffective of counsel; they run the risk of losing their license to practice law. Beginning in 2002 and ending in 2013 the 9th Circuit has reversed almost every death penalty case on grounds of "ineffective assistance of counsel" no matter how specious or tenuous.

Libberton v. Ryan(Warden, 583 F.3d 1147 (9th Cir. 2009)
Libberton and three other men drove the victim to a mine, where Libertine shot him, hit him over the head with a rock, dragged him over to a mine shaft and threw him down. The 9th Circuit reversed on grounds of "ineffective counsel."

Styers v. Schriro(Warden, 547 F.3d 1026 (9th Cir. 2008)
Styers planned and carried out the execution of his live-in girlfriend's four-year-old child, presumably to obtain insurance proceeds. The jury found him guilty, and the court sentenced him to death. The Arizona Supreme Court affirmed the conviction, as did the district court on habeas corpus. On appeal of that decision to the 9th Circuit, the court held that the doctors who testified on behalf of Styers in the trial court could not connect his alleged posttraumatic stress disorder to the killing. According to the 9th Circuit, this "nexus" test is Constitutional error, as the court must consider all mitigating evidence without considering its specific relationship to the crime.(childhood; family; psychological; religion). The Arizona Supreme Court did just that, as the 9th Circuit concedes, noting . . . the Arizona Supreme Court considered all of the proffered evidence." Despite that statement written by the Arizona Supreme Court, the 9th Circuit nevertheless reversed. Inexplicably, the Supreme Court denied review; *Ryan v. Styers).*

Secret v. Ignacio (Warden), 549 F.3d 789 (9th Cir. 2008).
"On May 14, 1983, twenty-two-year-old Ricky Secret kidnapped and murdered ten-year-old Maggie Weaver and nine-year-old Carly Villa. A few weeks later, two men found the girls' bodies in Logomarsino Canyon, a remote area east of Nevada." This "summary" of the evidence by the 9th Circuit panel is the only reference to the facts in this case. Unable to find any legal error during the trial, the 9th Circuit seized on statements by the prosecutor to the jury in the penalty phase correctly quoting Nevada law on the ability of the state to grant parole to any person convicted of murder. Because the prosecution had such an overwhelming case, including a confession of the defendant, the need to convince the jury to impose the death penalty did not require commenting on their concern about parole. The prosecutor could merely recite the evidence and any jury would have voted the death penalty.

The 9th Circuit seized on this allegedly "inflammatory" argument from the prosecutor to vacate the death penalty after the Nevada Supreme

Court and district court judges affirmed the conviction and penalty. And, without any authority, and absent any request from defense counsel, the 9th Circuit panel ordered the Warden to remove Secret from death row.

The district court held a subsequent hearing and resolved certain issues but asked counsel for additional argument in this 1983 case.

No doubt the prosecution will retry Secret. In the meantime, the Supreme Court refused to grant review of another 9th Circuit reversal of the death penalty.

Taylor v. Maddox, 366 F.3d 992 (9th Cir. 2004)
State and federal courts of appeal exist to review civil and criminal cases in order to determine whether any legal error occurred in the trial courts. Legal error is not factual error. Trial court judges and juries alike listen to the witnesses, consider the evidence, and resolve conflicts in the testimony.

The Supreme Court has repeatedly told the 9th Circuit to desist meddling in credibility findings. *Taylor v. Maddox* is an example of 9th Circuit evasion of this warning. A trial judge listened to the conflicting accounts of a detective and the defendant/prisoner who confessed to police in 1993. The state court trial judge specifically stated he did not assign credibility to the defendant. The jury convicted the defendant, and after the California Court of Appeal affirmed the conviction and a district court judge denied habeas corpus, the 9th Circuit on appeal eleven years later wrote that it preferred the defendant's version of the facts.

The federal courts sit as coequals to state courts, and under AEDPA are limited in their scope of review. When a state court affirms a conviction on appeal the federal courts owe deference, and AEDPA mandates a presumption of correct findings of fact. In *Taylor* the 9th Circuit completely ignores the role of a federal appellate court.

Shad v. Ryan (Warden), 131 S.Ct. 2092 (2011). Reversing the 9th Cir. 606 F.3d 102 (9th Cir. 2011) 2-1 judge opinion).

This case was prosecuted, and Shad convicted in 1982; it was reversed by the 9th Cir. The 9th Cir. reversed by the Supreme Court in 2011 in a decision citing its decision in *Cullen v. Pinholster*, 131 S.Ct 1388 (2011).

Ryan (Warden) v. Detrich, 131 S.Ct. 2449 (2011), Reversing the 9th Circuit decision in *Detrich v. Ryan*, 619 F.3d 1038 (2010).

The facts in this case are nauseating, but were reported by the 9th Circuit panel in its decision. Detrich picked up a woman who led him to a location allegedly a source of drugs. After acquiring cocaine, Detrich and the victim were unable to inject cocaine, Detrich blamed the woman. The 9th Circuit wrote,

"[Detrich] then told the victim they were going for a ride, and Detrich, and [one] Charlton, left in Charlton's car . . . Charlton drove, Detrich sat in the middle, and victim sat on the passenger side, against the door. Charlton testified that, while stopped at a red light, he saw Detrich humping the victim and asking her how she liked it . . . Soon thereafter, Charlton looked again and saw that [the victim's] throat was slit. Charlton further testified that Detrich then hit the victim and asked her who gave her the drugs, and that the victim only gurgled in response. Detrich asked twice more, and the victim again responded with only a gurgle . . . Charlton claims that he never saw Detrich actually stab the victim, but that he himself was poked in the arm with a knife several times. A pathologist established that the victim was stabbed forty times."

The jury convicted Detrich of this vicious and despicable crime, the death penalty was imposed, the Arizona Supreme Court upheld the conviction as did the district court on habeas corpus. The 9th Circuit reversed on grounds of ineffective assistance of counsel, ignoring deference to the Arizona Supreme Court and the district court judge. The 9th Circuit panel conducted an independent review of counsel's performance (a practice criticized by the Supreme Court and ignored AEDPA). Inexplicably, the 9th Circuit panel allowed Detrich to present evidence on appeal he had never submitted in any Arizona court.

The Supreme Court reversed this manifestly unjust and irresponsible decision peremptorily, citing another 9th Circuit case previously reversed on similar grounds; Cullen v. Pinholster; 131 S.Ct. 1388 (2011).

As the cases in this Chapter demonstrate, the Supreme Court has repeatedly reversed the 9th Circuit on the same ground: ineffective assistance of counsel. *Pinholster v. Cullen* and *Harrington v. Richter*, two death penalty cases decided by the Supreme Court in 2011, use the harshest and most emphatic language in ordering the 9th Circuit to discontinue its disobedience of the law. Yet even after these decisions, one judge of the 9th Circuit will never confirm the "effectiveness" of counsel in any death penalty case (or any other case, for that matter), no matter regardless of what counsel does; Leavitt v. Arave.

McMurtrey v. Ryan (Warden), 539 F.3d 1112 (9th Cir. 2008)

The 9th Circuit panel granted habeas corpus to a state prisoner thirteen years after the jury had convicted McMurtrey of murder, and the court had sentenced him to death. The state court judge subsequently held a six-day competency hearing, and found that the defendant was competent to stand trial. The Arizona Supreme Court affirmed the conviction. On habeas corpus the 9th Circuit panel, ignoring the state court findings and hearing no evidence from witnesses, found that McMurtrey was not competent to stand trial. The state court requested a second competency hearing, but the 9th Circuit panel held that the thirteen year period was too late. A convicted murderer escaped the death penalty.

U.S. v. Duncan, 643 F.3d 1242 (9th Cir. 2011)

In one of the most vicious crimes committed anywhere, Duncan prepared to kill a woman and her children.

Duncan entered the house wearing a mask and carrying duct tape; tied up the woman and her children; beat one of the occupants to death with a hammer; kidnapped the children for seven weeks, beating and molesting them; and was ultimately captured and tried in state court. He pled guilty but received a life sentence (presumably because the 9th Circuit invalidated the Idaho death penalty statute) in state court..

Originally he wanted no trial but acted strangely enough to warrant a hearing on his mental competence. The experts disagreed, but the trial judge held Duncan competent. He waived counsel, produced no evidence, was convicted, and the jury imposed the death penalty. He also waived his right to appeal, though the court did not hold a competency hearing on this issue.

The 9th Circuit held he was entitled to another hearing on competency to waive counsel on appeal of the death sentence. A petition for review in the Supreme Court has been denied.

This decision is an unprecedented waste of judicial resources.

Schad (Warden) v. Ryan, 606 F.3d 1022 (9th Cir. 2010)
The facts in this case are horrendous but it is the interminable delay in carrying out the death penalty that is important. The defendant was convicted in 1982 and the judgment affirmed by the Arizona Supreme Court. The Supreme Court denied a hearing in 1991. The district court denied a petition on habeas corpus, but the 9th Circuit reversed and returned the case to the district court on procedural grounds in 2010. In 2011 the Supreme Court reversed the 9th Circuit and returned the case to the court. In 2011 the 9th Circuit reversed its earlier opinion and affirmed the denial of habeas corpus. From a 1982 conviction to 2011 the 9th Circuit has delayed this case. Twenty nine years between trial and appeal.

Duncan v. Ornoski (Warden), 528 F.3d 1222 (9th Cir.2008)
A few days after the 9th Circuit wrote its indefensible opinion in *Belmontes v. Ayers,* the same judge who wrote the majority opinion in that case reversed the "special circumstances" finding by the jury of state court prisoner Henry Duncan on grounds his counsel was "ineffective" in defense of a murder charge.

In 1984, Duncan was employed as a cashier at a restaurant where the female victim worked as his supervisor. Employees found her repeatedly stabbed body the day after the murder. The room was covered with blood, and money as well as the key to the safe were missing. A broken knife handle lay next to her body and bloody shoe prints lay on the floor. Investigators removed fingerprints and palm prints from the scene but none matched Duncan's prints at that time.

Three months later a second entry and theft in the same room resulted in money stolen from the safe, presumably opened by the key previously removed by the thief on the night of the murder. Police arrested and printed Duncan again. This time his fingerprints and palm prints matched the bloody prints taken at the murder scene. The bloody shoe prints also matched Duncan's shoes. To explain the initial inability to match those found at the scene of the crime, an investigator testified Duncan's fingerprints originally taken after the murder were unreadable, The key to the safe was found in Duncan's car.

An expert prosecution witness testified the blood samples found at the scene of the murder could not be matched because Duncan had submitted no sample. When the prosecution sought a court order at trial to extract a blood sample from Duncan, his counsel objected and, inexplicably, neither side introduced evidence of blood sampling. Defense counsel, with indisputable evidence establishing his client's presence at the scene of the murder, unquestionably faced a challenge to avoid the death penalty. A matching blood sample would be indefensible. As anticipated, the jury found Duncan guilty of felony murder, a killing in the course of a robbery, and voted the death penalty.

At a subsequent hearing held after the trial, defense counsel testified he wanted the absence of any evidence of blood comparison test at the trial, fearing a positive result would doom his client who had admitted to him he was present in the room on the night of the murder. The risk of a "match" of blood samples was too great, and counsel wanted the jury to hear no more evidence of Duncan's presence at the scene than they had already heard. Or, if the blood sample did not match, the jury would want to know who else was in the room besides Duncan. No such evidence existed.

After failing to reverse his conviction in state court or the federal district court, Duncan appealed denial of his habeas corpus petition to the 9th Circuit. In an embarrassing display of trial inexperience, the court said the failure of defense counsel to obtain a blood sample, even surreptitiously if possible, qualified his representation as "ineffective assistance of counsel." Yet counsel, knowing his client had already discussed his presence at the murder scene, concluded the decision not to secure a blood sample was a risk a lawyer must take - other than in the 9th Circuit.

At a subsequent evidentiary hearing ordered by the 9th Circuit, counsel testified he had attempted to establish that a third person had committed the murder but, according to the panel in its decision, he offered no physical evidence tying anyone else to the scene. What physical evidence could counsel present? The evidence unequivocally established Duncan's fingerprints, palm prints, and bloody shoe print were found in the "money room." Duncan worked on the premises, knew the location of money, and returned to the restaurant a second time to steal more money with the key to the safe found in his car-a separate crime to which he pled guilty.

In fact, said the California Supreme Court in 1991 when it had reviewed the case on appeal, "All of the physical evidence that was presented at trial tied Duncan to the crime scene." The 9th Circuit panel says nothing about the fact that had Duncan testified, and presumably he did not, he could have identified the other party. For counsel, the only basis to escape his client's culpability lay in establishing Duncan did not personally kill the victim, or that he acted as an accessory. Duncan produced no such evidence because none existed.

The 9th Circuit panel repeatedly mentions the failure of counsel to obtain a blood sample ad nauseam and criticizes this strategic omission. The 9th Circuit again reweighed the evidence, speculated on the outcome, and chastised counsel who faced overwhelming evidence of guilt and presented no blood sample somehow inculpating a third party or excluding Duncan. The panel said the lack of testimony on blood samples made no difference on the issue of guilt because of the overwhelming evidence but the jury verdict of "special circumstances" necessary to qualify a defendant for the death penalty phase was prejudiced by ineffective assistance of counsel warranting reversal of that finding.

This distinction without a difference is ludicrous and nothing more than speculation. The Supreme Court denied a petition by the State for review and that decision is equally incredulous. Another death penalty stymied. The murder occurred in 1984. The prosecution must either retry the sentencing phase of the case or accept the reality of its inability to do so. The 9th Circuit panel did not close the door on other claims despite affirming the conviction on the merits of the case as distinct from the sentencing: "We need not reach Duncan's remaining claims as they pertain only to the penalty phase and our decision . . . vacating Duncan's sentence renders those claims moot." **In other words, this decision is not the end of the case.**

CHAPTER 7

THE FOURTH AMENDMENT

A. *Exclusionary Rule*

When members of the Continental Congress enacted the Fourth Amendment to the U.S. Constitution, their language reflected colonial resentment toward British troops searching houses for "seditious" papers and rummaging through vessels for smuggled goods. This conduct occurred in the shadow of English history and incurred a high degree of colonial wrath. In an attempt to prevent the federal government from replicating this conduct, the delegates - all former British subjects - wrote the Fourth Amendment to the U.S. Constitution. "The right of the people to be secure in their persons, houses, papers and effects against unreasonable searches and seizures shall not be violated, and no Warrants shall issue, but upon probable cause, supported by Oath or affirmation, particularly describing the place to be searched and the persons or things to be seized." As originally written, the Fourth Amendment did not apply to individual states.

Searching homes without warrants particularly alarmed the colonial population. The Fourth Amendment represented a prophylactic objection to the practice although the language of the clause contained no mechanism of enforcement. In 1787 federal law enforcement officers did not exist, and individual state militias enforced the law. When these organizations eventually disappeared and were replaced by states, counties, and cities, each formed local law enforcement agencies. The federal government expanded, and Congress ultimately enacted legislation applicable to federal law enforcement officers although constitutionally restricted by the Fourth Amendment.

In 1914 the Supreme Court reviewed a criminal case involving a warrantless search of a house conducted by federal law enforcement agents. The "victim" of the search could obtain no judicial redress in the lower federal courts and sought a ruling from the Supreme Court. In *Weeks v. United States* the court concluded that a warrantless search of a home in violation of the Fourth Amendment would result in the exclusion at trial of any evidence seized by federal agents despite its incriminating nature. In subsequent years the Supreme Court carved out exceptions to this judicially imposed "exclusionary rule," but the general principle of law remains today and is applicable not only to people but to houses, apartments, cars, and personal property.

The Fourth Amendment did not apply to the states, and the vast majority of criminal cases were prosecuted in state court. In *Mapp v. Ohio* the Supreme Court, without citing any authority or precedent other than the general "due process" language of the Fourteenth Amendment, "incorporated" the exclusionary rule of the Fourth Amendment into all state court prosecutions. A dissenting judge wrote critically of this judicial usurpation of authority.

Enforcement of the exclusionary rule forbidding the prosecution from introducing incriminating evidence at trial has levied incalculable harm to the American public. The "constable blunders and sets the criminal free," paraphrasing Supreme Court Justice Cardozo when he sat on the New York Court of Appeals (*People v. Defore*). In the years since the decisions in *Weeks* and *Mapp*, federal and state judges have repeatedly interpreted the Fourth Amendment in determining the "reasonableness" of a search and seizure (arrest) conducted by a law enforcement officer, or the circumstances requiring the police to obtain a search warrant. Their written decisions have savaged an inordinate number of forests.

California courts under the late California Supreme Chief Justice Rose Bird ruled against prosecutors for the State of California so frequently on Fourth Amendment issues that voters replaced her and two of her colleagues in a general election. The public subsequently repudiated search and seizure rules decided by the California Supreme Court, and mandated the state court to abide by federal rules decided under the aegis of the United States Supreme Court. The Justices wrote: "Although the primary justification of the exclusionary rule . . . is the deterrence of police conduct that violates Fourth Amendment rights . . . it is not a personal constitutional right . . . nor calculated to redress the injury to privacy of the victim of a search and seizure, for any reparation comes too late. The rule is a judicially created remedy . . . to safeguard Fourth Amendment rights generally through its deterrent effect," *Stone v. Powell*.

The Supreme Court in *Stone* recognized not only the inability to measure the "deterrence" value of the exclusionary rule but the inordinate damage to public safety caused by its invocation. The *Stone v. Powell* decision case was a 9th Circuit case excluding relevant and incriminating evidence in a state court trial on habeas corpus review in federal district court and rendered after the state court had already ruled. The Supreme Court concluded that the cost of an appeal in the state court and a second collateral habeas corpus attack in federal court on the same issue outweighed its value.in Fourth Amendment cases. The Justices said as long as the state court affords the defendant an opportunity to challenge an alleged violation of the Fourth Amendment, the state forum is sufficient. Although that rationale is sensible, one can argue the *Stone v. Powell* decision implicitly recognized the penchant for 9th Circuit anti government and anti-state court rulings. As a result of the Powell decision, only the Supreme Court can reverse a state court ruling on the Fourth Amendment.

Despite judicial invention of the exclusionary rule, its support is eroding among many courts, including the Supreme Court. Yet the 9th Circuit continues to exclude evidence seized by federal agents not only in *federal* criminal cases but indirectly when a party files a civil case in federal court against a state government official alleging Fourth Amendment violations. In that event, the 9th Circuit can collaterally invoke its own interpretation of the Fourth Amendment by excluding relevant evidence and disallowing officers immunity from lawsuits to which they are otherwise entitled in civil cases.

For our purposes, the Supreme Court has divided analysis of the Fourth Amendment prohibition against unreasonable searches and seizures (arrests and temporary detentions) into several categories as explained below:

B. Search & Arrest
"Search:"
1) "Searches" of the person, place, vehicle, or property pursuant to a warrant;
2) "Searches" of the person, place, vehicle, or property without a warrant;
3) Probation and Parole Searches;
4) "Special Needs" Searches (Railroad employees; vehicular checkpoints; airports);
5) Border Searches;
6) Administrative Searches
"Seizure:"
1) "Detention" of a person to investigate past, present, or future criminal activity;
2) "Arrest" of a person placed in custody;
3) "Seizure" of property (vehicles and/or personal effects);
Courts have imported numerous sub-divisions of each of these categories, be we focus on 9th Circuit and Supreme Court decisions.

Los Angeles County v. Rettele, 550 U.S. 609 (2007). Reversing the 9th Circuit decision 186 Fed. Appx. 765.
Sheriff's deputies obtained a valid search warrant to search a specific house. According to the affidavit in support of the warrant, the premises were occupied by African American males, one of whom possessed a registered firearm. The deputies conducted a background check to

confirm the location of the suspects but were unaware the house had been sold.

Entering the house pursuant to the warrant, the deputies discovered two Caucasian adults asleep in bed. The deputies ordered the occupants out of bed and requested them to dress quickly. In the absence of locating any of the named suspects in the house, the deputies departed within fifteen minutes. The Caucasian occupants of the house sued the deputies and the Sheriff's Department, filing a civil rights complaint (42 U.S.C. 1983) subsequently dismissed by the district court judge.

The two occupants of the house appealed, and a 9th Circuit panel of judges reversed the district court. The panel found that the absence of African American occupants on the premises should have alerted the deputies to their mistake, thereby entitling plaintiffs to recover monetary damages. In support of its unpublished decision, the panel cited a blatantly irrelevant Supreme Court case. The County of Los Angeles appealed to the Supreme Court, and one Justice thought the 9th Circuit so obviously wrong he would dispose of the case summarily without briefing (filing legal papers) or argument from the parties.

The Supreme Court said this: "Because the Caucasian adults were of a different race than the occupants the deputies were seeking, the [Ninth Circuit] Court of Appeals held that 'after taking one look at the Caucasian adults the deputies should have realized that the Caucasian adults were not the subjects of the search warrant and did not pose a threat to the deputies' safety. We need not pause long in rejecting this unsound proposition." The Supreme Court noted the deputies entered pursuant to a valid warrant and ordered the occupants out of bed on the established grounds that suspects sleep with guns concealed by bed covers and pillows.

The Supreme Court recognized the need for deputies to control the situation, assure their personal safety, and reduce the prospect of flight. This common sense observation reflects a sensible decision by the Supreme Court. And justice John Paul Stevens, noting the two-to-one split among the panel of judges in the 9th Circuit decision, added this comment: "The fact that judges of the Court of Appeal disagreed [on the search issue] convinces me they should have not announced their decision in an unpublished decision."

Justice Stevens is correct. The 9th Circuit panel did not publish this case in the conventional volume of the *Federal Reporter*. Instead, the court buried its decision in an unpublished opinion that only lawyers or those familiar with legal research could find. And not only had the 9th Circuit panel indirectly invalidated the search, its decision also denied the officers immunity from a civil judgment. Had the 9th Circuit opinion gone unchallenged, the deputies and the County were subject to liability for money damages.

This case illustrates how a federal court, forbidden to review state court decisions on search and seizure, indirectly invalidates the search and concurrently confirms the right of the parties to file a civil suit in federal court exposing the officers and the County to liability for payment of money.

U.S. v. Grubbs, 547 U.S. 90 (2006); Reversing the 9th Circuit decision in 389 F.3d 1306 (9th Cir. 2004).

Pursuant to the language of the Fourth Amendment that "no warrants shall issue but upon probable cause particularly describing the place to be searched and the persons or things to be seized" the Supreme Court has encouraged law enforcement officers to obtain search warrants issued by a judge. If the judge signs the warrant, the Supreme Court instructed state and federal courts to extend deference to the prosecution in interpreting a challenge to the search if an arrest and prosecution ensue.

In some cases, the judge issues a warrant to seize weapons, clothing, stolen property, or other evidence of criminal conduct. In crimes without a specific victim, such as those involving drugs, contraband, or computer drives, the contraband is more readily concealed, and the scope of the search extends more intensively. In another class of crimes, the officers expect a specific act, event, or condition to occur prior to their entry to a dwelling house. In other words, the "things" subject to search under the Fourth Amendment need not be on the property until a "triggering" event occurs. The court classifies this category as an "anticipatory warrant." In most cases, this kind of warrant applies to drug sales or possession of drugs or weapons.

In U.S. v. Grubbs, postal inspectors investigating sexual crimes against minors allegedly committed by Grubbs prepared to surreptitiously mail a package to him at his home depicting sexually perverse conduct with a minor. The package was not delivered until after the inspectors presented an affidavit reciting the relevant facts of the investigation to a federal magistrate and obtained "an anticipatory search warrant," its service on Grubbs to be triggered only upon receipt at Grubb's house. The package was delivered and accepted by his wife. The inspectors entered the house, recovered the package, and arrested Grubbs.

Subsequently prosecuted and convicted, Grubbs appealed and contended that the failure to include the triggering condition (delivery of the package) in the language of the warrant itself, despite its inclusion in the affidavit in support of the warrant, invalidated the search. The 9th Circuit agreed. According to the 9th Circuit panel, the absence of notice of the triggering condition in the warrant disabled the occupant of "no real chance of policing the officer's conduct . . ." and to "be on the lookout and to challenge officers."

The Supreme Court dismissed this comment summarily. Aside from noting the Fourth Amendment contains no language requiring officers to exhibit the warrant at the outset of the search, the Supreme court said:. "[T]he Constitution protects property owners not by giving them a license to engage the police in a debate of the basis for the warrant . . . The Constitution permits a judge to determine whether to issue a warrant and to review it in the event of prosecution."

Reversing the 9th Circuit, the Supreme Court commented, "Because the Fourth Amendment does not require the triggering condition for an anticipatory search warrant be set forth in the warrant itself, the Court of Appeals erred in invalidating the warrant at issue . . . and the case is [returned] to the 9th Circuit for further proceedings consistent with this opinion."

The date of this Supreme Court reversal of the 9th Circuit panel is March 21, 2006. The panel rewrote its decision two years later within two weeks of that date. The panel wrote: "The order for publication [of the 9th Circuit decision] is hereby withdrawn. The panel will take up the remaining issues on appeal under consideration. The parties will be notified if supplemental briefing or additional argument is required;" U.S. v. Grubbs. The order contains neither a word about the Supreme Court reversal of the 9th Circuit panel decision nor an explanation of the "withdrawal" of the order. The court has not published any further decision.

In a subsequent case, U.S. v. Hector, the defendant also objected to the failure of the officer to exhibit the search warrant to the occupants during a search of a house. The district court judge excluded evidence found during the search, but the 9th Circuit reversed, undoubtedly warned by the language of the Supreme Court in the *Grubbs* case and the absence of any Constitutional requirement to exhibit the warrant on the occupant of a house. Hector filed a petition for review in the Supreme Court. Denied.

Muehler v. Mena, 544 U.S. 93 (2005); 156 Fed.Appx. 24. Reversing the 9th Circuit decision in Mena v. City of Simi Valley, 332 F.3d 1255 (9th Cir. 2003).

When the 9th Circuit wants to reverse its district court judges, or a state supreme court, or state court of appeals, the search of the trial record in quest of error is relentless. In criminal cases, the 9th Circuit panel: 1) seeks evidence the prosecution erroneously excused minority jurors during jury selection; (2) challenges jury instructions; (3) determines ineffective assistance of counsel; (4) cites prosecutorial misconduct; (5) scours the record for evidentiary errors and, when all else fails, (6) announces violation of some variety of "due process."

In civil cases, when police officers are sued for alleged violation of civil rights the analysis changes in favor of the plaintiff. Officers are denied immunity (to which they are otherwise entitled) from litigation against them and their public employers. Or, in some cases, the 9th Circuit panel cites inapplicable Supreme Court case law as authority for its decision, as it did in *Carey v. Musladin* (see the explanation in chapter 4), a case illustrating this judicial quest for error.

Part of any decision by an appellate court includes recitation of the facts elicited from witnesses who testified in the trial court. Here is the factual recitation of a 9th Circuit three-judge panel who wrote the original decision in the *Mena* case, subsequently reheard by the 9th Circuit's full panel, in reviewing the search and arrest of the occupants of a dwelling during service of a search warrant:

> "[The affidavit in support of the warrant stated]: The house located at 1363 Patricia Ave., which Anthony Romero [Raymond Romero's brother] described as a poor house, was owned by Jose Mena. Although Jose Mena lived at the Patricia Avenue residence only part-time, his daughter, Iris, was a full-time resident. In addition, several other unrelated boarders lived in the Menas' home, renting rooms in the house, space in the garage, and a motor home and vans parked in the backyard."

> "Officer Muehler wrote an affidavit in support of a warrant to search the Mena house for [deadly weapons], specifically firearms, and including ammunition, casings, holsters and cleaning equipment, knives and accessories such as sheave; [and] evidence of street gang membership or affiliation with any other street gang . . . [It was] a 'poor house' meaning "a residence with a large number of suspects in a residence designed for one family."

Apparently the officer had been to the residence before and had observed all the doors inside were shut and some padlocked. This information was not included in the warrant, but reflected an unusual provision for security in the context of the affidavit. According to the evidence, sixteen officers were involved in the investigation. The original three-judge 9th Circuit panel confirmed the validity of the search and the search warrant. Mena sought a rehearing of the decision.

Let's compare the language of the full 9th Circuit panel in *Mena* that reheard the case and reversed the original decision of the three-judge panel who had upheld the search warrant and subsequent search of the house. The full panel wrote: "Just before 7:00 a.m . . . several officers from the Simi Valley Police Department . . . executed a valid search warrant at 1363 Patricia Avenue. [Officers] Brill and Muehler [who had been sued], were directly responsible for supervising the search. The police officers searched the residence as part of their investigation of a gang-related drive-by shooting. The officers believed that Raymond Romero, the officer's primary suspect, was in the house, a single-family dwelling housing many unrelated suspects."

How placid and misguided this statement. This recitation of the facts by the full panel of 9th Circuit judges sounds as though the affidavit describes a routine search devoid of potential resistance or violence in a bucolic location occupied by numerous individuals. A brief single paragraph describes a perfunctory description of the premises, ignores the circumstances confronting the officers, and omits the extent of the evidence sought. The recitation sets the tone of a relatively harmless search and is a charitable characterization of the court's factual description.

The original 9th Circuit three-judge panel decision set the stage more realistically. The panel described innumerable occupants of a single family dwelling, a search for weapons, ammunition, knives and gang paraphernalia. The very language of the original court decision forecasts danger to the officers conducting the search. That sixteen officers participated in the search does not suggest a routine and harmless investigation.

And now this treacle from the 9th Circuit full panel: "Pursuant to the warrant, police forcibly entered the house, placed the plaintiff Iris

Mena [who subsequently sued the officers] in handcuffs, along with three other suspects, and transferred them to the garage . . . [T]he officers led Mena barefoot and still wearing her pajamas outside through the rain to a cold garage for personal surveillance while other officers searched the premises." The search yielded weapons, ammunition, and gang paraphernalia.

This sympathetic and pathetic summary, irrelevant and unrelated to any legal issue, serves as the basis for the civil case under the civil rights statute (42 U.S. C. 1983) alleging violation of the Fourth Amendment prohibition against unlawful seizures. This case, more than any other, confirms the thesis of this text. Apparently pity trumps gang violence.

During the search, immigration agents accompanying police questioned Iris Mena about her immigration status, but ultimately released her. Mena subsequently sued the city police department and the officers for violation of her civil rights by restraining her for an unreasonable amount of time. In her civil case she alleged that police should have neither handcuffed her nor questioned her immigration status.

The 9th Circuit full panel agreed with Mena because the affidavit in support of the warrant did not include her as a suspect. The result: exposing the officers and City to money damages. The State of California sought review of this decision in the Supreme Court. In reversing the 9th Circuit full panel decision, the Justices disposed of Mena's argument by ironically citing the same case law as authority for support of its decision as the 9th Circuit wrongly cited in its decision. The Supreme Court said, "the police have the right to detain suspects [and handcuff them] while conducting a search of the premises," and reversed the 9th Circuit with this language: "[T]he Court of Appeals [9th Circuit] improperly relied upon the fact that the warrant did not include [plaintiff] as a suspect. The warrant was not concerned with individuals but with locations and property . . . [the] connection of an occupant to [a] home alone justifies a detention of that occupant during a search."

The 9th Circuit full panel also determined the immigration agents violated Mena's Fourth Amendment rights by questioning her immigration status during her detention. Said the panel: "On these facts alone, we observe that Mena has alleged a violation of Constitutional rights." The Supreme Court dismissed this contention: "[We] have held repeatedly that mere police questioning does not constitute a seizure of the person [arrest or detention]...[E]ven when officers have no basis to suspect a particular individual, they may generally ask questions of that individual, [or] ask to examine the individual's identification... No independent basis for a Fourth Amendment violation occurred."

To add to the Supreme Court reproach, the Justices criticized the 9th Circuit for wrongly relying on a previous Supreme Court decision that summarized evidence necessary for border patrol agents to detain individuals attempting to enter the country illegally. The Supreme Court wrote: "We certainly did not, as the [9th Circuit] Court of Appeals suggested, create a requirement of particularized reasonable suspicion for purposes of inquiry into citizenship status." In essence, the full 9th Circuit panel had cited a border patrol case in their decision entirely unrelated and inapplicable to the officer's search of a gang-related location pursuant to execution of a valid search warrant.

The Supreme Court returned the case to the 9th Circuit. True to form, the panel conceded its reversal but reviewed the evidence and held in a subsequent case Mena was restrained *after* the search was completed, not during the search as written by the Supreme Court; *Mena v. City of Simi Valley*. The panel buried this sophistry in an unpublished decision and apparently the U.S. Attorney General did not seek review in the Supreme Court. The authors of the unpublished opinion have been reversed more that anyone on any federal appellate court.

The Supreme Court decision in *Mena* is eminently reasonable. But as one judge of the 9th Circuit panel noted, the Supreme Court case in Mena reversed three prior 9th Circuit decisions previously decided mandating "officers to restrict the questions [asked] during the stop (of a pedestrian or motorist) to those that are reasonably related to the justification for the stop." In a word, three individuals in those cases were released improperly on grounds attributable to erroneous 9th Circuit decisions. Because those cases were mandatory authority in the 9th Circuit for subsequent decisions predicated on the same factual basis, or applied by federal trial court judges to similar factual situations, it is impossible to calculate the damage to the public.

Tekle v. U.S., 511 F.3d 839 (9th Cir. 2007)

Despite the Supreme Court decision in *Muehler v. Mena* approving the right of officers to handcuff occupants of a house while conducting a search pursuant to warrant, the 9th Circuit ignored that Supreme Court decision in *Tekle v. U.S.* In fact, the court wrote its original decision in August 2006, granted a rehearing, and filed its amended decision in December 2007, almost fifteen months later.

In this case, federal agents executed a search warrant and briefly handcuffed an eleven-year-old child during the search of a house. His guardian sued, alleging violation of the Federal Tort Claims Act (a federal statute imposing civil liability on law enforcement officers under certain circumstances), and a federal claim for use of excessive force under the Fourth Amendment. The trial court granted summary judgment (dismissed the case) for the government, but the guardian of the minor appealed to the 9th Circuit, although this time ignoring any reference to the Tort Claims Act in his papers ["briefs"] filed in the court. "No matter," said the majority of the 9th Circuit panel, "we can exercise our discretion to hear the claim"-ignoring the opportunity for the government to respond.

The 9th Circuit judges took in excess of one year to rewrite the opinion without any explanation, deprived the government of an opportunity to respond to a claim never asserted in plaintiff's written argument, and ignored the *Mena* decision. For an unknown reason, the government did not seek review in the Supreme Court.

Entry to Search (Knock & Notice)
U.S. v. Banks, 540 U.S. 31 (2003); Reversing the 9th Circuit decision in
Banks v. U.S., 282 F.3d 699 (9th Cir. 2002).
Under federal law, federal agents serving a search warrant must announce
their presence prior to forcibley entering a dwelling place ("knock and
notice").

In U.S. v. Banks, the 9th Circuit reversed a criminal conviction and suppressed the evidence seized by police and FBI agents inside a house during
their search pursuant to a search warrant. The 9th Circuit panel based its
decision on a list of factors that determine when officers can dispense with
the knock-notice requirement if certain exigent circumstances exist such as
the presence of a fugitive, or a known armed suspect, or possible destruction
of evidence. According to the 9he Circuit, the facts in this case did not fit
the list. The State of California sought review in the Supreme Court.

The Supreme Court dismissed the 9th Circuit rationale. "We disap-
prove of the [9th] Circuit Court of Appeals [multiple] scheme for vetting
knock-and-notice announcements . . . [the] demand for enhanced evidence of exigency before a door can reasonably be damaged by a warranted knock-notice intrusion was already bad law before the [Ninth
Circuit] decided this case." In fact, said the Court, the 9th Circuit ignored
two Supreme Court cases (both reversing the 9th Circuit) [in which] "[w]
e recently disapproved a framework for making a 'reasonable suspicion'
determination that an attempt to reduce what the Ninth Circuit describes
as 'troubling uncertainty' in analysis."

The Supreme Court actually reversed the 9th Circuit three times (two
prior decisions on the same issue) in addition to the instant case. The 9th
Circuit panel, on return of the Supreme Court reversal in the *Banks* case,
transferred the case to the district court judge to comply with the Supreme
Court order.

In the event any ambiguity remained in the "knock and notice" cases,
the Supreme Court in a later decision removed all doubt by criticizing the

exclusionary rule requiring suppression of evidence. The court refused to apply Fourth Amendment analysis in knock and notice cases.

In *Hector v. U.S.* a 9th Circuit panel, sensing the displeasure of its previous rulings by the Supreme Court, did not suppress the evidence seized during the search although the officers did not display the warrant to the occupants. Hector filed a petition for review in the Supreme Court in September 2007. It was denied.

U.S. v. Black, 482 F.3d 1035 (9th Cir. 2006)

In addition to police officers' attempts to arrest suspects for investigation of criminal activity, they frequently must respond to domestic abuse calls. Experience confirms this fact situation is among the most dangerous activity confronting officers, and their presence frequently precipitates violence.

In *U.S. v. Black*, the officers responded to a domestic abuse telephone call from a woman who said she was threatened by a man with a gun. Police officers arrived at a pre-prearranged location recommended by the caller, but they saw no one. Unable to enter the locked apartment the woman had identified on the telephone, and concerned about her absence, officers searched the area and discovered Black in the backyard. A search of his person revealed a key to the locked apartment. Officers entered and saw no one, but observed a gun lying on the bed. The officers exited and obtained a search warrant for the gun.

The case was filed in federal court, and the district court judge ruled the evidence was admissible. The defendant appealed. Not all 9th Circuit judges are oblivious to reality, and can understand the world of criminal law. The common sense police decision in the *Black* case to determine whether the woman was alive or injured in her apartment was confirmed by two judges of a three-member 9th Circuit panel. One judge dissented, arguing with the facts and concluding the officers should not have entered the apartment at all. The reader can only imagine public reaction if police walked away without entering the apartment only to discover later that the victim had been found dead or seriously injured inside.

This three-judge panel subsequently wrote an amended opinion, but the dissenting judge continued her naïveté (*U.S. v. Black*). Unfortunately, other 9th Circuit judges share her views.

C. Arrest & Detention (Seizure of the Person)

The Supreme Court has categorized two categories of the word "seizure" of the person within the meaning of the Fourth Amendment: arrest and detention. An arrest occurs when officers take custody of a person for the purpose of charging a criminal offense. Detention occurs when officers temporarily stop a person to determine whether a crime has been committed, is being committed, or is about to be committed. In some cases, a crime has already been committed by someone and the officers are attempting to determine if the person detained is responsible.

Whether an "arrest" of a person by a law enforcement officer is a Constitutionally "reasonable" seizure is evaluated under the standard of "probable cause," a broad category applicable to an infinite variety of facts. The standard requires a review of the totality of circumstances to determine whether the officer had "probable cause," as required by the Fourth Amendment, that is, an "objectively reasonable: basis to arrest someone for commission of a crime. The officer can consider different types of "direct" evidence: conduct of the person; a reliable source of information from another person or officer; circumstantial evidence; and expertise. Court cases are endless and disagreement abounds among them.

Or, in the case of a detention," the officer must have a reasonable basis to interfere with the liberty of an individual on less than probable cause but based upon suspicious conduct, past, present or future. Cases in state and federal courts on this topic are also endless, but the penalty for lack of probable cause to arrest, or a reasonable basis to detain, is draconian:

inadmissibility at trial of any evidence found on the person during the arrest or detention process, and in some cases, additional evidence discovered in a car or house occupied by a person.

Stone v. Powell, 428 U.S. 465 (1976). Reversing the 9th Circuit decision in 507 F.3d 93 (9th Cir.1974) and noted earlier in this Chapter.
Powell was arrested by local police for vagrancy and convicted in a California court. After unsuccessful appeals in state court, Powell filed a petition for habeas corpus in federal court. The district court judge denied the petition, and Powell appealed to the 9th Circuit. In December 1974, the 9th Circuit reversed Powell's conviction on grounds the vagrancy ordinance was unconstitutionally vague and Powell's arrest was therefore illegal. The court commented, "The Fourth Amendment exclusionary rule serves no deterrent purpose with regard to police officers who were enforcing statutes in good faith, [but] *exclusion [of the evidence] would serve the public interest by deterring legislators from enacting unconstitutional statutes."* Italics added.

No decision could more forcefully express the frustration of the Supreme Court than this 9th Circuit opinion expressing judicial arrogance by instructing legislators in performance of their job. Without singling out the 9th Circuit, the Supreme Court decision in *Stone v. Powell* eliminated any further federal court habeas corpus review of search and seizure issues previously decided by state courts. *Stone v. Powell* was decided in 1976, but in 2009 the 9th Circuit continues to interfere with state legislatures in contexts unrelated to search and seizure. For example, in 2011 the Supreme Court removed habeas corpus jurisdiction from the 9th Circuit in all cases involving parole decisions made by state courts.

After thirty years of experience reviewing search and seizure cases from federal and state courts, the Supreme Court ultimately realized the horrendous damage imposed on society as a consequence of the rule excluding relevant and incriminating evidence when a court held that officers lacked "probable cause." In many cases, the officer's good faith was never in question, only the legal conclusion of a court prevailed.

In *Hudson v. Michigan*, the Supreme Court relented, and ruled that the "exclusionary rule could-and should-be inapplicable when balancing the gravity of the crime with "probable cause."

. . . Suppression of evidence, however, has always been our last resort, not our first impulse. The exclusionary rule generates 'substantial social costs which sometimes include setting the guilty free and the dangerous at large. We have therefore been 'cautious' against expanding [the rule], and have repeatedly emphasized, that the rule's 'costly toll' upon truth-seeking and law enforcement objectives presents a high obstacle for those urging [its] application. We have rejected '[i]ndiscriminate application' of the rule, and have held it to be applicable only 'where its remedial objectives are thought most efficaciously served', that is, 'where its deterrence benefits outweigh its 'substantial social costs.'" The judges in the 9th Circuit should read this case.

Aside from the damage caused by invocation of the exclusionary rule, the Supreme Court fashioned a civil remedy to ameliorate violations of the Fourth Amendment. Having invented the exclusionary rule in the first place, the Court approved a potential money damages remedy also without any statutory authority to do so. In addition, a federal statute specifically allows a civil lawsuit against the officers and the employing agency for alleged violation of civil rights, including those of the Fourth Amendment.

Fisher v. City of San Jose, 519 F.3d 908 (9th Cir. 2008): [on rehearing, 558 F.3d 1069 (9th Cir. 2009)]
"As judges, we should not armchair quarterback a crisis from the safety of our chambers. Such post-game analysis is disconnected from reality"

What facts induced this 9th Circuit judge, dissenting from a court decision written by two other judges on the panel, to write this scathing remark? What follows is an abbreviated version of the evidence in a civil case filed against the City of San Jose and several of its police officers alleging civil rights violation by a man named Fisher.

A security guard responding to a complaint of excessive noise in an apartment complex contacted Steven Fisher, an intoxicated tenant in the process of cleaning a rifle, and invited him outside to talk about the source of the noise. Fisher exited his apartment carrying the rifle. The guard, frightened by Fisher's menacing demeanor and intoxication during their conversation and fearing for his safety, contacted the San Jose Police Department. Police officers arrived shortly before 2:00 a.m. to investigate, but Fisher had returned inside his apartment and refused to open the door. He responded incoherently to the officers and cited the Second Amendment right to bear arms. He invited one of the officers into his apartment but threatened to shoot her if she entered.

Patrol officers called for support from an experienced team of officers. After the team arrived, officers observed Fisher walking around inside the apartment carrying a rifle. For several hours following and throughout the morning, he continued to walk around with the rifle. One officer testified at a subsequent trial that Fisher pointed his rifle at the officers, and at another time apparently loaded the weapon in their sight. For a period of six hours the officers could not see whether Fisher was armed or had other weapons accessible to him. Attempts to contact him by telephone were unsuccessful. Other uncontradicted testimony at trial established that Fisher had eighteen rifles in his apartment.

Police evacuated the entire apartment complex, extinguished electric power inside Fisher's apartment, broke its glass door and tossed in a "throw phone" to talk to him in lieu of the regular telephone line that had repeatedly emitted a "busy" signal. Officers threw a "flashbang" device into the apartment in an attempt to disorient Fisher, and subsequently they hurled tear gas canisters through the broken glass door. All tactics were to no avail. Ultimately police established contact with Fisher using the "throw phone," and he agreed to leave the apartment unarmed. Upon his exit, officers arrested Fisher although they never requested an arrest warrant from the court.

Fisher sued the City and several police officers in district court alleging the warrantless arrest entitled him to money damages. At the trial, the jury unanimously found in favor of the City and its police officers-including a verdict rejecting Fisher's claim that officers arrested him unlawfully without a warrant. Despite the jury verdict, the district court judge invoked a federal rule granting Fisher's motion for judgment in his favor as a matter of law, and ruled the arrest conducted without a warrant violated his rights. In an exercise of judicial hubris, the court awarded Fisher one dollar in damages and ordered the police department to conduct training on the law of arrest and search. On appeal by the City and its police officers, the two-to-one judge majority of the 9th Circuit panel affirmed the trial court ruling. The dissenting judge's words are quoted in the first paragraph above.

The 9th Circuit's two-member panel majority ruled that officers can only enter a house to effect an arrest if they have obtained an arrest warrant from a magistrate unless precluded by exigent circumstances or an emergency. According to the panel majority, the truncated version of the facts recited above does not constitute an emergency dispensing with the warrant requirement. In their opinion, evidence that an incoherent and intoxicated individual in possession of multiple firearms who threatened to shoot an officer, and avoided every attempt inducing him to exit the apartment, does not constitute an emergency dispensing with the need to obtain an arrest warrant.

Here is the panel majority rationale: the arrest warrant requirement "does not evaporate the moment officers surround a home with weapons and begin to take measures to induce an individual to leave his home . . . Rather, officers must obtain a warrant before any additional intrusions into the home if the initial exigency 'dissipates' sufficiently to allow the police to obtain a warrant."

The dissenting judge replies

> "What we have here is a very dangerous situation that was resolved safely for all concerned [including] Fisher, the public, and the

police, because of good police work. Nevertheless, the majority decision penalizes the police by announcing a new warrant requirement and imposing civil liability upon them for failing to obtain a telephonic arrest warrant in the midst of a police standoff that could have turned deadly at any moment . . . Armed standoffs are fluid and dangerous situations that are stressful, tense, and require difficult decisions to resolve peacefully . . . Armed standoffs always require [complex] tactical decisions that attempt to balance the safety of all involved."

The Fisher case is not prosecution of a criminal case initiated by an arrest conducted by officers who mistakenly concluded they had probable cause to arrest or lacked an arrest warrant. Fisher filed a civil case against the City of San Jose and its police officers exposing them to liability for alleged violation of his Constitutional rights. The jury verdict in favor of the City and its officers validated the propriety of the arrest, including a jury decision that police did not need an arrest warrant. The trial judge overruled the jury verdict and imposed his own version of the legal consequences of the arrest.

Neither the 9th Circuit panel majority nor minority panelists disagreed the officers had probable cause to arrest Fisher. They disagree as to the point in time the arrest triggered the necessity for a warrant, whether at the time of the initial confrontation when Fisher refused to emerge from his apartment, or when the officers physically took him into custody. The standoff took place from the initial nighttime contact at 2:00 a.m. until 2:30 p.m. the next day. Despite the trial record, the majority decision writes that during the entire time of the standoff the police never personally saw Fisher armed, (the security guard told them he possessed a rifle) allowing ample time to obtain a warrant, although he ignored repeated attempts to flush him out. Had the officers tried to enter the apartment, the court failed to recognize that Fisher could have quickly concealed himself, ambushed anyone who entered, and had the ability to stave off police with multiple firearms.

Fisher caused the six-hour period of time to elapse, not the officers, but according to the court majority, this period of time "dissipated" the emergency and permitted officers time to seek a warrant. The *Fisher* case stood for the proposition that when the initial emergency event is "dissipated," the justification for a warrantless arrest no longer exists. To avoid civil liability, the officers must seek judicial authorization for an arrest warrant, contact a judge, contact an officer to prepare papers or recite the facts telephonically to the judge in support of the affidavit, wait until the administrative process necessary to obtain the warrant concludes, review the accuracy of the warrant and affidavit, and notify relevant department personnel the arrest warrant has been issued.

The panel majority decision is replete with legal discussions of the Fourth Amendment prohibiting unlawful searches and arrests potentially imposing civil penalties on police officers. But in the *Fisher* case, academic hairsplitting confirms the dissenting judge's opinion of the panel majority decision: "disconnected from reality." As the minority judge panelist notes, officers will now have to determine when "dissipation" occurs - at their own risk. Fortunately, the full panel of 9th Circuit judges reheard the case and reversed the panel majority who wrote the decision described above. In the end, the City and its officers prevailed.

This case is reviewed in detail to illustrate the lack of ordinary common judicial sense and bias of 9th Circuit judges. A jury heard the case and delivered the correct verdict. The trial judge reversed the jury - the group selected to determine liability-upon his own initiative and found two other appellate judges with equally incoherent decisions. Had the Supreme Court read the decision of the majority original panel it would have verbally raked the district court judge and majority of the 9th Circuit panel.

County of San Francisco v. Rodis, 129 S.Ct. 1036 (2009). Reversing *Rodis v. City & County of San Francisco,* 499 F.3d 1094 (9th Cir. 2007); reheard after reversal; 558 F.3d 964 (9th Cir.2009). The Supreme Court vacated the original decision and returned it to the 9th Circuit for reconsideration.

As noted above, thousands of state and federal courts have wallowed in the "probable cause" to arrest requirement of the Fourth Amendment. As noted earlier, the Supreme Court imposed the exclusionary rule to prevent abuses of the Fourth Amendment and to deter police misconduct. But in untold numbers of cases, the officers acted in good faith, no abuse occurred, yet the court excluded the evidence. No court responded as eagerly to finding the officers lacked probable cause than the 9th Circuit. Here is an example of a case involving no harassment, no force or duress, in which the officer acted reasonably to an unusual set of circumstances, all of no concern to the 9th Circuit panel on appeal.

The precise legal issue in the *Rodis* case is "qualified immunity" which police officers and the City alleged as a defense to a civil rights suit filed against them. "Qualified immunity" is a legal defense to cases filed by person(s) alleging public officials violated their Constitutional rights. Public officials, usually police officers, are entitled to urge this defense and terminate the lawsuit (immunity from litigation) prior to trial as long as no Constitutional law violation occurred. Although the qualified immunity defense is more legally complicated, public officials must be able to perform their duties with considerable discretion and not be the subject of frivolous litigation in performance of their duties. The *Rodis* case illustrates the complete indifference to this defense by some of the 9th Circuit judges.

Rodis entered a drugstore to purchase miscellaneous items and paid for them with a one hundred dollar bill. The cashier examined the bill, became concerned that it might be counterfeit, and called the manager to inspect it. After testing the bill, the manager told Rodis "he was going to call the police." Officers arrived and inspected the bill but were uncertain of its authenticity and called Secret Service. Prior to their arrival, the officers arrested Rodis. Upon arrival of Secret Service agents and after listening to the officers, the agents concluded the bill was authentic. The officers drove Rodis home. Rodis was never jailed, abused, or threatened. Naturally, Rodis sued for false arrest and violation of his civil rights. In a

2-1 decision the 9th Circuit panel concluded the officers lacked "probable cause" to arrest him.

It is obvious that city police officers do not confront counterfeiting every day. In fact, even the average citizen cannot distinguish counterfeit bills. The officers in *Rodis*, cognizant that they lacked expertise, contacted Secret Service to validate or reject their suspicion. What alternatives did they have other than to arrest? Release Rodis and hope they would find him again? The 9th Circuit panel said Rodis was well known in the community. What relevance is that? Had officers released him and he fled the scene, who would be held responsible no matter how well Rodis was known in the city? Or, had they released Rodis earlier but Secret Service confirmed the bill as counterfeit, the cry of "favoritism" would emerge.

But the 9th Circuit panel concluded that police should not have arrested Rodis because they did not have evidence of all the elements of the crime of counterfeiting to establish probable cause. How often do city police officers have knowledge of the elements of the federal crime of counterfeiting? They obviously confronted a highly unusual set of circumstances and acted professionally. The exclusionary rule was completely absent from its philosophic base (deterrence of police misconduct) in this case, but invoked by the court to deny officers immunity and expose them and the city to money damages.

As the dissenting judge in *Rodis* explained, "The Supreme Court has long held that 'probable cause' [to arrest] does not require the same type of specific evidence of each element of the offense as would be needed to support a conviction (citing cases)." Citing another Supreme Court decision reversing the 9th Circuit, the dissenting judge then lists a host of other Circuit Court decisions disagreeing with the majority panel of judges in *Rodis*. The Supreme Court agreed to review the *Rodis* case and reversed the 9th Circuit, ordering it to reconsider its decision. Pursuant to that order the 9th Circuit reversed itself, but from the language of that decision you would never know the Supreme Court had reversed the 9th Circuit. In effect, the 9th Circuit had to repudiate its own decision.

The Fourth Circuit Court of Appeals, in an unpublished decision, wrote this language in a case involving similar circumstances: "We have previously rejected the argument that an item's illegality must be apparent to the searching officer at the precise moment that he spots it. [The Fourth Amendment] only requires that 'the incriminating nature' of the item . . . becomes apparent during the course of the search, without the benefit of information from any unlawful search or seizure."

D. Probation Searches
U.S. v. Knights, 534 U.S. 112 (2001)
Reversing the 9th Circuit decision *in U.S. v. Knights,* 219 F.3d 1138 (9th Cir. 2000).
Under California law, any person on probation for commission of a crime must "submit his person, property, residence, vehicle, and personal effects to search anytime with or without a search warrant, warrant of arrest or reasonable cause by any probation officer or law enforcement officer."

State and local law enforcement officers initiate the vast majority of detention, arrest, and search cases, and the Supreme Court has ruled in *Stone v. Powell* that the federal courts cannot review state court decisions in criminal cases on Fourth Amendment grounds. Although state officers may arrest a person for committing a crime, the Attorney General of the United States may file the ensuing prosecution under a federal statute. Possession of firearms by felons is the most common example. Thus, an arrest by state officers may result in a federal trial in district court in which case the defendant, if convicted, can appeal the arrest and search to the 9th Circuit.

This scenario occurred when state police officers arrested Knights, a man already on probation, but his prosecution and conviction occurred in federal court for commission of a federal offense. After the arrest, officers had searched probationer Knights' house without a warrant based on reasonable suspicion he was using drugs. Convicted in federal court,

Knights appealed to the 9th Circuit. The 9th Circuit suppressed evidence seized during the search on grounds the search was "investigatory and violated the Fourth Amendment." The court refused to enforce California law allowing warrantless searches of probationers. The Supreme Court reversed, characterizing the 9th Circuit decision as consisting of "dubious logic."

E. Parole Searches

U.S. v. Crawford, 323 F.3d 700 (9th Cir. 2003); on rehearing, *U.S. v. Crawford*, 372 F.3d 1048 (9th Cir. 2004).

Despite public sentiment evidenced by California voters who have repeatedly supported the death penalty and the "Three Strikes" Law (increasing sentences for defendants with prior convictions), state law establishes the right of a convicted felons to be released on parole (remaining theoretically in "custody" but released from prison and supervised by a parole officer) prior to completion of their sentence. Under this condition, a state may impose limitations on the terms of parole.

Two legal issues arose from state imposed restrictions prior to releasing a prisoner on parole: 1) the parolee must consent in writing to a search of his person, residence, or vehicle without a warrant; 2) no arrest warrant is necessary to restrain the parolee. In a federal conviction, a 9th Circuit panel invalidated both these restrictions in *U.S. v. Crawford*. The panel held that the state could not impose a waiver of the right to be free from searches, and the parole or arresting officer must establish probable cause to arrest a parolee.

The full 9th Circuit panel reheard the case, and affirmed Crawford's conviction, but reversed the earlier panel ruling on grounds other than the validity of the search. The majority of judges in the rehearing decision avoided the issue of parole searches. In concurring with the majority decision, Judge Trott wrote a comprehensive review of parolees and the danger of their reentry into society thereby justifying warrantless searches in achieving public safety. The judge cited the previous California Supreme Court ruling confirming the right of officers to search parolees without a warrant or evidence of "probable cause" unless the arresting officer acted arbitrarily or capriciously.

As discussed in the context of the Section on "Prisoners' Rights," the solicitude of the 9th Circuit for parolees (supervised release) in federal courts is unparalleled. In *Williams v. Alameida* [director of the Department of Corrections and Rehabilitation) the parolee Williams sued the California Department of Corrections and Alameda County for allegedly confining him beyond the terms of his sentence before his release from prison. But Williams was a fugitive on parole at the time and the district court judge dismissed his claim. The 9th Circuit allowed dismissal of the claim but the court panel "conditionally" dismissed the appeal on December 28, 2007 and allowed Williams sixty days to submit himself to the State and file a motion to reinstate his appeal. On June 1, 2008, the same panel issued an identical order ostensibly filed December 28, 2007, bearing the same file number but entitled "subsequent determination" giving Williams sixty days to make an appearance, presumably after his arrest on the parole warrant. What possible rationale justifies this pandering to a fugitive violating his parole? The California Attorney General (Jerry Brown) did not seek review in the Supreme Court.

The Supreme Court denied review of the *Crawford* case at that time, skirting the parole issue. But three years later in *Samson v. California* the justices solidly rejected any theory requiring probable cause, or officers obtaining an arrest warrant for a parolee who had signed a written statement surrendering Fourth Amendment rights. Although the Supreme Court did not discuss the original 9th Circuit decision in *Crawford* invalidating warrantless arrest and search of parolees, the Justices unequivocally confirmed the right of parole agents and law enforcement officers to search parolees without a warrant and without "probable cause."

In the *Samson* case, building on its *U.S. v. Knights* decision permitting warrantless searches of probationers, the Supreme Court explained the public danger of releasing parolees and the likelihood of their inability to remain crime free. Recidivism is rampart among parolees, and few can reintegrate into society as evidenced by California statistics on their high degree of repeated commission of crimes or parole violations.

That a three-judge panel of the 9th Circuit in *Crawford* would display an indifference to public welfare, and override the overwhelming majority of California voters and Legislature, is another example of judicial arrogance. The 9th Circuit panel apparently ignored the Supreme Court decision in the *Knights* case permitting warrantless probation searches as governing the rule in *Samson*. The Supreme Court in *Samson* also indirectly rejected another 9th Circuit case, *U.S. v. Foley*, a previous decision also requiring "probable cause" to search probationers who had waived their Fourth Amendment rights as a condition of probation.

U.S. v. Mendez, 476 F.3d 1077 (9th Cir. 2007)

The facts in this case are routine. Mendez appealed his federal district court conviction of a "felon in possession of a firearm" to the 9th Circuit on grounds that other than for an expired license plate the officers/detectives working "gang related" activities did not have a reason to stop his vehicle. He argued that the officers could not question him on any topic other than the license violation during the ensuing delay in determining whether he had an outstanding warrant. The two detectives noted that Mendez bore tattoos identifying a local gang, but upon police questioning he stated he had terminated his membership. In further questioning by police, he disclosed his prior prison record and admitted a weapon was concealed in his car. Police seized the weapon and arrested him as a felon in possession of a firearm.

Tried and convicted in federal court, he appealed. The original 9th Circuit majority decision (2-1) suppressed the evidence in an excruciatingly lengthy opinion concluding that officers could only question a person on the basis of the facts justifying the reason for the original detention. In other words, only the expired license plate.

Here is the language of the dissenting judge: "Here we go again. The Supreme Court has told us repeatedly that the Fourth Amendment protects against unreasonable searches and seizures. It does not declare inviolate the sanctity of a suspect's personal security when a police officer has reasonable concerns for his safety. The [Supreme] Court unanimously reversed and rejected 'as contrary to our prior decisions' the divide and conquer technique employed by the Ninth Circuit in U.S. v. Arvizu, (reversing a 9th Circuit opinion in another case)." The Justices returned the case to the 9th Circuit.

The 9th Circuit 2-1 majority subsequently revised its original *Mendez* decision, upheld the stop (detention) of Mendez, and confirmed the right of police to question him during this "seizure," (of the person) citing the Supreme Court decision in *Muehler v. Mena* (discussed earlier). It conceded under *Muehler* that police questioning does not constitute a "seizure" of the person unless it unnecessarily prolongs the detention of the individual. No "reasonable suspicion" is required to justify questioning.

Only the Supreme Court's decision in *Muehler v. Mena* compelled the 9th Circuit's panel to reverse itself. But in its revised opinion, the 9th Circuit panel also conceded that *Muehler* overruled a host of 9th Circuit opinions as far back as 2001, proving once again its unjustified rules in previous cases had freed guilty defendants

F. Border Searches

This Section notes that the Supreme Court has repeatedly chastised the 9th Circuit for refusing to acknowledge the reality of illegal aliens attempting to enter the United States. Presuming the Fourth Amendment applied to those illegally entering the country, the 9th Circuit applied the rules of search and seizure by excluding evidence to preclude border patrols agents from exercising their training and expertise in detaining suspected illegal aliens. Working on a specific goal, border patrol agents acquire expertise in recognizing conduct imperceptible to the uninformed observer, and often interpret superficially innocent conduct as indicative of illegal activity. This factor completely escapes the majority of 9th Circuit judges, who exhibit no comprehension of border security.

U.S. v. Arvizu, 534 U.S. 266 (2002)
Reversing the 9th Circuit decision in *831 F.3d 1413 (9th Cir. 1987).*
On an unpaved remote Arizona road frequently used by smugglers, a border patrol agent signaled Arvizu to stop driving a minivan. Arvizu slowed down, but ignored the agent's presence. Children inside the vehicle waived mechanically as though instructed, and all sat uncomfortably with their knees raised. The agent testified he was alone during shift changes, a fact known to smugglers. The district court judge enumerated ten factors warranting the agent to stop the vehicle. A search revealed one hundred pounds of marijuana. Arrested and convicted in district court, Arvizu appealed.

The 9th Circuit isolated all the factors described above, individually asserted each constituted innocent conduct, and suppressed the seized evidence. The State of Arizona appealed. Here is the language of the Supreme Court reversing the 9th Circuit:

> "We hold that the Court of Appeals' methodology was contrary to our prior decisions and that it reached the wrong result in this case When discussing how reviewing courts should make reasonable suspicion determinations, we have said repeatedly that they must look at the "totality of the circumstances of each case". . . This process allows officers to draw on their own experience and specialized training to make inferences from and deductions about the cumulative information available to them that might well elude an untrained person."

"We think the approach taken by the [9th Circuit] Court of Appeals here departs sharply from the teachings of [our] cases which preclude this sort of divide and conquer analysis. The 'totality of the circumstances,' not the individual factors, is the test of reasonable suspicion to warrant stopping an individual or vehicle."

The court concluded with this opinion of its decision in the *Arvizu* case, which the 9th Circuit repeatedly ignores in other contexts: "[T]he Court of Appeals should [acknowledge] the district court [judge's] superior access to the evidence and the well recognized inability of reviewing courts to reconstruct what happened in the courtroom." On return of this case to the 9th Circuit, the court affirmed the conviction.

The Supreme Court, in reversing the 9th Circuit in *Arvizu* and its analysis reproached by the Justices, reversed another 9th Circuit decision. In 1989 case entitled *U.S. v. Sokolow* the Supreme Court criticized that 9th Circuit decision in this language: "We think the Court of Appeals' effort to refine and elaborate the requirement of 'reasonable suspicion' in this case created unnecessary difficulty in dealing with one of the relatively simple concepts embodied in the Fourth Amendment." Sokolow is another example of the 9th Circuit rejection of Supreme Court precedent as far back as 1989.

U.S. v. Flores-Montano, 541 U.S. 149 (2004). Reversing a case unreported by the 9th Circuit.

Border Patrol agents stopped the car driven by Flores-Montano who attempted to enter the United States from Mexico. Directing the vehicle to a secondary inspection, the agent tapped the fuel tank and heard a solid sound rather than a hollow one, indicating the content was not gasoline. With the assistance of a mechanic, the agents disassembled the gas tank and discovered over one hundred pounds of marijuana. Flores-Montano was arrested. The district court judge suppressed the evidence on the grounds of unlawful search (the agent lacked "probable cause"). The 9th

Circuit held that the removal of the gas tank was not a "routine" search and also suppressed the evidence. The U.S. government sought review in the Supreme Court.

Writing an impatient decision, the Supreme Court reversed and reminded the 9th Circuit that the Justices had repeatedly approved intensive border searches of vehicles with no particular level of suspicion needed. The 9th Circuit judges had relied on their own prior decisions to reach the conclusion that the search was intrusive, and, under the Fourth Amendment, "unreasonable."

Thus, any border searches conducted after its previous (now erroneous) decisions rendered before Flores-Montano were not in violation of the Fourth Amendment, and the 9th Circuit had suppressed evidence wrongfully by applying its own rule. An exasperated Chief Justice wrote: "Time and again, we have stated that searches made at the border, pursuant to a long-standing right of the sovereign to protect itself by stopping and examining persons and property crossing into this country, are reasonable simply by virtue of the fact they occur at the border. Congress has always granted the Executive plenary authority to conduct routine searches and seizures at the border, without probable cause or a warrant, in order to regulate the collection of duties and to prevent the introduction of contraband into this county." Reversed.

On return of the case to the 9th Circuit, the panel barely cited reversal of its decision by the Supreme Court. But in a new hearing, Flores-Montano offered an issue he never raised at trial, or on appeal to the 9th Circuit, or the Supreme Court. Ordinarily, the government argued, failure to present a claim on appeal constitutes a waiver of the issue and cannot be raised. This issue posed no hurdle for the 9th Circuit panel. This is not a "new claim," said the panel, only a new argument. Of course.

Flores-Montano now contended a federal statute, not the Fourth Amendment, governed his case. After dutifully reviewing the newly discovered statute, the 9th Circuit panel confirmed the conviction and denied his appeal. Despite the ultimate 9th Circuit decision after Supreme Court reversal confirming the validity of the arrest, search, and conviction of Flores-Montano, the history of this case is interesting. As noted above, the district court judge had originally suppressed the evidence and the government appealed; *U.S. v. Flores-Montano.* The 9th Circuit panel dismissed the government appeal of that decision as "frivolous;" U.S. v. Flores-Montano. The Supreme Court upheld that "frivolous" government appeal, obviously not the 9th Circuit's flippant and condescending remark.

Luz Lopez-Rodriguez & Gastelum Lopez v. Mukasey, 536 F.3d 1012 (9th Cir. 2008)

In October, 2000, Immigration & Naturalization Service agents received information that Lopez- Rodriguez had entered the country illegally and was living at a specific address. At an immigration hearing the agents testified they entered the house without force, and after she lied to them about her nationality and birthplace, they learned that she and another woman living in the house, were in the country illegally. Lopez-Rodriguez signed a declaration admitting her illegal entry, and the agents filled out forms for deportation. The immigration judge ordered removal of both women.

On appeal of the Immigration Court decision to the 9th Circuit, a 2-1 majority panel agreed that the agents had entered the home without a warrant and lacked consent of either woman to enter. Under the Fourth Amendment, an illegal entry to a residence causes any evidence thereafter seized inadmissible in a criminal proceeding, but the Supreme Court has ruled the Fourth Amendment exclusionary rule does not apply in deportation proceedings where the sole issues are identity and alienage-unless an "egregious" violation of the Fourth Amendment occurs.

That decision did not deter the 9th Circuit panel. Finding the entry to the residence in violation of the Fourth Amendment "egregious," the panel excluded from evidence the deportation form provided by the agents and Rodriguez's declaration admitting she entered the country illegally. The court dismissed the immigration proceedings against both women. The immigration form was neither contraband, drugs, stolen property, weapons, nor instrumentalities of crime as required for issuance of a search warrant. No evidence of a crime was seized from anyone or anywhere.

The 9th Circuit panel court cited no precedent for this decision, in effect, allowing two admittedly illegal aliens to continue to reside in the United States. And the court does not question why a simple arrest in 2000 was decided eight years later.

In this case, the judicial use of the exclusionary rule to exclude the evidence (INS forms and a declaration) is another example of 9th Circuit abuse already criticized by the Supreme Court. The only issue in deportation proceedings is identity and alienage. Identity in this case was undisputed and Rodriguez not only lied to the agents but admitted her ineligibility to remain in the United States. According to the 9th Circuit panel, the Fourth Amendment violation was "egregious." This word lacks verbal boundaries, is highly subjective, and establishes no standards here other than the 9th Circuit's definition: "evidence obtained by deliberate violations of the Fourth Amendment, or by conduct a reasonable officer should [have known] is a violation of the Constitution."

This statement will cause a chilling effect on immigration enforcement agents because it mirrors the law conferring immunity from litigation on government officials in civil cases. Immunity is invoked by public officials in proceedings alleging statutory violation of civil rights, not deportation proceedings. The dissenting judge in the case sounds this alarm, aware of the 9th Circuit predilection for reversing immigration cases and denying immunity to police officers in cases alleging violation of Constitutional rights. The judge wrote: "The Supreme Court [has] determined that the high costs of the exclusionary rule rendered it too costly to apply in immigration proceedings . . . Our case law appears destined to import the exclusionary rule, with all of its attendant costs, back into immigration proceedings."

This is not the first case the 9th Circuit has written adopting an exception to a Supreme Court unambiguous rule. Here is its explanation in the case evading the Supreme Court rule that the exclusionary rule is inapplicable in deportation proceedings: "agents committed the violations deliberately or by conduct a reasonable officer should have known". Given the number of 9th Circuit Fourth Amendment decisions reversed by the Supreme Court, and innumerable decisions written by state and federal courts disagreeing on whether officers committed a violation of the Fourth Amendment, this statement is absurd. And the immigration judge also saw no "egregious" violation when she ordered deportation. Nor did the lawyers who filed her appeal cite this rule to the Board of Immigration Appeals.

The record does not reflect any request by the administrative agency (BIA) or the U.S. Attorney requesting the Supreme Court to review this indefensible decision.

G. Jail Searches

Bull v. City and County of San Francisco, 539 F.3d 1193 (2008); rehearing ordered in 558 F.3d 887 (2009); the full court reversed the panel in 595 F.3d 964 (9th Cir. 2010). See, 758 F.Supp.2d 925 for further proceedings.

The City of San Francisco produced extensive and overwhelming evidence of drug smuggling in its jails and cited its inability to exercise control in the absence of full searching authority. Nevertheless, the author of the three-judge panel of the 9th Circuit majority opinion in the original *Bull* case denied San Francisco authorities the right to conduct body cavity searches ("strip searches") of pre detention arrestees before transferring them to the general jail population in the absence of evidence of "reasonable suspicion" or other limited conditions justifying a search.

The second judge in the panel concurred with the author of the decision in *Bull* but wrote, "[]By disregarding the jail administrators' urgent concerns about serious contraband smuggling problems, I agree with the [dissenting judge] that we are potentially putting lives in the San Francisco detention system at serious risk. By effectively eliminating security concerns from our calculus, we contradict Supreme Court precedent and common sense and take upon ourselves a rule unsuited for the courts . . . [J]udges must guard against the all-too-human tendency to believe that their individual solutions to often intractable problems are better and more workable than those of the persons who are actually charged with and trained in the running of the particular institution under examination."

This quote reflects the opinion of a 9th Circuit judge reluctantly concurring with the decision of another judge on the three-judge panel. No one doubts the serious invasion of privacy implicit in "strip searches." But the privacy factor in jails and prisons differs substantially from any other category of search by public officials. The dissenting judge in *Bull* writes of the 9th Circuit's serious departure from the Supreme Court acknowledgment of this factor in its Fourth Amendment jurisprudence.

"The Fourth Amendment requires all searches conducted by public officials to be "reasonable," but that word and its application are contingent on the context. The Supreme Court in Bell v. Wolfish balanced "the significant and legitimate security interests of the institution (jail) against the privacy interest of the inmates," and held a "visual cavity inspection . . . can be conducted on less than probable cause." Other language in Bell clearly recognizes the need for strip searches in jail facilities."

Despite the clear approval of this type of search by the Supreme Court, the 9th Circuit undertook its own analysis of institutional privacy interests and basically ignored the *Bell* decision. Strip searches of this type, according to the majority panel, violate our clearly established (by the 9th Circuit) Fourth Amendment rights. The author of the lead opinion in Bull disposed of the *Bell v. Wolfish* case in one paragraph and cited contrary 9th Circuit precedent as authority for the following rule: "Unless the predetention inmate was arrested for weapons violations, drug offenses, violence, violation of probation or parole, or manifests 'individualized suspicion,' and despite eventually housing them in the general jail population, jailors may not conduct strip searches."

The majority opinion in *Bull* ignores the fact that those arrested in categories unrelated to those arrestees named by the judge subject to search can also conceal weapons or contraband. The criminal record of an arrestee jailed for any offense is often unknown at intake. Similarly, jailers often do not know the status of a parolee or probationer until time develops a record match. Gangs are notorious for intimidating other inmates in the prison population, regardless of the reason for their arrest, or in some cases demanding narcotics from them. The concurring judge in *Bull* is correct. The judiciary is the least equipped institution to render the kind of decision in *Bull* that was made in the case.

A request in the *Bull* case for rehearing or rehearing *en banc* (full court) ensued, undoubtedly based on the language of the concurring judge who felt bound by 9th Circuit precedent, but clearly expressing disagreement with the result. *Bull* squarely contradicted Supreme Court precedent.

It is also important to note that this case was submitted November 6, 2007 and decided August 25, 2008 - nine months later. The 9th Circuit ordered rehearing by the full court, and in reversing the three-judge panel quoted the Supreme Court from the *Bell* case as follows: "Rather, courts owe corrections officials deference on the grounds that 'the realities of running a corrections institution are complex and difficult, courts are ill equipped to deal with these problems, and the management of these facilities is confided to the Executive and Legislative Branches, not to the Judicial Branch.'" The concurring opinion in Bull was even more to the point: "If plaintiffs here succeed, every strip search will become a potential federal case. Federal judges will start running the jails, along with pretty much everything else."

H. School Searches
Camreta v. Greene, 131 S.Ct. 2020 (2010). Reversing the 9th Circuit decision in *Green v. Camreta*, 588 F.3d 1011 (2009).
This case decided by the 9th Circuit is not only incomprehensible but illustrates the manipulation of a court in attempting to fashion a rule avoiding

Supreme Court review. Not only is the decision irresponsible, the attempt to undercut the Supreme Court is reprehensible.

Police received information that a student in a local school had been subjected to a sexual violation. To investigate the allegation, officers arrived at the school and interviewed the student. Incredibly, the student's parents subsequently sued the officers for interviewing the child without a warrant. The district court judge dismissed the case, and the parents appealed to the 9th Circuit.

The 9th Circuit held that the Fourth Amendment required police to obtain a search warrant before interviewing a student in school who had alleged a sexual violation, but no civil liability attached on grounds the officers were entitled to qualified immunity. Nevertheless, the officers sought and obtained review in the Supreme Court, despite having prevailed in the case. The Justices, stunned at oral argument of the case in court to understand the Fourth Amendment basis for the 9th Circuit decision requiring a warrant, realized if they refused to decide the case already resolved in favor of the officers by qualified immunity, the principle announced by the 9th Circuit requiring a search warrant before interviewing a student would stand.

Carving an exception to its general rule in avoiding Constitutional issues unless necessary, the Supreme Court vacated the entire case, despite the officers having prevailed on immunity, in order to avoid the underlying 9th Circuit rationale to become precedent in this case for future cases mandating a search warrant.

Upon remand, the 9th Circuit returned the case to the district court after vacating that portion of its decision applying to the Fourth Amendment. All that is left of the case is the immunity officers have been awarded

1. The Scope of the Fourth Amendment
Ninth Circuit case law and its frequent reversal record is not a recent development. As long ago as 1991, a 2-1 majority panel excluded $277,000.00 recovered by police officers from a vehicle parked in a backyard with

Mexican license plates obscured by a tarp covering the vehicle. The officers removed the tarp and discovered an illegal VIN (vehicle identification number) number on the car. A search of the unoccupied car revealed the money obtained from narcotic sales. The 9th Circuit excluded the evidence.

Is this what the Fourth Amendment protects? Does this rule deter police misconduct? Is this evidence of a police state? A quarter million dollars of drug money cannot be seized from an unoccupied car parked in a yard, covered with a tarp, and displaying Mexican license plates? And this in the year 1991. Remarkably, the government did not seek review in the Supreme Court. In 2008 the Supreme Court affirmed a police search under almost the same circumstances. *Allen v. Arizona.*

This Chapter reviewed only a small portion of Fourth Amendment decisions written by the 9th Circuit but illustrates the repeated erroneous mistakes of law written by those judges. The cost to taxpayers is one thing, the cost to the public is another. Invoking the exclusionary rule to prevent the prosecution from presenting incriminating evidence, or in the alternative, compelling the state to offer the defendant a plea to a lesser offense, is the price society pays for 9th Circuit decisions repeatedly denounced by the Supreme Court. Fortunately the Supreme Court withdrew the right of federal courts to review state court convictions based on searches and seizures, but searches by federal officers remain under 9th Circuit jurisdiction on appeals from district courts. In a Supreme Court case reviewing another federal Circuit decision (*Davis v. United States*), the Justices explain the purposes of the exclusionary rule of the Fourth Amendment and the cost to society. The 9th Circuit repeatedly ignores the rule.

The Supreme Court itself has foretold the narrowing of the exclusionary rule. In *Hudson v. Michigan*, a decision by a different federal appeals court, the Supreme Court reviewed a state case in which law enforcement officers had entered a house without identifying themselves prior to their forced entry (noted earlier in this Chapter). The Supreme Court detached the Fourth Amendment from the so called "knock and notice rule" requiring officers to identify themselves before entering forcibly. For police to comply with that statute guaranteed that the occupants would either flush narcotics down the toilet or offer armed resistance. The Supreme Court refused to allow such a result and concluded the price of the exclusionary rule too steep to warrant its imposition. As noted in the text, the Court reversed a 9th Circuit case in reaching this result.

In an unrelated case (*Herring v. U.S.*, not a 9th Circuit case) the Supreme Court finally acknowledged the cost of the exclusionary rule had exacted too great a price on society. Officers arrested Herring after having been informed that a warrant for his arrest was outstanding. Minutes later the clerical staff in another city informed the officers that the warrant had been recalled but this fact had not been entered into the computer. The district court and federal circuit court denied defendant's motion to dismiss. The Supreme Court affirmed, refusing to exclude evidence seized contingent on a computer error.

Despite the *Herring* decision, the 9th Circuit reversed another obviously guilty defendant in *U.S v. Gonzales*. Under long-established Supreme Court decisions on Fourth Amendment issues, the Justices had allowed police to search an occupied vehicle as long as the officer had probable cause to arrest an occupant, or probable cause to search the car itself. Relying on this well-established rule, an officer lawfully stopped Gonzales in his car and, with good cause, was arrested and subsequently convicted of a crime.

Prior to his arrest, the Supreme Court had specifically approved the scope of vehicle searches to include glove compartments, but in a later case (*Arizona v. Gant*) the Justices changed their minds and limited vehicular searching authority conducted by police officers. But the Supreme Court refused to exclude evidence discovered in those searches under some circumstances if the officer acted in good faith or in relying on a statute or a warrant.

Despite the *Herring* case admonition not to invoke the exclusionary rule inappropriately and originally designed to "deter" police misconduct, the 9th Circuit ruled in the *Gonzales* case the officer's reliance on "well-established" case law was not allowed. Another guilty party temporarily went free, not because of police misconduct but because the 9th Circuit said so.

The dissent in *Gonzales* strongly disagreed with the majority opinion. In denying a petition for rehearing the majority said this: "Judge Bea's dissent presents a *distorted view* of what this case is all about. It requires a response that can be part of the public record. Otherwise our *panel's reasoned response* to the [full 9th Circuit court] call would remain hidden from public view."

The answer to that "distorted view" by Judge Bea [dissenting judge] is evidenced by the Supreme Court reversing "the 9th Circuit panel's 'reasoned response' of the court majority." This case was reversed by the Supreme Court based on the rule in *Davis v. U.S.* preventing courts from applying the new rule on vehicular searches retroactively. On remand from the "distorted view" of the dissent announced by the majority in *Gonzales*, the 9th Circuit buried its decision reversing itself.

CHAPTER 8

THE FIFTH AMENDMENT & THE *MIRANDA* RULE

The Self-Incrimination Clause of the Fifth Amendment to the U.S. Constitution provides: "No . . . person shall be compelled in any criminal case to be a witness against himself," U.S. Constitution, Fifth Amendment. "The core protection afforded by the Self Incrimination Clause is a prohibition on compelling a criminal defendants to testify against themselves; *U.S. v. Patane.* As the Supreme Court explained, "the Self-Incrimination Clause prohibits extracting words from the lips of the accused which would take the place of other evidence." The Fifth Amendment limits testimonial evidence, but does not limit non testimonial evidence (e.g., blood samples).

The courts originally struggled with cases involving allegations of confessions attributable to police use of threats, force, coercion, and other attempts to induce arrestees to incriminate themselves. Because the cases involved conflicting testimony between police and suspect, the court experienced difficulty in determining the truth, and whether the statements obtained were "involuntary" under the Fifth Amendment. Instances of alleged "involuntary confessions" continued to exist, but the Supreme Court ultimately decided to eliminate, or at least reduce, disputes on the voluntariness of confessions (*Brown v. Horell*).

In an attempt to rectify the confusion, the Supreme Court crafted judicially imposed rules designed to protect the Privilege Against Self Incrimination Clause by precluding evidence from someone whose answers to questions posed by police could be introduced at trial. In the case entitled *Miranda v. Arizona* the Supreme Court concluded the danger of coercion inherent in police custodial interrogation is a risk potentially violating a suspect's privilege against self-incrimination. In the future, a law enforcement officer must advise a person in custody, or deprived of his freedom of action in a significant way, of the right to an attorney and the right to remain silent before any questioning can proceed.

However, the Court added if "any further extension of the *Miranda* rules and its [subsequent cases] sweep beyond the actual protection of the Clause, these rules must be justified by its necessity for the protection of the actual right against compelled self-incrimination (citing the *Patane* case." The *Miranda* rule is a right exercised at trial, and any "constitutional violation occurs only at trial." *Withrow v. Williams.* It is not for this [Supreme] Court to impose its preferred police practices on either federal law enforcement officials or their state counterparts."

The 9th Circuit has never quoted this rule.

The admonition to inform arrestees of the right to counsel and silence became a cult phrase in every cop show despite the fact *Miranda* applies only if police ask questions of a suspect in custody - a fact ignored by writers of police drama series. The *Miranda* rule is neither textually required by the Fifth Amendment to the U.S. Constitution applicable to federal courts nor applicable textually to individual states. The rule is judicially invented, with no precedent for its adoption, regardless of its well intentioned purpose to avoid coercive police interrogation. But the rule has also prevented introduction of highly relevant and otherwise admissible evidence in trial despite the otherwise "voluntary" nature of a confession.

Application of the *Miranda* rule has been repeatedly invoked in courtrooms and the results are not pleasant. The *Miranda* admonitions only apply to suspects in "custody," or deprived of their "freedom of action in a significant way," and each case is obviously factually driven. Federal and state court decisions are replete with inconsistencies. The Supreme Court has clearly held that whether a person is in "custody" is an objective test, not the subjective perception of the person questioned.

Chavez v. Martinez, 538 U.S. 760 (2003). Reversing the 9th Circuit decision in 270 F.3d 852 (9th Cir. 2001).

Federal statute 42 U.S.C. Section 1983, known as a federal civil rights statute, allows lawsuits against police and/or their public employers for violation of Constitutional rights. In *Chavez v. Martinez*, the Supreme Court reviewed an encounter between Martinez and Officer Chavez who was conducting an investigation of a shooting. Martinez filed his Complaint in federal court alleging the officer brutally choked him causing severe physical injuries. According to Martinez, the officer failed to give him the *Miranda* warning of his right to silence and counsel before questioning him in violation of the Fifth Amendment privilege against self-incrimination, although the prosecutor had filed no charges against him. The 9th Circuit ruled on appeal from the district court that the failure to advise a witness (Martinez) of the *Miranda* admonitions deprived Officer Chavez of any immunity (in litigation) for injuries he allegedly caused during questioning.

The Supreme Court gave the 9th Circuit a lesson in Constitutional law, reminding the court that the privilege against self incrimination applies to trials, not arrests, and any statements without a *Miranda* admonition are only inadmissible at trial. The *Miranda* decision is a judicially invoked rule to protect the Fifth Amendment at trial. The Court wrote: "The 9th Circuit's view that mere compulsion violates the Self-Incrimination Clause finds no support in the text of the Fifth Amendment and is irreconcilable with our case law. We reverse the 9th Circuit's Fifth Amendment claim."

The Supreme Court also reminded the 9th Circuit that Martinez was not a suspect, only a witness to a shooting. "[We] can find no basis in our prior jurisprudence . . . or in our nation's history and traditions to suppose that freedom from unwanted police questioning is a right so fundamental that it cannot be abridged absent a 'compelling state interest.' The lack of guideposts for our oft stated reluctance to expand the doctrine of substantive due process further counsel against recognizing new 'fundamental liberty interests.'"

But the Court did note that Martinez might have a Fourteenth Amendment right (applicable to states) of freedom from police coercion and sent the case back to the 9th Circuit for development of the court record. In one long paragraph the 9th Circuit held the *Martinez* Complaint "shocks the conscience" and allowed the qualified immunity issue to proceed to trial. The court wrote, "Under the facts alleged by Martinez, Chavez violated "clearly established due process rights;" *Martinez v. City of Oxnard*. A concurring judge wrote, "We should have [returned the case to the trial court] with instructions to proceed in a manner consistent with the Supreme Court when it said . . . 'Nor can the Ninth Circuit's approach be reconciled with our case law.'" In other words, the 9th Circuit panel majority ignored the Supreme Court's direction to order a hearing in the district court to determine the facts, not just accept allegations of misconduct in order to determine whether to subject the officer to potential monetary liability.

Although this case affirms the right of Martinez to go to trial and support his allegations, the 9th Circuit decision denies the officer immunity to terminate the case. The chastising language of the Supreme Court demonstrates the refusal of the 9th Circuit to adhere to the law in general and Constitutional law in particular. Incidentally, the trial judge who originally ruled against the officers is also accustomed to reversals, as in this case.

The Supreme Court has ruled in other contexts that the "liberty interests" protected by the Fourteenth Amendment Due Process Clause reflect traditions rooted in our history, and courts should be reluctant to announce new rights. Under the Martinez case decided by the Supreme

Court, a witness has no fundamental Fifth Amendment Constitutional right to freedom from coercive police interrogation although the party may file a civil suit seeking money damages.

Despite the Supreme Court language, on return of the *Martinez* case by the Supreme Court, the 9th Circuit panel noted, "A clearly established right, fundamental to ordered liberty, is freedom from coercive police interrogation." For reasons unknown, the Supreme Court denied review.

U.S. v. Caruto, 526 F.3d 445 (9th Cir. 2008); amended, 532 F.3d 822 (9th Cir. 2008). retried, convicted, and affirmed on appeal; 627 F.3d 759 (9th Cir. 2010).

Anyone charged with smuggling contraband from Mexico into the United States in a vehicle usually defends on grounds of lack of knowledge that the gas tank or a false compartment contained narcotics. Caruto attempted to enter the United States in a vehicle, and border agents found approximately one million dollars worth of cocaine in its gas tank. In an interview with the agents, Caruto stated she had lent the truck to three unknown persons who returned it on the date of her arrest and told her to drive to Los Angeles to help a friend. Minutes into the interview she invoked her *Miranda* rights and the agents terminated the interview. Prosecutors charged her with narcotic violation laws.

At trial, Caruto testified she had shown the truck in Mexico, potentially for sale, to one Jiminez who was interested in buying it. He agreed to pay her a deposit of $1,000.00 and the balance of the purchase price in Los Angeles, but she did not accept the money and was not specifically going to Los Angeles. She was unable to contact Jiminez after her arrest. On cross examination she conceded speaking to agents at the border, but at that time said nothing to them about Jiminez, or her intended sale of the truck. In closing argument to the jury, the prosecutor told jurors that none of the statements Caruto made to the agents at the time of her arrest contained any reference to Jiminez or the sale of the truck.

The Supreme Court had ruled in prior cases that a prosecutor at trial cannot introduce evidence of "silence" of a suspect in response to police questioning on the ground that comment to the jury would penalize a suspect for exercising the right to remain silent. But the Court has also held that any statements made by an arrestee at the time of the arrest, and after a *Miranda* admonition, inconsistent with trial testimony is admissible to impeach (contradict) the defendant.

In *Caruto* the defendant made statements to the border agents and then invoked her right to silence after initially having been advised of her *Miranda* rights. The 9th Circuit panel held that the difference at trial between admissible evidence of statements made by an arrestee after agents informed her of *Miranda* warnings, and inadmissible statements after a Miranda advisory, is based on prosecutorial comments that focus only on the inconsistency between the two statements rather than a failure to include facts. Assuming this hairsplitting is correct, Caruto's testimony at the trial (about Jiminez) and the sale of the truck) and the statements to the border agents (nothing about the truck having been returned by Jiminez and the money to go to Los Angeles) were not inconsistent - just incomplete. The 9th Circuit panel concluded that Caruto's exercise of her right under *Miranda* prevented her from further explanation of her conduct to the agents. But she told the agents one version at the border, invoked *Miranda*, said no more, then testified at trial inconsistent with what she originally told the agents.

Her silence after invocation of *Miranda* is irrelevant. Caruto is another example of academic hairsplitting distinctions no one else would make. The dissenting judge wrote: "Her 'explanations' are, simply, inconsistent." Incidentally, the prosecution also offered evidence that the truck contained a false compartment. Then came this observation by the prosecutor: "No drug smuggler would secrete one million dollars worth of cocaine in a car driven by someone they don't know."

The purported policy justifying *Miranda* is to avoid the potential of coercion during interrogation of individuals either in custody or deprived of their "freedom of action." But Caruto was at a border inspection station to determine if she had the right to enter the United States, not an intimidating examination of a suspect in a police facility. In other words, the rationale for the Fifth Amendment is entirely different. If the border agents had simply told Caruto she could not enter the United States unless as a citizen, they would be correct. The jury did not believe her manufactured story, and neither would anyone else.

The *Miranda* decision guaranteed judicial savaging of forests to write decisions importing complexity into a superficially simple advisement of suspects in custody of their right to counsel and the election not to answer questions. From 1981 to 1994 the 9th Circuit misconstrued the *Miranda* decision. The Supreme Court attempted to clarify the language of the *Miranda* advisement in *Florida v. Powell*, but the 9th Circuit is likely to be oblivious to whatever the Supreme Court decides.

Berghuis v. Thompkins, 130 S.Ct. 2250 (2010)

This case is a decision by the Supreme Court reviewing a decision of the Sixth Circuit Court of Appeals.

Although not a 9th Circuit case, the decision seriously undermines 9th Circuit cases on the role of "silence" by an arrestee during custodial interrogation. According to the Supreme Court, any person under arrest must clearly and unequivocally invoke right to silence just as they must clearly invoke the right to counsel.

U.S. v. Rodriguez, 518 F.3d 1072 (9th Cir. 2008)

In 2008, the 9th Circuit wrote a decision in an appeal from a conviction of Rodriguez, lawfully arrested for possessing firearms in a federally supervised park. The Ranger read Rodriguez his *Miranda* rights and he responded, "I'm good for tonight." Did this constitute a waiver of the right to counsel? Under the *Davis v. U.S.* case, officers who have advised suspects of their *Miranda* rights need not clarify an ambiguous statement and may resume questioning. But in Rodriguez the 9th Circuit held the *Davis* case only applies after a suspect has been advised of his right to counsel and silence. An ambiguous answer before agreeing to talk requires clarification.

What possible rationale warrants another hairsplitting decision? Ambiguity is ambiguity. And the absurdity of this decision lies in its inapplicability to the facts. Rodriguez was lawfully arrested with two firearms in his truck when stopped by Rangers for driving under the influence of alcohol. If the statements he made to Rangers are inadmissible, what difference does it make in finding him guilty? Knowingly possessing restricted firearms (one had a silencer) is sufficient for conviction. The legal error, if any, is harmless and irrelevant.

Anderson v. Terhune (Director), 516 F.3d 781 (9th Cir. 2008)
When state court convictions are affirmed on appeal and the defendant files a habeas corpus petition in federal court, the latter is bound by the statutory restrictions of the federal statute (AntiTerrorism and Death Penalty Act; AEDPA). From the 9th Circuit perspective, these restrictions only cause the court to find ways to avoid the statute. *Anderson v. Terhune* (Director) illustrates this strategy. In an *en banc* (full court) habeas corpus decision from a state court, the 9th Circuit panel majority emphasized that after a two hour of unquestionably non coercive questioning by state officers in a nonviolent environment, Anderson said "I plead the Fifth" but later resumed talking The officer asked him "what he meant" but Anderson did not explain and continued to answer questions about his use of drugs.

The district court denied the petition for habeas corpus, but on appeal from that decision the 9th Circuit panel majority immediately announced this "unequivocal" comment ("I plead the Fifth") should have ended the questioning. But the dissenting judge explains that after two hours, despite what Anderson said-not the police – he unilaterally resumed the conversation. And what the majority ignores, of course, is AEDPA, the federal statute requiring federal courts to give deference to state court findings.

The California Court of Appeal in this case upheld the conviction and had construed the four word statement comparable to the dissenting 9th Circuit judges, as did the district court judge. Under AEDPA the federal courts owe deference only to an "incorrect" state court decision, not an "unreasonable" one, and can only reverse an "unreasonable" decision. Given the potential of multiple interpretations of the phrase "I plead the Fifth," in the context of Anderson discussing drug use (not the murder to which he confessed), the Court of Appeal may have been "incorrect" but not "unreasonable." The 9th Circuit ignored this requirement and arrogantly announced, "The state court's characterization is a fanciful imagination of the colloquy between Anderson and the officer, and under AEDPA, an unreasonable determination of the facts."

Note that this is also another death penalty case reversed on spurious grounds.

U.S. v. Velarde-Gomez, 269 F.3d 1023 (9th Cir. 2001)
Cases in federal and state courts interpreting *Miranda* are legion, and the 9th Circuit is at the forefront of reversals. In *U.S. v. Velarde,* several border patrol agents discovered sixty pounds of marijuana in suspect Velarde's gas tank, as noted in the *Caruto* case above, a common place to conceal drugs. Questioned by agents about his knowledge of marijuana, the agent testified Velarde just "sat there, unsurprised, calm and silent." At trial, Velarde apparently decided to testify to his innocence, and the government impeached (contradicted) him by asking questions about his nonresponse to questions posed by the agents at the time of his arrest. The jury convicted Velarde and he appealed to the 9th Circuit.

The 9th Circuit panel ruled there is a distinction between a suspect's "silence" and his "demeanor." Prosecutors cannot comment on "silence" in response to police questioning on the theory the suspect is invoking his *Miranda* rights, but can comment on "demeanor" (i.e. conduct). In a rambling linguistic explanation, the majority of the panel concluded Velarde's responses to questioning were "silence," not demeanor. The dissenting judges dismissed this questionable distinction. In any event, this same word - play is also applicable in the *Rodriguez* decision, discussed above.

The issue of the correct analysis of "silence" or "conduct" is irrelevant. The full 9th Circuit court on rehearing the case confronted a patently frivolous claim, fact specific, and insubstantial. As the dissenting judges point out, Valerde's "concocted" version of the events at trial was ludicrous. And what difference does his "silence" make, write the dissenting judges, since Velarde was apprehended "red handed" and now must be retried without the inconsequential evidence of "silence."

The *Miranda* decision originally applied to interrogations conducted in law enforcement facilities where the atmosphere was arguably intimidating. But instances of police questioning in various locations or under different circumstances emerged, and courts were confronted with innumerable issues on the time and place when officers must warn people of their right to silence and counsel. Of course every case is fact specific but the 9th Circuit provides a litany of factors it considers in determining whether *Miranda* warnings are necessary.

Although the 9th Circuit embraces the *Miranda* rationale and would immediately endorse it in principle without the Supreme Court decision, the genesis of all the confusion in applying this exclusionary rule is attributable to the Supreme Court during its Constitutional reconstruction years. In *U.S. v. Williams* the 9th Circuit panel struggled to explain two Supreme Court cases that illustrate the incoherence and confusion of the *Miranda* decision, and they cannot decide the controlling Supreme Court case. The court returned the case to the district court, and no further action is reported.

What needs to be understood is that every exclusion of relevant and incriminating evidence benefit the defendant in criminal cases. In federal court cases, the exclusionary rules of the Fourth and Fifth Amendments are often applied by the 9th Circuit in the absence of any threat of force or violence by police, or in a good-faith misunderstanding by the officer(s) of the rule. In addition, the frequent disagreement with state and federal courts encourages endless appeals and the disappearance of finality in criminal cases.

No other country enforces the unique *Miranda* Fifth Amendment rule by excluding voluntary confessions or the exclusionary rule of the Fourth Amendment. Unlike demands in the United States to abolish the death penalty in conformity with the rest of the world, the 9th Circuit and its supporters never seek withdrawal of these two American rules.

Arrest & *Miranda*
Yarborough v. Alvarado 541 U.S. 652 (2004)
Reversing the 9th Circuit decision in 316 F.3d 841 (9th Cir. 2003).
As noted, the Supreme Court has held that if police question anyone in custody or are "deprived of their freedom of action in a significant way" they must advise that person of their right to silence and counsel. A person in "custody" is usually established by an arrest evidenced by restraining suspects, transporting them to a police facility and placing them in confinement. But "freedom of action restrained in a significant way" refers to prolonged detention of a suspect at any location.

Yarborough v. Alvarado exemplifies the difference in evaluation of whether custody attaches to a person detained by police. Without recounting the evidence in the *Alvarado* case, the average person would agree that the questioning of an eighteen-year-old man at a sheriff's office (and transported to this location by his parents), asked about witnessing a murder in an interview conducted without pressure or interrogation of him as a suspect, and released without arrest, arguably would result in his status as having been in "custody." The California Court of Appeal held it did not; the district court on a habeas corpus hearing agreed; on appeal from the district court the 9th Circuit disagreed; *Alvarado v. Hickman* (Warden). The State of California sought review in the Supreme Court.

On review of the 9th Circuit decision in *Yarborough v. Alvarado* the Supreme Court reversed the 9th Circuit after recounting the facts surrounding the questioning and said: "The state court application of our ['custody' standard for arrest] was reasonable. The [9th Circuit Court] of Appeals was nowhere close to the mark when it concluded otherwise." Because *Yarborough v. Alvarado,* a state court case, came to the federal court on habeas corpus rather than direct appeal from the district court, the Supreme Court applied the AEDPA standard of deference prohibiting a federal court from substituting its judgment for that of a state court merely because it disagrees with the state court's decision. The Supreme Court noted the "custody" requirement is an objective test, not subjective, test and the "9th Circuit Court of Appeals ignored this rule." Reversed.

Ryan (Warden) v. Doody, 131 S.Ct. 456 (2011); *Doody v. Schriro,* 548 F.3d 847 (9th Cir. 2008); rehearing denied, 596 F. 3d 620 (9th Cir. 2010)

In August 1991, Phoenix, Arizona, was rocked by nine brutal murders at a Buddhist temple. The victims, including six Buddhist monks, lay face down in a circle, each shot execution style in the head. Several of the victims had sustained additional, nonfatal shotgun wounds. Living quarters inside the temple had been ransacked, and items of personal property, including money, cameras, and stereo equipment, were missing. A massive police investigation followed.

Eventually police arrested Doody, who was subsequently tried and convicted in an Arizona state court of *nine counts of murder, nine counts of robbery, and one count of burglary* (the 9th Circuit panel omits that facts in its decision). The trial judge admitted Doody's incriminating statements to police, the jury convicted him, and the Arizona Court of Appeals affirmed the conviction. Doody filed a petition for habeas corpus in federal court alleging violation of his *Miranda* rights. The district court denied the petition, and Doody appealed to the 9th Circuit.

Although the facts depict a vicious murder, the case represents another misguided decision not only on application of the *Miranda* rule but the record of the 9th Circuit in particular. The jury resolved the voluntariness of the confession against Doody and convicted him. The Arizona Court of Appeals issued a lengthy decision affirming the conviction in general and the *Miranda* admonition in particular. The district court affirmed the conviction. On habeas corpus in federal court the 9th Circuit majority reversing the Arizona court literally retried the case, ignored AEDPA, misread the record and reversed the conviction. The Supreme Court vacated the 9th Circuit decision in October 10, 2010 and ordered the 9th Circuit to consider a recent Supreme Court case entitled *Florida v. Powell*. On May 5, 2011 the 9th Circuit rewrote the same opinion as in its original decision, contending it had read the Supreme Court decision and it made no difference to its decision.

As the dissenting 9th Circuit judge points out, the Supreme Court had reversed the 9th Circuit repeatedly on their indefensible application of AEDPA, and this case was no exception. Here is his comment after citing all the cases decided by Supreme Court decisions.(Names and citation of the cases are omitted):

> "The Supreme Court has repeatedly told us not to [avoid AEDPA] in this language: [T]he 9th Circuit] Court of Appeals' discussion of the . . . evidence departed from the deferential review that . . . AEDPA demand[s]. The [9th Circuit] Court of Appeals reached [the wrong] result based, in large measure, on its application of an improper standard of review . . . The question is not whether a federal court believes the state court's determination . . . was incorrect but whether that determination was unreasonable-a substantially higher threshold. The reasoning of the [Ninth Circuit] Court of Appeals . . . failed to review the state courts' resolution of this question through the deferential lens of AEDPA. The requirements of [AEDPA], of course, provide additional, and binding, directions to

accord deference . . . By not according the required deference, the [Ninth Circuit] Court of Appeals failed to respect the limited role of federal habeas relief in this area prescribed by Congress and by our cases. An unreasonable application of federal law is different from an incorrect application of federal law. The Ninth Circuit did not observe this distinction, but ultimately substituted its own judgment for that of the state court in contravention of [AEDPA].).''

"But we are unrepentant and this court once again substitutes its judgment for the judgment of a state trial court and a state court of appeals. Because it does so, and because I believe that the Arizona courts' determinations were neither contrary to clearly established federal law as declared by the United States Supreme Court, nor an unreasonable application of it, I respectfully dissent.''

In compliance with the 9th Circuit decision, unchanged despite the subsequent reversal by the Supreme Court, the prosecution will never be able to retry Doody. Part of the prosecution's case consisted of testimony from an accomplice who pled guilty and was sentenced. Now in prison, the accomplice will not testify again in the absence of any incentive.

The Supreme Court inexplicably denied a hearing in the *Doody* case. The injustice perpetrated by the 9th Circuit is inexcusable. Repeated admonitions by the Supreme Court to apply deference to state court decisions goes inexcusably ignored in the 9th Circuit. The Supreme Court warned all federal courts when it originally decided the *Miranda* decision not to expand its scope. No court has jettisoned this rule of law more than the 9th Circuit.

Miranda cases will forever be litigated no matter what the officers say to an arrestee. The detectives in the Doody case tried to explain *Miranda* to Doody so he would understand. According to the 9th Circuit, the explanation was unclear. What should the officer say when a suspect states he does not understand? Just repeat the formula? And, as the dissenting judges wrote, the majority completely ignores AEDPA.

CHAPTER 9

VINDICTIVE PROSECUTION

U.S. v .Jenkins, 504 F.3d 694 (9th Cir. 2008) amended decision; original decision: 494 F.3d. 1135 (9th Cir. 2007); Rehearing denied; 518 F.3d 722 (2008)

Vindictive prosecution is a judicially invented remedy to prevent the prosecution from filing charges against a defendant in retaliation for committing some act or conduct allegedly affecting a prosecution.

On two consecutive days in October, border patrol agents stopped Jenkins and arrested her each time for concealing illegal aliens in her car. No charges were filed although Jenkins admitted to the agents she was paid to smuggle aliens. Three months later she and her husband attempted to enter the United States in a vehicle but border patrol agents searched their vehicle, discovered marijuana, and arrested them for importing marijuana.

Indicted for importation of marijuana, Jenkins testified at trial she was unaware of the contraband concealed in the car because she believed she was smuggling illegal aliens. Based on this testimony, and while the jury was deliberating, the U.S. Attorney indicted her for smuggling aliens based on the October events when no charges had been originally filed despite the evidence.

The district court judge dismissed the indictment, citing his decision as "prophylactic" to prevent a "chilling" of the defendant's right to testify at trial. The court then said the government did not do "anything wrong," but the timing of the alien smuggling charges did not pass the "smell test." Unsurprisingly, the court cited no authority for this unusual opinion. The district court dismissed the indictment on grounds of "vindictive prosecution." The government appealed.

In a 2-1 decision, a 9th Circuit panel majority in *Jenkins* cited its own case law as precedent for its decision and included a Supreme Court case discussing vindictive prosecution. The 9th Circuit panel majority decision, without reviewing decisions of other courts on this vague and clearly subjective judicial evaluation of evidence, affirmed the decision of the district court trial judge. This decision by the trial judge and the 9th Circuit panel demonstrates their lack of any trial experience, exhibits their embarrassing naïveté, and cites no legal authority for its decision.

The panel opined that the U.S. Attorney should have filed the smuggling charges against Jenkins at the time of her original arrest. Apparently the case load of the U.S. Attorney's Office is irrelevant. Is filing smuggling charges against a woman who unsuccessfully attempted to smuggle a sum total of four men into the country worth prosecuting? That fact pattern is not a priority for federal prosecution. Whether to prosecute is a prosecutorial decision.

According to the panel majority, the original arrest in the smuggling case was "complete" and the U.S. Attorney penalized the defendant for testifying in the marijuana importation trial. In the real world, any case that appears "complete" can dissolve in a heartbeat based on a number of factors: the border agent has retired; was terminated; moved out of the country and not subject to subpoena; died; some jurors are sympathetic to the alleged plight of aliens; no tape recording to corroborate the admission of smuggling sets up a test of credibility; or *Miranda* rights not read or read improperly. All these events can occur in a routine case as well as retrials in death penalty cases.

As the dissenting judge observes, the decision whether to prosecute, and when to prosecute, is an executive function, not a judicial one, absent malice, of which the panel found none, and the trial judge said the prosecution did "nothing wrong." The defendant did not have to testify at trial but offered a clever defense to the marijuana charge that she was basically a smuggler of aliens and unaware of contraband concealed in her car.

Here is what the majority of the panel says about its decision: "We are sensitive to the government's concern that the dismissal of charges resulting from a defendant's in-court admission may hamstring prosecutorial efforts." Yes, that insight is real a possibility.

The 9th Circuit circulated this decision to the full court but a majority of judges declined review. Seven judges dissented. These judges castigated the panel opinion for its failure to honor the difference between judging and advocacy. The Supreme Court has warned lower courts to remember the distinction and had written, "Judges cannot feasibly determine how best to allocate prosecutorial resources, let alone weigh the strength of the prosecution's evidence against such consideration,"

CHAPTER 10

QUALIFIED IMMUNITY

Law enforcement officers enjoy unprecedented, but not unlimited, discretion in performing their duties. The Supreme Court has repeatedly ruled that officers are entitled to immunity from a lawsuit for conduct in the line of duty if acting reasonably and unless they violated " well-established" law as determined by the Supreme Court; *Anderson v. Creighton.* For example, in cases alleging unlawful search or seizure, the Supreme Court noted, "Even law enforcement officials who reasonably but mistakenly conclude probable cause to arrest or search is present are entitled to immunity."

The legal doctrine is labeled "qualified immunity," and also applies to other public officials, for example, prison officials sued by inmates. The onetime leading Supreme Court case on qualified immunity, *Saucier v. Katz,* required the plaintiff who filed the lawsuit to establish the officer or public officials violated a "clearly established" Constitutional right, and that the officer knew his conduct was unlawful. This test is as verbally malleable as any other Constitutional rule.

The Saucier case is another 9th Circuit case reversed during the 2010 term of the Supreme Court. At that time, the Supreme Court noted, "The Ninth Circuit's approach to [qualified immunity] . . . could undermine the goal of qualified immunity to avoid excessive disruption for government and permit the resolution of many insubstantial claims." Several years later, the Supreme

Court reconsidered the procedural rules of the *Saucier* case in *Pearson v. Callahan* and modified its earlier decision in order to give trial courts more flexibility in applying the doctrine of qualified immunity and enabling public officers to do their jobs without responding to frivolous lawsuits.

The Supreme Court, during its realignment of the Constitution in 1960–70, found a "liberty interest" that precluded prison officials from censoring incoming mail and ordered a "review" process within the prison system; *Procunier v. Martinez.* This decision, although subsequently narrowed by the Supreme Court, generated numerous 9th Circuit opinions meddling with the prison system, a practice that continues unabated in California and in some cases imposes civil liability on prison officials.

See for cross-reference the chapter on Prisoner's Rights.

Hunter v. Hydrick, 129 S.Ct. 2431 (2009); Reversing the 9th Circuit decision in 500 F.3d 978 (9th Cir. 2007)

In a case unrelated to *Hunter v. Hydrick* entitled *Ashcroft v. Iqbal,* a Muslim sued former U.S. Attorney General Ashcroft (see Chapter 7) for detaining him as a "material witness in a pending case against another person." The Attorney General's Office never utilized Iqbal's testimony at a subsequent trial. The Supreme Court found the allegations in the Complaint Iqbal filed insufficient to warrant trial and dismissed the case.

When the 9th Circuit wrote its original decision in *Hunter v. Hydrick* denying immunity to state officials, it considered the allegations (written claims of inmates) as follows: "Indeed, we do not see how . . . [inmates] could plead the individual roles of each state officer with any more specificity." The Supreme Court in reviewing the 9th Circuit decision n *Hunter* did not share the clarity of vision perceived by the 9th Circuit. The Supreme Court reversed the *Hunter* case based on its *Ashcroft* decision and returned it to the 9th Circuit in May 2009 to clarify its "specificity of the allegations in the claim." On its return to the 9th Circuit the court reversed its original decision.

Robinson v. Lehman, 552 U.S. 1172 (2008). Reversing the 9th Circuit decision in *Lehman v. Robinson*, 228 Fed. Appx. 697; 346 Fed. Appx. 188 Buried in an unpublished decision, a 9th Circuit panel reviewed a district court ruling in a civil case denying a motion for summary judgment (request for dismissal) filed by police officer defendant Robinson. The plaintiff (Estate of deceased Joshua Lehman) who filed the suit alleged that Officer Robinson unlawfully used lethal force against the deceased in violation of his civil rights. The officer asserted immunity from suit. Denied immunity in the district court, the officer appealed to the 9th Circuit.

The 9th Circuit panel began its analysis with this quote from *Tennessee v. Garner*, a case decided several years ago by the Supreme Court: "The Fourth Amendment prohibits police from employing lethal force against a suspect who poses no immediate threat to the officer and no threat to others." From that quotation the reader can predict the result of this case, as factually described below.

Officer Robinson filed a motion to dismiss the case contending he was immune from civil liability despite causing the death of Lehman whom he had shot after the culmination of a car chase. In denying the motion, the 9th Circuit panel described deposition testimony from other officers to establish Officer Robinson was not shielded from liability. The 9th Circuit panel selectively summarized some unfavorable deposition pretrial testimony elicited from other officers on the scene but ignored qualifications in their answers to questions.

The court summarized evidence that police had pepper-sprayed, Tasered, and "partially subdued" a recalcitrant Lehman, who refused orders to exit his damaged truck after he lost control during a police chase. According to testimony from one of the officers at the scene, said the court, "negotiations between other officers and Lehman were in progress." The "negotiations" consisted of attempts to order the defiant Lehman to exit his damaged vehicle. The 9th Circuit panel wrote: "The officer [Robinson] . . . shot and killed Lehman as he sat in his car, with all the tires shot out, surrounded by at least ten armed police officers and numerous police vehicles." Not a word about Lehman's prior conduct warranting justification for police presence at the scene.

The reader wonders why the tires were shot out and why Lehman was alone in a disabled vehicle surrounded by armed police officers and numerous police vehicles. That a pepper-sprayed and Tasered Lehman was "partially subdued" is hyperbole, if not a misstatement. What does that phrase mean when Lehman refused to exit his truck upon orders from police and was personally struck with incapacitating devices? How do you "negotiate" with the driver of a vehicle who refuses to exit his vehicle after engaging in a harrowing car chase by police? How do you know if he is armed?

In contrast, here is a truncated summary of other police witness testimony, as paraphrased by the State of Nevada in support of the motion to dismiss the lawsuit, and completely ignored by the 9th Circuit panel:

> "Earlier that day [of the incident], sheriff's deputies on patrol had encountered Lehman. Lehman repeatedly rammed their vehicle, disabling it, and fled in his pick-up truck. One deputy fired shots into all four tires but Lehman escaped. During a car chase by other officers, Lehman continued to drive his vehicle on deflated tires. Officers unsuccessfully attempted to intercept his vehicle by initiating a spin maneuver with their patrol car, but Lehman never stopped until forced into oncoming traffic. Officers broke a window on Lehman's car and fired pepper spray and Taser inside when Lehman refused to exit the vehicle.
>
> Officer Robinson, arriving at the scene in response to a radio call, saw Lehman briefly emerge from his vehicle. Lehman then engaged in several chopping motions with a knife directed toward other officers. Vehicular traffic was backed up for miles and drivers

had stopped their cars to observe the scene. Robinson mistakenly believed Lehman had fired shots at officers (originally, deputy sheriffs had fired shots at Lehman's truck) but he had enough information to reasonably conclude Lehman was involved in the earlier event with sheriff's deputies.

Despite the presence of several police vehicles, Robinson could see Lehman had an escape route along the highway in the direction of officers standing in his path. Robinson saw Lehman look around as though assessing whether he could hit the officers. Although Robinson did not know the officers' precise location from his vantage point, he believed additional officers had arrived and were concealed from his view behind Lehman's truck. Lehman accelerated his vehicle toward the officers, compelling one officer to jump aside to avoid being crushed. In an attempt to protect other nearby officers from injury by the moving vehicle, Robinson fired at Lehman. Because of crossfire issues, Robinson believed he was the only person in a position to fire his weapon, and that shooting Lehman was the only way to stop his flight. A videotape illustrated this version of the facts.

This testimony, summarized by the State of Nevada in its petition for review of the 9th Circuit decision to the Supreme Court, obviously differs significantly from the description of the events written by the 9th Circuit panel. The 9th Circuit decision concedes that police officers must make split-second decisions in circumstances that are "tense, uncertain and rapidly evolving" but in the opinion of the panel, the Lehman confrontation apparently did not involve any of those conditions. In their view, the "suspect pose[d] no immediate threat to the officers and no threat to others." Apparently a moving vehicle aimed toward officers poses no threat.

In a gratuitous concession to confer qualified immunity on police officers in other cases who do confront "tense, uncertain and rapidly evolving circumstances," the 9th Circuit panel cites one of its own cases refusing to permit the defense of qualified immunity when an officer shot the driver of a "slow-moving car because 'the [the officer] could avoid being injured by simply stepping aside'" (*Acosta v. San Francisco*). That naïveté speaks for itself. Vehicles do accelerate and are capable of swerving. After that, the 9th Circuit panel denied the Robinson motion to dismiss the lawsuit on grounds the officer was entitled to qualified immunity.

The obvious alternative in the *Robinson* case is to let the jury decide the facts. However, the Supreme Court carefully read the State of Nevada's request to review the 9th Circuit decision, and the Justices agreed and reversed. The Supreme Court vacated the 9th Circuit decision and ordered that court to reconsider its decision in light of a previous Supreme Court decision in *Scott v. Harris*. In fairness to the 9th Circuit, the panel wrote their unpublished opinion in *Robinson v. Lehman* on April 16, 2007, and lacked the benefit of the *Scott v. Harris* decision, which was written by the Supreme Court on April 30, 2007.

The Supreme Court decided the *Scott v. Harris* case after viewing the videotape of a horrific car chase. The Justices compared the testimony of the driver (who subsequently sued the police) with the tape. The Supreme Court held a trial court can grant a motion for summary judgment sustaining qualified immunity for officers despite disputed facts if one version is so inconceivable no jury could find against them. The scenario in *Scott* is strikingly comparable to the evidence in *Robinson v. Lehman*.

The Justices could have simply reversed the 9th Circuit panel and granted the motion for summary judgment but exercised their discretion to allow that court to reconsider its decision. The Supreme Court rendered its reversal and returned the case to the 9th Circuit in February 2008. On September 19, 2009, one year and six months later, this is what the 9th Circuit panel wrote in an unpublished decision entitled *Lehman v. Robinson*:

> "This case was [returned] to us by the United States Supreme Court following the Court's decision in *Scott v. Harris* . . . Following

Scott, we asked for supplemental briefing [legal papers] from the parties. In *Scott v. Harris*, the Supreme Court cautioned that 'we are not required to accept [a] version of events when it is 'clearly contradict[ed]' by a video in the record and the accuracy of the video is not disputed."

The Supreme Court returned the case to the 9th Circuit, and here is what that court said:" "Unlike a [different] federal court of appeals in Scott, we reviewed the video that captured the events at issue in this case. The video did not 'clearly contradict' the plaintiffs' version of events. Because the video does not 'clearly contradict' the version of events recounted by the plaintiffs, and for the reasons stated in our prior memorandum disposition . . . the district court's denial of Robinson['s]motion for summary judgment based on qualified immunity is affirmed" (Bolded in the original).

This simplistic, almost rude, sentence is an excellent example of 9th Circuit ideology calculated to ignore the Supreme Court. The panel agreed to allow the Lehman case to continue to trial because they watched a video. Too bad they didn't consider the evidence.

Hunter (Warden) v. Bryant, 502 U.S. 224 (1991). Reversing the 9th Circuit decision in 903 F.2d 717 (9th Cir. 1990). Dismissed upon return to the 9th Circuit; 396 F.3d 1036 (9th Cir. 1991).
Secret Service agents arrested Bryant who had sent a letter threatening the President of the United States. Although the document was admittedly ambiguous, Secret Service agents arrested him after receiving other information from a third party; questioned Bryant and seized a copy of the letter. The U.S. Attorney subsequently dismissed the case and Bryant sued the agents. Each agent alleged immunity from litigation.

The district court denied the agent's claim to immunity, and the 9th Circuit affirmed the decision on appeal. On review by the Supreme Court, the Justices wrote:

"The decision of the Ninth Circuit ignores the import of [our prior decisions]. The Court of Appeals confusion is evident from its statement that [whether] a reasonable officer could have believed he had probable cause is a question for the trier of fact . . . This statement is wrong for two reasons. First, it routinely places the question of immunity in the hands of the jury. Immunity ordinarily should be decided by the court long before trial; Second, the court should ask whether the agents acted reasonably under settled law in the circumstances, not whether another reasonable, or more reasonable, interpretation of the events can be constructed [by a court] five years after the fact."

In other words, the 9th Circuit judges were guessing. The Supreme Court returned the case to the 9th Circuit and that court, in effect, dismissed the case.

Brosseau v. Haugen, 543 U.S. 194 (2004). Reversing the 9th Circuit decision in *Haugen v. Brosseau,* 339 F.3d 857 (9th Cir. 2003); amended 351 F.3d 372 (9th Cir. 2003).

With few exceptions, judges on the 9th Circuit have never served as police officers, prosecutors, criminal defense attorneys, or even criminal trial judges. They have no understanding of violence in the street and the constant stress of working with mentally deranged, homicidal, and brutal people. Many of the 9th Circuit judges who write decisions in criminal cases specialize in punctilio and a quest for error. They are indefatigable in refusing to accord law enforcement officers' immunity for allegedly conducting unlawful arrests, as discussed in Chapter 4 on Arrest & Search. And in death penalty cases, no court refuses to confirm decisions of state courts more than the 9th Circuit.

When violence occurs in a confrontation between police and a civilian, many of the 9th Circuit judges expect officers to act in accord with all Constitutional protections - but only as the court interprets them. Consider the facts in *Brosseau v. Haugen*: Two men began fighting with Haugen in a residential neighborhood, and a neighbor reported the brawl to police. Officer Brosseau arrived as the two men attempted to force Haugen into a truck. The officer's arrival and distraction enabled Haugen, wanted on a felony warrant, to flee. Officer Brosseau ordered the two men to wait in a nearby truck.

Other officers arrived with a K-9 dog in the search for Haugen when he suddenly appeared nearby and jumped into a Jeep parked near the truck occupied by the two waiting men. Haugen attempted to start the Jeep and refused to obey Brosseau's order to exit. The officer smashed the window, but an undeterred Haugen started the car, drove between the occupied truck and another car, "stepping on the gas," and swerved across a lawn. Officer Brosseau, concerned for the occupants in the truck and another nearby car, fired a shot hitting Haugen in the back but he continued down the street, stopping only when he discovered he had been shot.

Case Summary: A man wanted on a felony warrant refused to obey an order to exit a truck, weaved through two parked vehicles, swerved across a lawn with the accelerator floored, continued his flight and was frustrated in his escape only because of an incapacitating wound. Incredibly, he sued the officer who shot him.

According to the 2-1 majority of a 9th Circuit panel on appeal by the officer from the district court, she is not entitled to immunity because it is a question of fact whether the officer was reasonable in shooting at a fleeing suspect. Apparently the officer should ignore the danger to occupants of other vehicles or other officers and let the felon escape. According to a concurring judge, it is better to just let the felon escape without further injury to other officers and the public.

The dissenting judge skewers the majority decision and its evident departure from reality. He writes: "Nor can I accept the majority's holding that because police can reduce the danger of a high-speed chase by letting a felon escape they may never use deadly force to protect the public from the danger posed by a felon's reckless flight in a vehicle. The majority's sweeping holding, which promises an easy escape to any felon willing to threaten innocent lives by driving recklessly, is *indefensible as a matter of law and policy*, and it conflicts with our [other] circuits' holdings that police officers do not violate the Fourth Amendment by using deadly force to stop a fleeing felon who appears likely to drive an automobile with willful disregard for the lives of others."

The naïveté of two (out of three) federal judges who wrote the original decision in *Haugen* is appalling. You do not let a felony suspect who refuses to obey a simple order, drives a car wildly across a lawn between occupied cars, and flees down the street, to escape. According to the judge concurring in the majority decision, Haugen was a non-dangerous suspect. In support of his opinion, this judge cited *Harris v. Roderick*, (another 9th Circuit decision) denying qualified immunity to an officer in the Ruby Ridge case who shot a suspect that had previously shot and killed a U.S. Marshall. Apparently officers should just stand around and hope no one else gets executed.

In reviewing this case, the Supreme Court found the facts so easy to decide that the Justices signed a unanimous opinion reversing the 9th Circuit. Reversed by the Supreme Court, the 9th Circuit sent the *Haugen* case back to the district court for "further proceedings." No further action was taken by the court.

Kennedy v. Ridgefield City, 440 F.3d 1091 (9th Cir. 2006).
Eight 9th Circuit judges in this case dissented from the opinion of the majority.
In this case, Kennedy contacted police to inform them that a neighbor had molested her child. An officer subsequently notified her that he had contacted the neighbor. The following day the neighbor murdered Kennedy's husband and attempted to murder Kennedy. She filed a lawsuit against the City and police officers.

Under unquestioned Supreme Court law, the City and the officers are not civilly liable for the death of the husband, or the attempted murder of his wife, because neither the officer nor the police department did anything to endanger their lives. Police would have inevitably informed Kennedy of the investigation of the neighbor and their investigation of the alleged molestation. The 9th Circuit three-judge panel disagreed, and denied the City and the officer immunity in response to a lawsuit filed by Kennedy. According to the panel, the state (City) and the officer had "created a dangerous situation."

Although the facts are extensive, here is what eight dissenting judges said in a rehearing of the previous three-judge panel imposing potential liability on the City and the officer:

> "It is regrettable the court declines to hear this case en banc (full court). Contrary to Supreme Court precedent, the *Kennedy* opinion expands the judge-made 'state created danger' doctrine to impose impermissibility broad . . . civil rights liability on police officers under circumstances that at most are evidence of negligence. Its expansive new holding opens the floodgates to . . . lawsuits by citizens who will claim 'deliberate indifference' following any failure on the part of the police to adequately protect them from harm after they report a crime notwithstanding the danger of retaliation by criminal suspects often exists when citizens report a crime.
>
> *Kennedy* will foreclose officers from invoking qualified immunity before trial; a jury will have to decide whether to impose liability and damages. The slippery slope of liability created by the court's opinion cannot be confined to extraordinary cases. This unjustifiable expansion of the 'state-created danger' doctrine raises the possibility of liability every time a person dials 911 or reports a crime to law enforcement and the police are delayed in their response or follow-up investigation."

The eventual decision is curious. The 9th Circuit full court denied a rehearing of the case, with eight judges dissenting, but the majority of the court withdrew its original decision and stated it was no longer good law.

County of Sacramento v. Lewis, 523 U.S. 833 (1998). Reversing the 9th Circuit decision in 98 F.3d 434 (9th Cir. 1996).

The 9th Circuit suffered another ignominious reversal in *County of Sacramento v. Lewis.*

In a wild high-speed chase with police, the passenger of a fleeing vehicle fell, or was thrown, from his seat onto the street and run over by a pursuing police car. The 9th Circuit refused qualified immunity to the officer who had driven the police vehicle in pursuit. The Supreme Court, in a unanimous decision, reversed the 9th Circuit. In an incisive comment, Supreme Court Justice Scalia decried, indirectly, the 9th Circuit decision and wrote that the officer's conduct, if anything, was negligence, not a Due Process Clause violation. And this case arose in 1996.

The ideological imbalance among 9th Circuit judges is apparent from a reading of these cases and not confined only to its opinions on the death penalty, the Fourth Amendment, the Fifth Amendment, and immunity. These cases not only confirm antigovernment bias but also illustrate the damage to public safety. When you exclude relevant and incriminating evidence, a guilty person goes free. When you deny immunity to officers, you subject them to financial liability and create a genuine concern on their future ability to do their job.

CHAPTER 11

PRISONERS' RIGHTS

Frustrated by federal court intervention in court decisions, Congress enacted the following laws: Antiterrorism and Effective Death Penalty Act (AEDPA) to rein in federal courts on habeas corpus; the REAL ID Act to withdraw immigration court jurisdiction from district courts; require immigration court decisions appealed only to U.S. Courts of Appeals, simultaneously limiting jurisdiction of those courts; enacted the Prison Litigation Reform Act to restrict frivolous appeals of prisoners in the wake of a sharp rise in prison litigation. These Congressional enactments unequivocally reflect Congressional displeasure with federal courts and their decisions, particularly in federal habeas corpus cases.

To reduce prisoner litigation, Congress statutorily imposed an "exhaustion" of remedies requirement compelling state prison inmates to assert all post conviction complaints administratively to prison officials before seeking federal court review. The California Department of Corrections and Rehabilitation drafted a grievance policy for prisoners requiring them to initially file their complaint with prison officials and receive an answer within a short time frame before the inmate initiated litigation. The statute also provides for an internal administrative appeal procedure if requested by a prisoner.

Woodford (Warden) v. Ngo, 548 U.S. 81 (2006). Reversing the 9th Circuit decision in *Woodford v. Ngo,* 403 F.3d 620 (9th Cir. 2005).

In *Woodford v. Ngo,* the prison inmate filed a civil rights lawsuit against prison officials without fulfilling any of the time guidelines required in the prison administrative regulations. The district court dismissed the complaint, and Ngo appealed to the 9th Circuit. According to the 9th Circuit panel, failure to comply with timeliness requirements of prison regulations did not disqualify the prisoner from filing litigation. The court said noncompliance with internal procedural timeliness could be ignored and the prisoner proceed in court in the absence of any further administrative action. The government sought review in the Supreme Court.

The Supreme Court reversed and dismissed the 9th Circuit decision as ludicrous. The Justices noted that Congress had intended to restrict prisoner filings in federal court by allowing state correction officers the opportunity to remedy or deny a complaint and prepare an administrative record for review before the prisoner sought litigation in federal court. To ignore procedural guidelines frustrates that objective, and the Supreme Court wrote: "[A] prisoner must complete the administrative review process in accordance with the applicable procedural rules, including deadlines, as a precondition to bringing suit in federal court."

The procedure of complying with timing guidelines is obvious: to establish an efficient record - keeping system on prisoners. To allow a prisoner to ignore simple rules undermines the Congressional objective to limit frivolous litigation, frustrates an internal mechanism for addressing any complaints, and undermines the administrative process. No organization, particularly the Department of Corrections & and Rehabilitation, can function without a system of rules and guidelines. Inexplicably, and in the face of numerous other federal Court of Appeals decisions to the contrary, the 9th Circuit approved of a judicial indifference to practicality and control of inmates.

In reversing the 9th Circuit, the Supreme Court in *Ngo* wrote this comment: "[The prisoner] failed to point to any statute or [court] case that purported to require exhaustion [of administrative remedies] while at the same time allowing a party to bypass deliberately the administrative process by flouting the agency's procedural rules." The Court returned the case to the 9th Circuit, and the panel concluded Ngo had not exhausted his administrative remedies. Even so, one judge complained that the timelines instituted by prison officials for prisoners to file complaints was too short. Ngo, after ignoring any deadlines, filed his petition five months after the deadline. Despite that, this judge nevertheless complained.

Barrett v. Belleque (Warden), 544 F.3d 1060 (9th Cir. 2008)
It is unsurprising that the 9th Circuit case load is backlogged given its antipathy to immigration judges, federal agents, and law enforcement officers. Barrett, a state prisoner, filed a civil rights action against prison officials for censoring his racist, vulgar, and offensive tirades levied against prison officials. The trial court summarily dismissed the case. On appeal, the 9th Circuit took the time to actually consider this silly case and reversed the trial judge on First Amendment grounds. This kind of judicial time wasting on a state prisoner's frivolous complaint answers a number of questions about the 9th Circuit. When the case was returned to the district court, the judge granted the Department of Corrections & Rehabilitation summary judgment (a dismissal), but it took two written decisions by the district court to say so. In effect, this court reversed the 9th Circuit.

Pierce v. County of Orange, 526 F.3d 1190 (9th Cir. 2008)
The 9th Circuit employs a wide range of devices interfering with state courts, law enforcement personnel, jails, prisons, and lawyers. As reviewed in the Chapter on Lawyers, these judges think they know more about the right to represent defendants without ever having tried a criminal case. Of course they know how to enforce the law better than law enforcement by denying immunity to officers, even though few of the judges have any law enforcement experience. They know how to run prisons and manage jails

despite lacking any administrative experience. And no one will ever be executed in California regardless of how many times the Supreme Court reverses the 9th Circuit on grounds of "ineffective assistance of counsel."

Pierce provides an example of judicial imposition of managerial tasks on correction officers or jail officials who supervise inmates who have murdered, raped, robbed, lied, and are hopelessly undisciplined. Managing a jail or prison facility differs significantly from a business - but not according to the 9th Circuit. *Pierce v. Co. of Orange* is an example of a court order served on county jail officials mandating compliance with certain conditions imposed by the court as to each item: Reading material sent by mail; Sending mail; Mattresses/ beds; Law books; Population cap; Sleep Blanket; Telephone access; Jail communication with lawyers; Seating/ holding cells; Mealtime; Administrative segregation; Religious services; Day room; Exercise; Visitors. In addition to this prolix and lengthy order, the court (in this case a district court, not the 9th Circuit) included in its decision an endless number of footnotes.

As the 9th Circuit court decision in *Pierce v. County of Orange* notes, this case required supervision of the jail by the district court from 1975 to 2008 at an enormous cost to taxpayers. That a federal court would undertake to supervise the entire jail population of Orange County from 1975 to 2008 without any apparent objection by the Attorney General (Brown) or the County is inexplicable. To its credit, the 9th Circuit in *Pierce* finally agreed to terminate all but two of the orders. A decision rendered about thirty three years too late.

Kane v. Espitia (Warden), 546 U.S. 9 (2005). Reversing the 9th Circuit decision in *Kane v. Espitia*, 113 Fed.Appx. 802.Reversing also the 9th Circuit decision in *Bribiesca v. Galaza*, 215 F.3d 1015 (9th Cir. 2000).
Espitia, convicted in California state court, had elected to represent himself in filing a petition seeking habeas corpus despite the obvious disadvantages of prison confinement. All California courts had denied Espitia's argument that the Sixth Amendment to the Constitution right to an attorney

included the right of access to a law library and its legal resources. A district court judge also denied the petition for habeas corpus on the same grounds, but in Espitia's appeal to the 9th Circuit a panel of judges agreed with him.

In reversing the district court judge, the 9th Circuit cited an earlier Supreme Court decision that purportedly held that the "lack of access to law books violated his [Espitia's] right to represent himself as established by the Supreme Court."

The State sought review from the 9th Circuit decision, and the Supreme Court reversed on the first day of its 2005-06 term in abrupt and censorious language decrying the absence of any legal basis for the 9th Circuit decision. In a cursory one-page opinion, the Justices rejected the 9th Circuit decision, informing the appellate court that no Supreme Court authority existed for ordering self-represented prisoners access to legal material and, in fact, no other federal Circuit Courts had held to the contrary.

The summary disposition of *Espitia* is only another example of Supreme Court displeasure with the 9th Circuit. The Justices' curt reversal speaks more loudly than the reproach. During the course of its decision in Espitia the Supreme Court also criticized a previous 9th Circuit decision written five years earlier on the same issue: *Bribiesca v. Galaza*. In other words, the *Espitia* decision in 2005 overruled the 2000 decision in *Bribiesca*. For five years (2000-2005) the 9th Circuit had been applying the wrong law.

Undeterred, the 9th Circuit held in *Mendoza v. Carey* that the inability of a Spanish-speaking inmate to obtain legal materials "tolled" (suspended) the filing deadlines applicable to petitions for writs of habeas corpus filed in prison. The district court had sentenced Mendoza after his plea of guilty in 2001. Mendoza filed three petitions for habeas corpus in state court and one in federal district court. Under federal law the petition exceeded the statutory time limitation for filing petitions. But a 9th Circuit panel, ignoring the Supreme Court cases in *Kane* and *Espitia* which had ruled there is no *per se* (of itself) right to anyone for access to legal materials, and, without any evidence Mendoza could read Spanish, allowed him to file his petition.

Although the 9th Circuit insists that a prison is not necessarily required to maintain a library in Spanish, German, French, or any other foreign language, the force of the decision is obvious.

The Attorney General of California (Lockyer) sought no review in the Supreme Court. The ruling in this case has been almost universally rejected by other courts.

Prison Legal News v. Lehman, 397 F.3d 692 (9th Cir. 2005)

Only in America could inmates confined in prison attempt to form a labor union, and the 9th Circuit agreed to this preposterous request. The Supreme Court squelched this bizarre attempt by prisoners who asserted violation of the First Amendment and its protection of free speech. In *Jones v. North Carolina Prisoner's Labor Union, Inc.* the Supreme Court had reminded lower federal courts (read 9th Circuit) that prisons are different, and inmates are not accorded the rights of citizens. Inmates in prison are incarcerated for brutal, heinous, despicable crimes. Having tortured victims, strangled them, raped, and robbed, remorseless and incapable of rehabilitation, this human detritus is the core of prison life. No one denies that prison officials should feed and house inmates, but otherwise we owe them nothing but the absence of intentional and willful misconduct by their captors. Those who ruin or deprive people of their lives do not warrant sympathy or seek recognition of a labor union.

Intent on meddling with prison administration, the 9th Circuit does not want prison officials to interfere with delivery of mail, including bulk packages and catalogs. In *Prison Legal News v. Lehman* the 9th Circuit ordered prison officials to process not only first class mail and subscriptions (apparently someone is paying for it) but also non subscription bulk mail. The court rejected prison officials' contentions that sorting, searching, and delivering bulk mail prevents the introduction of contraband and diverts personnel from more important duties. Moreover, the court failed to award qualified immunity to prison officials who had been sued by inmates. Surprisingly, the State of Washington sought no review in the Supreme Court.

Phillips v. Hust, 129 S.Ct. 1036 (2009); Reversing the 9th Circuit decision in 507 F.3d 1171 (9th Cir. 2007).

For another example of wasting judicial resources and ignoring AEDPA, this case arrived on habeas corpus to the 9th Circuit from a Washington state court decision.

In *Phillips v. Hust* a 9th Circuit panel criticized the state prison librarian (Hust) for denying inmate Phillips use of a copying machine to file a petition for review of his case in the Supreme Court. Phillips sued the librarian who denied the allegation. Although the 9th Circuit never identified a date of Phillips's imprisonment, the district court referenced "the eighteen years of his [Phillips's] litigation" in the court system. Moreover, the 9th Circuit denied the librarian qualified immunity and sent the case back to the district court for computation of damages to Phillips: $1500.00.

The dissenting judge in the 9th Circuit deplored the majority reasoning and its refusal to allow the librarian qualified immunity. Here is the language of the dissenting judge:

> "All I can add to [the dissent of another judge] is my utter astonishment that we're leaving an opinion on the books that not only denies the prison librarian qualified immunity but actually holds her liable. Her transgression? Failing to help a prisoner bind a brief [legal file] in a way that's not even permitted by the Supreme Court's rules. It's perfectly clear that a timely petition, bound or unbound, would have been accepted by the Supreme Court. How the prison librarian violated any of his rights, let alone his "clearly established rights," is a mystery that repeated readings of the majority opinion do not dispel . . ."

The dissent was signed by a total of nine judges. The full 9th Circuit court declined rehearing.

The Supreme Court granted review, reversed the 9th Circuit, and ordered that court to reconsider its application of AEDPA to the case. Complying with that order, the 9th Circuit panel reversed its decision and held the librarian immune from civil liability.

Foster v. Runnels (Warden), 554 F.3d. 807 (9th Cir. 2009)
Under prison policy, a prisoner who interferes with a Corrections Officer in the service of meals is disqualified from certain benefits, including receiving his own meals.

When Foster refused to remove paper obscuring observation from a window of his cell, the Corrections Officer reported the violation and imposed prison policy depriving him of a few meals. Foster, a state court prisoner filed a civil rights case (42 U.S.C. § 1983) in district court against the warden and a corrections officer. Denied by the district court, Foster appealed. According to the 9th Circuit, the prison officers' decision deprives the prisoner of his Eighth Amendment Right not to be subjected to cruel and unusual punishment.

In a case that should have been dismissed in one paragraph, the 9th Circuit panel writes endlessly about prisoners' rights, and particularly the right to meals, and said: "This right is 'clearly established,'" and therefore the corrections officer is was denied immunity. It is difficult to characterize this decision. The word "incomprehensible" comes to mind. The 9th Circuit, of course, assumes judges know how to manage prisons, including a frivolous charge such as this, better than those who do manage prisons and prisoners like Foster. As noted in *Bull v. City & County of San Francisco* (see chapter 7), the 9th Circuit also knows how to manage jails. The 9th Circuit agreed to rehear that case and reversed its original decision; *Clement v. California Dept. of Corrections & Rehabilitation*, 364 F.3d 1148 (9th Cir. 2004)

The California Dept. of Corrections & Rehabilitation introduced a policy of restricting Internet access to prisoners on grounds of inordinate monitoring time spent by staff and, more importantly, the ability to send coded messages. It is a well-known fact that many prisoners continue to manage drug operations despite their confinement, and allowing Internet access facilitates an ability to communicate with those outside the prison. Apparently this concern is of no moment to the 9th Circuit judges who enjoined (prohibited) the Department from enforcing its policy.

The Attorney General of California (Brown) sought no review in the Supreme Court.

Crickon v. Thomas, 579 F.3d 978 (9th Cir. 2008)

Federal prison officials have also suffered under the "expertise" of 9th Circuit management. The Bureau of Prisons (BOP), an administrative agency of the U.S. Government, published a regulation offering prisoners an opportunity to shorten their sentence if they successfully completed a drug rehabilitation program. The BOP excluded any inmate convicted in state or federal court who had been sentenced for homicide, robbery, rape, or aggravated assault. Presumably the BOP assumed all these offenses included violence, and convicts sentenced for those crimes should not receive a shortened sentence available to nonviolent offenders. The BOP submitted no justification for this exclusion for these obvious reasons.

The premise excluding violent offenders from the program is so obvious that only the 9th Circuit could not understand it. Yet a three-judge panel held that a failure of the BOP to explain the rationale excluding those convicted of crimes of violence eligible for a shorter sentence rendered the regulation unenforceable. Given the opportunity for prisoners to achieve shorter sentences for good conduct and other sentencing credits, and the accelerated time for parole, additional sentencing reductions of those convicted of inexcusable crimes is indefensible.

One sentence should be enough.

Norwood v. Vance (Warden), 591 F.3d 1062 (9th Cir. 2009)
Not all judges in the 9th Circuit repeatedly vote against the government or
law enforcement. *Norwood v. Vance* is a case reflecting the division existing
among 9th Circuit judges. The facts are lengthy, but illustrate the incredulous reasoning of the dissenting judge. The court wrote:

> "One Gregory Norwood was incarcerated at CSP-Sacramento, a
> maximum security prison, during a particularly violent period in
> the prison's history. Norwood brought this [lawsuit] alleging that
> prison officials violated the Eighth Amendment prohibiting cruel
> or unusual punishment when they denied him outdoor exercise
> during four separate extended lockdowns over the course of two
> years.
>
> The prison initiated these lockdowns after serious inmate
> assaults on staff. During the lockdowns, inmates were confined
> to their cells, and normal programs were suspended while offi-
> cials investigated the violence. Contingent on what they learned,
> officials gradually eased restrictions on specific gangs and eth-
> nic and racial groups. Officials restored outdoor exercise sooner
> for inmates whom they believed would pose less risk of further
> violence. Norwood was not a gang member, but gang members
> often pressured unaffiliated inmates of the same race or ethnicity
> to assist them. Prison officials therefore believed that limiting the
> scope of lockdowns to known gang members would be inadequate
> to ensure safety.
>
> During this two-year period, there were also numerous
> inmate-on-inmate attacks. Officials did not always initiate total
> lockdowns after such attacks. According to one prison staff mem-
> ber, the prison's response to inmate-on-inmate violence '[d]epends
> on the circumstances of the assault. [I]f it's fisticuffs, and it's a

one-on-one situation, no, we wouldn't lock down for that. If it's a slashing assault, or a stomping, or multiple inmates involved in a melee, then yes, we would lock down . . . '

Officials initiated the first lockdown in early 2002 after eleven Hispanic inmates attacked four correctional officers, nearly killing one of them. Prison officials did not know if the attack was planned or isolated. They were also unaware, and were never able to ascertain, who provided the weapons. The weeks following the attack brought a series of inmate-on-inmate attacks, including a homicide, as well as another attempted murder of a corrections officer. Nevertheless, officials eventually decided it was safe to begin restoring normal programs, beginning with 'critical workers.' Norwood was in the second group of workers to resume outdoor exercise. His exercise had been suspended for about three months.

In May 2002 a black inmate stabbed an officer in a dining hall. Officials initiated a second lockdown but began restoring normal programs by the end of the month. By mid-July, prisoners other than blacks had resumed outdoor exercise. Even so, attacks on officers occurred during this lockdown, including a battery and an attempted battery. Norwood, who is black, was denied exercise for three months.

In the waning days of 2002, black inmates attempted to murder a correctional officer, and a number of black Crips attacked staff members. Officials initiated a third lockdown, but during its duration several inmates committed four batteries or attempted batteries of officers and five batteries or attempted murders of inmates. During this lockdown, Norwood's outdoor exercise was suspended for four and a half months.

In September 2003, a black Crip attempted to murder a corrections officer. Because of the seriousness of the incident and the fact that
it was the fourth major assault on staff in a nineteen-month period,
officers locked down all inmates and declared a state of emergency.
Officers eventually determined that the attacker had acted alone and
began restoring outdoor exercise. But the violence continued. Certain
white inmates, and those celled with them, were locked down because
of an attempted murder of an inmate in November, and certain Crips
and their cellmates remained on lockdown initiated from earlier violence. Norwood was denied outdoor exercise for two months."

A jury found that prison officials violated Norwood's Eighth
Amendment right to outdoor exercise but concluded that he suffered no
harm and thus awarded no compensatory damages. The jury did award $11
in nominal damages and $39,000 in punitive damages. The district court
awarded $23, 875.55 in attorney's fees. The Corrections Officers appealed."

How a jury could even award eleven dollars is questionable, but the
answer lies in the ability of the attorney to obtain attorney fees if a client prevails no matter how insignificant the kind of litigation. How any
reasonable observer, who knew nothing about the law, could possibly fault
prison staff under the circumstances recited above is incomprehensible.
The majority of the 9th Circuit three-judge panel correctly reversed the
eleven-dollar verdict after an exhausting legal analysis, and also afforded
prison staff qualified immunity.

The dissenting judge argued a jury instruction at the trial was incomplete and that the failure to permit exercise was a violation of the prisoner's
rights. The trial record is replete with evidence of recurring violent prison
inmates, and yet this judge who worries about a failure to allow a prisoner
proper exercise displays a pathetic and a complete misunderstanding of
prison life. The worst part of this case is the ability for a prisoner to even
file a lawsuit of this type. And we wonder about the cost of prisons when
the judges allow these absurd and frivolous lawsuits to proceed.

The court filed an amended decision to include only modest changes in the language. The request for a full hearing by the other members of the court was denied. Although the 9th Circuit ultimately affirmed prison officials, the case illustrates the frivolous litigation, the time it took, and the cost of the trial.

Carver v. Lehman (Dept. of Corrections & Rehabilitation), 528 F.3d 659 (9th Cir. 2008); decision withdrawn, 540 F.3d 1011 (9th Cir. 2008); amended, 550 F.3d 883 (9th Cir. 2008); amended 558 F.3d 869 (9th Cir. 2009)

A State of Washington sentencing law provided release of inmates from prison into the community who establish fulfillment of certain preconditions during imprisonment. Carter filed a petition for release under this program. A district court judge concluded Carver did not establish his qualification for release under this program, and denied the petition. On appeal, the 9th Circuit panel decided the State of Washington had created a "liberty interest" under the Due Process Clause of the Fourteenth Amendment in the sentencing law, and on June 9, 2008, ordered Carver's enrollment in community release with this language: "We acknowledge our holding is inconsistent with the [previous] dispositions of this court, as well as the unpublished decisions of several district courts that have addressed this question." This haughty June 9, 2008 opinion was written by judge who had sworn to uphold the law.

On August 26, 2008, approximately two months later, in responding to the State of Washington's request for rehearing, the 9th Circuit wrote this: "The opinion filed on June 9, 2008 . . . is withdrawn. It may not be cited as precedent by or to this court or any district court of the Ninth Circuit." This is not the first time the 9th Circuit withdrew decisions without explanation. Finally, in another amended decision, the court held that Carver had no judicially invented "liberty interest," without any legal support, and in defiance of existing law.

Warsoldier v. Woodford (Warden, 418 F.3d. 989 (9th Cir. 2005)

Nothing escapes the scrutiny of the 9th Circuit in managing prison life, not only in federal prisons but in state prisons as well. In *Warsoldier v. Woodford* the incarcerated Warsoldier contended his religious membership in an Indian tribe forbade hair cutting. California prison policy required prisoners to cut hair short in order to prevent concealment of contraband, masking their identity, experiencing lice or evidencing membership in a gang. None of these restrictions is "reasonable" said the 9th Circuit, arguing that other state or federal prisons did not require this restriction.

That other states and the federal government adopt different grooming policies is irrelevant. Now, in California state prisons, as a matter of exercising religious convictions, prisoners can wear their hair at any length. Only in the 9th Circuit does the court micromanage prisons. Note that a federal court in this case is establishing prison policy for all California state prisons.

California Attorney General (Jerry Brown) sought no review.

Krug v. Lutz (Director of Department of Corrections & Rehabilitation, 329 F.3d 692 (9th Cir. 2003)

In a federal district court, the Arizona Department of Corrections entered into a consent decree between the Arizona State prison system and its inmates in 1973. The order established rules for Department of Correction officials in reviewing obscene publications addressed to prisoners. Under the terms of the decree, a disatisfied inmate could appeal a rule issued by one prison official to a second official other than the one making the original decision. In 1997 the Department changed the rule, and the same prison official who initially reviewed a publication could also decide the appeal.

Inmate Krug filed a complaint in the district court contending this single decision maker violated his "liberty interest" by not complying with the rule requiring a different person to process his appeal. Incredibly, the district court granted his petition for an injunction although granting immunity to prison officials. The 9th Circuit agreed.

Aside from the absurdity of the claim, and the time taken by the courts to deal with it, during its decision the 9th Circuit panel cited numerous other cases it had previously decided interfering with prison administration. No one denies the general obligation of prison officials to provide humanitarian living conditions to inmates, even for those violent and irresponsible. But to spend time and money on determining whether an inmate can demand that a different prison official must review the decision of another prison official is ludicrous.

City of Reno, Nevada v. Conn 131 S.Ct. 1812 (2011)
Reversing *Conn v. City of Reno, Ashton, and Robertson*, 572 F.3d 1047 (9th Cir. 2009). (Original decision); *Conn v. City of Reno, et al.*, 591 F.3d 1081 (9th Cir. 2010 (dissent)
Although the underlying event in this case was an unfortunate death, extensive factual recitation is not the issue.

Police detained an intoxicated woman who threatened to commit suicide while in their custody. She was examined, treated, and released but arrested the next day. While in custody she committed suicide. The family sued the arresting officers and the City of Reno in federal court for "deliberate indifference" of her constitutional rights. The officers and the City asserted qualified immunity but the 9th Circuit three-judge panel denied their defense. The City of Reno and the two arresting officers petitioned for review of the decision by the entire 9th Circuit judges of the court (rehearing). An insufficient number of judges agreed to a rehearing but the dissent from that decision is signed by seven judges.

The dissent is important because of its criticism of the role of police mandated by the majority panel, and judicial imposition of duties imposed on the City at the expense of individual responsibility. The dissenting judges wrote:

"Until this opinion came along, police officers weren't required to serve as babysitters, psychiatrists or social workers, and judges didn't run suicide-prevention programs. Responsibility for preventing suicide rested with the individual and the family, not the state. But the panel has discovered that the Constitution demands a change in job description: Judges will henceforth micro manage the police, who in turn will serve as mental health professionals. The panel's reasoning has no stopping point, and our decision to let it stand threatens unprecedented judicial intervention in our local institutions."

"At bottom, this case raises the question of whether the state has a legal (as opposed to moral) obligation to provide for the health of its citizens. We have repeatedly rejected the idea that such an obligation exists. This is in part because the benevolent welfare state is in tension with our tradition of liberty and individual dignity: What the state provides for you, you do not provide for yourself, and as the sphere of public largesse grows, the realm of private initiative retreats. It also reflects a judgment that any redefinition of the role of the state should occur under the supervision of democratically elected officials, not unaccountable federal judges. States may obligate themselves, but they should not have novel duties thrust upon them by judicial fiat.

In the panel's hands, standards that are meant to limit liability to all but the most extreme cases become tools for imposing the policy preferences of unelected federal judges. This combination of errors amounts to a toxic recipe for judicial micro management of local institutions."

This quotation from a dissenting judge (later agreed to by the Supreme Court) confirms the premise of this text. The 9th Circuit majority decision is purely a matter of imposing policy on the police. As the dissent points out, any policy decision should be exercised by a democratically elected citizenry. This observation would apply to innumerable decisions summarized in the text.

Here is what the 9th Circuit majority of judges said when the Supreme Court returned the case to it after summarily reversing the court in three lines. "Based on the Supreme Court decision (in light of [another Supreme Court case]) . . ." the 9th Circuit affirmed the district court judge who had granted dismissal of the case against the City of Reno for municipal liability. But the Supreme Court had not addressed the issue of liability alleged against two individual officers who had also been sued despite an almost equal ruling in favor of the City for the same conduct. This strategy is indefensible.

A. Parole

Under federal and state law the sentence imposed by the judge does not assure a prisoner will serve the stated time in state or federal prison. Federal and state law mandate that after a certain percentage of time spent in prison the prisoner is eligible for parole or, in federal courts, "supervised release." The term "parole" defines the release of a prisoner from actual custody but who continues to serve the balance of the sentence outside prison walls under supervision of a parole officer. The ostensible purpose is to reintegrate the prisoner into society by releasing inmates under certain conditions (e.g., submit to warrantless searches of the person, house, vehicle) and orders to report regularly to the parole officer.

The debate on whether the system accomplishes its goal of reintegration is ongoing. Recidivism is patently high, and most parolees, unable to comport with societal norms, are returned to prison for parole violations. The Supreme Court has issued few decisions on the rights of parolees but, unsurprisingly, the 9th Circuit has written its own laws. But that practice will no longer continue in state courts. The Supreme Court has removed all state court parole decisions from the jurisdiction of federal courts.

B. Prisoner Voting Rights

Farrakhan v. State of Washington, 338 F.3d 1009 (9th Cir. 2003); 590 F.3d 989 (9th Cir. 2010) returned from district court). Ordered reheard *en banc* (by full panel): 623 F.3d 990 (9th Cir. 2010); original decision, and appeal decision, vacated and reversed by the 9th Circuit panel, 623 F.3d 990 (2010).

Farrakhan, an incarcerated prisoner in the state of Washington, filed a lawsuit in 1996 alleging the disproportionate ratio of black prisoners in custody deprived them of race-based voting rights under the federal Voting Rights Act. The district court summarily denied this absurd request but the prisoner appealed, requesting the 9th Circuit to repeal the Washington statute prohibiting felons from voting. Despite this ludicrous allegation, the 9th Circuit agreed (sort of) and sent the case back to the district court to render additional findings of fact.

Here is an excerpt from one of the dissenting judges in the appeal of the 9th Circuit decision from the original Farrakhan case ruling that the case could continue in litigation: "This is a dark day for the Voting Rights Act. In adopting a constitutionally questionable interpretation of the Act, the [majority] panel lays the groundwork for the dismantling of the most important piece of civil rights legislation since Reconstruction. The panel also misinterprets the evidence, flouts our voting rights precedent and tramples settled circuit law . . . all in an effort to give felons the right to vote. The court (three-judge panel) should have taken this case en banc (full court)] and brought order back into our case law. I dissent from the court's failure to do so."

As noted by the dissenting judge, every state in the union forecloses convicted felons from voting, and Washington had enacted the statute in 1866 prior to enactment of the Fourteenth Amendment. Nothing in the Voter Rights Act remotely adverts to felony voting disenfranchisement and Congress has never considered enacting such legislation.

The dissenting judge was not finished with his criticism:

> "Farrakhan has no evidence of a history of official discrimination in voting, no evidence of racially polarized voting, no evidence of

voting practices or procedures often used to discriminate against minorities, no evidence of discrimination in candidate slating, no evidence of discrimination in health, education or employment, no evidence of racial appeals in campaigns, no evidence that minorities have a harder time winning elections, no evidence that representatives are unresponsive to minority communities and no evidence that felon disenfranchisement is an unjustified policy. Plaintiffs [Farrakhan] have utterly failed to meet their burden of producing evidence showing vote denial on account of their race.

Every state in [9th Circuit] jurisdiction bars felons from the voting booth. The panel's decision will change all that. It contradicts our case law and the law of at least four other circuits, making us an outlier in voting rights jurisprudence. It does so without so much as acknowledging congressional approval of felon disenfranchisement and without any consideration of the grave constitutional consequences of its actions. I am troubled not only by my colleagues' insistence on an indefensible interpretation of the Voting Rights Act, but also by their utter disregard for our precedent. I dissent."

As noted, the 9th Circuit panel sent the case back to the district court for additional findings. After holding hearings on the case, the district court again ruled in favor of the State of Washington. Farrakhan appealed the decision, and again the 9th Circuit panel (2-1) reversed and found in his favor and sent the case back to the trial court; *Farrakhan v. State of Washington.*

The 9th Circuit found that discrimination exists in the Washington State criminal justice system and that evidence constituted a violation of the Voting Rights Act disenfranchising minority voters. In support of its allegations, Farrakhan introduced two statistical reports from "experts" concluding minorities accounted for a disproportionate number of prisoners attributable to discriminatory police and prosecution practices.

As the court points out, the State offered no contradictory evidence and argued Farrakhan's evidence legally insufficient. Without knowing the State of Washington legal strategy, criticizing their lawyers is difficult. But the 9th Circuit panel repeatedly referenced the absence of this evidence constituted a failure to contradict plaintiffs' case. Despite that, the district court dismissed the case again, and on appeal the 9th Circuit reversed again, ordering the case to continue litigation. The full court reheard the case and dismissed the lawsuit reversing the three-judge appellate panel.

The routine complaint that minorities are stopped, searched, and charged disproportionately is evidenced only by speculation. Every arrest is different, and no one denies the crime rate in minority communities is higher than elsewhere. Reactions of drivers or pedestrians stopped by police vary, and statistics do not account for their demeanor, conduct, attitude, outstanding arrest warrants, or a variety of other factors. That alleged discrimination in minority communities supported by two experts paid by plaintiffs (*Farrakhan*) to render their opinions (*Farrakhan*) is tenuous at best. Even assuming the accuracy of the reports, that the criminal justice system is allegedly infected with discrimination is irrelevant in determining whether someone can vote under the Voting Rights Act. That statute was never intended for use in this case.

The original decision, later reversed by the full panel of 9th Circuit judges, is at odds with every other Court of Appeals, and its decision is best expressed by the dissent written in the original case (above). And once again, this case evidences federal court interference in state issues.

Hebbe (Warden) v. Pliler, 627 F.3d 338 (9th Cir. 2010).
A prison inmate Pliler) alleged in his habeas corpus petition that prison officials had prevented him from the timely filing his petition challenging his confinement due to a lockdown. According to the 9th Circuit panel majority, the delay tolled (suspended) the provisions of AEDPA. The concurring judge notes the California Court of Appeal appointed counsel who

could find no error; nor does the record show any evidence in support of the claim. And you wonder why the 9th Circuit docket is so crowded.

The California Attorney General (Brown) sought no review in the Supreme Court.

Interference with the California prison system by federal courts continues to exist. In 2013 a three-judge federal court panel, all of whose members have antigovernment records, ordered the release of prisoners on grounds of overcrowding. The history of this case is extensive and ongoing. A court indifferent to public safety and ignoring prison management hardly fits the prediction of the founders of the Constitution that the judicial branch is the weakest.

PART II: THE "CULTURAL" DECISIONS

In the formative years of the United States, individual states remained the most visible and active political legislative and judicial entity. Federal courts, with some exceptions, existed principally to resolve disputes between citizens of different states. Congressional arguments during these years mired in disputes over admission of new territories. The Louisiana Purchase, the Mexican-American War, and slavery dominated politics. The Civil War dramatically changed the political landscape and altered the federal government's role in the postwar period. With some exceptions, not until the beginning of the twentieth century did American courts, and the Supreme Court in particular, play a significant role in American cultural life.

From 1865 to 1918 the country moved west while the East Coast developed an industrial powerhouse. After the conclusion of two world wars, the United States emerged as a leader internationally and domestically. But in the 1960s, as noted in Part I, the courts began to play a larger role not only in criminal law but in the daily lives of the people. When the Supreme Court decided *Brown v. Board of Education* striking down educational disparity between black and white students in public schools, the country felt a judicial earthquake. With no precedent to support the case, and universal education practices to the contrary, the Supreme Court unleashed unprecedented power.

In the years since *Brown*, the Supreme Court has written other decisions profoundly changing the "cultural" landscape. Endless litigation now exists in employment and housing cases amid clashes between "affirmative action" and "racial preference." The Supreme Court has drastically curtailed symbols of Christianity in the public square; approved burning the American flag as a derivative of "free speech"; invalidated the law of every state prohibiting abortion; ordered the busing of schoolchildren; and approving same-sex marriage.

Equally auspicious are Supreme Court decisions reversing the 9th Circuit. To some extent, the Supreme Court has modified its previous "cultural" decisions but more conspicuous are its innumerable reversals of 9th Circuit decisions and the curious lack of then - California Attorney General (Brown) to seek review in the Supreme Court. The current Supreme Court, once at the vanguard of changing the political landscape, has ameliorated some of the excesses of the 1960s and '70s. Yet its opinions continue to rile advocates of one philosophic position or another, and the detritus of those decisions continues to affect cultural life. No court has engaged in correcting alleged "social injustice" and challenging tradition more than the 9th Circuit.

Part II identifies these cases decided by the 9th Circuit contradicting the belief system of the vast majority of men and women living in the eight western states and two U.S. Territories under the jurisdiction of the 9th Circuit. Congress resisted an attempt to geographically split the 9th Circuit because the majority political party (in 2009) engaged in a similar political agenda. The 9th Circuit invokes legal language in its decisions to mask social goals by reweighing the evidence, disregarding Supreme Court precedent in rhetoric clothed in verbose and complex writing, and inventing new "rights," under the rubric of "liberty interests" inherent in the Fourteenth Amendment of the U.S. Constitution.

When we talk about courts, we ask, "who are these judges?" What kind of people do citizens want to make decisions impacting our lives? Most people want fair-minded, honest, and impartial judges. In the 2008 presidential campaign, one candidate wanted " . . . "somebody who's got the heart, the empathy to recognize what it's like to be a young teenage mom, the empathy to understand what it's like to be poor, or African American, or gay, or disabled, or old." If courts are to decide disputes contingent on "who" is the party in litigation instead of what are the facts and the law, we can dispense with the law and decide on the basis of status.

Illustrative of "who" should sit as federal court judges are the U.S. Senate hearings on selection of Supreme Court judges. The nominees are subjected to uninformed questioning by Senators who lack any legal experience and seek an ideological compatriot who will vote in accord with their political philosophy. The current composition of the Supreme Court consists of those who are considered "liberal" or "conservative." In other words, policy trumps merit. The last two Supreme Court appointments by the Obama administration confirm this observation.

One principle objective of any government is public safety. In Part I we canvassed the 9th Circuit record on public safety and found it deplorable. But the American people in general, and the men and women who live within the jurisdiction of the 9th Circuit in particular, also expect recognition of traditional loyalties to their country, state and family. Living in a democracy requires restraint from preventing certain distasteful practices or deplorable conduct we strongly dislike, but the alternative is autocracy, a philosophy foreign to the American experience. "Freedom of speech" has almost become a license for indecency and hate. Allowing dissidents to burn the American flag, undermining a national symbol, angers the American people who identify with the life of a free people and the privilege of living in this country. Curtailing modest displays of Christianity has resulted in endless litigation and distorts the religious history of the United States.

Early arrival of Pilgrims to America included people unprepared for an environment decidedly different from lives they led in their former countries. Colonial America provided none of the advantages of living in a country of their birth, and immigrants could only survive if they intrinsically believed in their own personal strength and character. We stare with amazement at primitive tools used in the seventeenth century that require considerable strength to operate and without availability of easy replacements for broken parts. Nonetheless, the eastern coast of the United States grew, and people moved west with the same spirit of independence their forefathers had forged. The Civil War split the country, but slowly the people began to mend as a nation. Although the vestiges of that war still remain, time has dimmed their memory for most people.

Of course critics of the United States abound, always seeking to criticize the country for a variety of reasons and, according to pundits, we are "polarized." The vast majority of American people, regardless of their political divisions, recognize the superiority of this nation despite any historical faults. Unfortunately, some Americans can only find criticism no matter where they look. They ignore the spirit of a country that won two world wars, salvaged a torn South Korea, tore down the Berlin wall and beckoned thousands of immigrants motivated by their quest for liberty and independence. For some people though, it is never enough to right the wrongs.

Until the 1960s, federal judges focused on business disputes, labor law, trust cases, patents, and bankruptcy of little or no interest to the vast majority of people. The Supreme Court began to change during this period, and from that point on wrote its revolutionary decisions on education, abortion, sodomy, race, and religion. Invoking the vague Constitutional phrases of "due process" and "equal protection," the Court sundered state law under the broad aegis of the Fourteenth Amendment originally adopted only to end slavery.

Since that time, the Court has modified its approach although the detritus of the Warren court (Chief Justice Earl Warren) remains. But that body of law, no matter the more recent dilution of its scope, serves as the kindling for the 9th Circuit attack on American culture. The cases in Part II will develop this theme. The 9th Circuit consists of life-tenured judges, many who came to the bench with a political agenda. They invoke judicial rules to achieve goals unattainable by a legislature, knowing that the Supreme Court can review few cases to stem the tide. The Supreme Court itself has made that point clear.

For our purposes, a case arrives directly on appeal from the district court judge who presided over the trial in the federal system, or on habeas corpus collaterally from state courts in criminal cases. The text excludes bankruptcy, patents, admiralty, foreign laws, and business cases within the scope of our analysis except to identify another 9th Circuit reversal. The entire federal court system is cumbersome, but included in the text are the most obvious legal machinations invoked by the 9th Circuit.

CHAPTER 12

EDUCATION

The legal and political skirmishes between school administrators, teachers, unions, and parents continue to entangle themselves in arguing the proper role of educating children and are a constant source of conflict among the parties. Inevitably these disputes surface in the courts, and judges at the state and federal level become immersed not only in educational theory disputes but in confronting basic principles of federalism (the legal relationship between state and federal legislatures and courts). Federalism, as noted earlier, is not confined exclusively to federal and state courts, but confronts the role of federal courts in deciding issues quintessentially state responsibilities.

A. Schools and Federalism

The federal courts in general, and the 9th Circuit in particular, have imposed "structural reform" in numerous state public activities. *Horne v. Flores*, the first case in this Section, is a dramatic display of federal arrogance and interference in public functions specifically under state control. Paradoxically and disturbingly, the case also discloses the efforts of state officials to endorse federal interference to achieve objectives otherwise unattainable. Excerpts from *Horne v. Flores* are extensive because it is a summary of federal intervention condemned by the Supreme Court, and a warning to other federal courts to be responsive to the role of federalism.

Horne v. Flores, 129 S.Ct. 2579 (2009), Reversing the 9th Circuit decision in *Flores v. State of Arizona,* 516 F.3d 1140 (9th Cir. 2008).

The Supreme Court wrote this introduction to the case in 1992:

> [This case arises] from litigation that began in Arizona in 1992 when a group of English Language-Learner (ELL) students in the Nogales Unified School District (City of Nogales in Arizona) and their parents filed litigation alleging the State of Arizona was violating the federal Equal Educational Opportunities Act (EEOA; citation omitted) requiring a State "to take appropriate action to overcome language barriers that impede equal participation by its students in its instructional programs." In 2000, the federal district court entered a declaratory judgment (declaration of rights) with respect to Nogales ordering the School District to comply with certain 'judicial instructions.' In 2001, the district court extended the order to apply to the entire State. Over the next eight years, [the School District] repeatedly sought relief from the district court's orders, but to no avail. We [Supreme Court] granted [review] after the Court of Appeals for the 9th Circuit affirmed the denial of [State of Arizona's] motion for relief under Federal Rules of Civil Procedure and we now reverse the judgment of the Court of Appeals and [return] for further proceedings.
>
> The district court and the Court of Appeals misunderstood both the obligation that the EEOA imposes on States and the nature of the inquiry that is required when parties . . . seek [modification of the court order]. Both the [district court and the 9th Circuit] focused excessively on the narrow question of the adequacy of the State's incremental funding for ELL instruction instead of fairly considering the broader question whether, as a result of important changes during the intervening years, the State was fulfilling its obligation under the EEOA by other means. The question at issue

in these cases is not whether Arizona must take 'appropriate action' to overcome the language barriers that impede ELL students. Of course it must. But [the School District] argues that Arizona is now fulfilling its statutory obligation.

For nearly a decade, the orders of a federal district court have substantially restricted the ability of the State of Arizona to make basic decisions regarding educational policy, appropriations, and budget priorities. The record strongly suggests that some *state officials have welcomed the involvement of the federal court as a means of achieving appropriations objectives that could not be achieved through the ordinary democratic process* (emphasis added). Because of these features, these cases implicate all of the unique features and risks of institutional reform [police departments; schools; prisons; jails]; litigation."

Second, institutional reform injunctions often raise sensitive federalism concerns. Such litigation commonly involves areas of core state responsibility, such as public education. [O]ur cases [Supreme Court] recognize that local autonomy of school districts is a vital national tradition, and that a district court must strive to restore state and local authorities to the control of a school system operating in compliance with the Constitution.

Federalism concerns are heightened when, as in these cases, a federal court decree has the effect of dictating state or local budget priorities. States and local governments have limited funds. When a federal court orders that money be appropriated for one program, the effect is often to take funds away from other important programs. A structural reform decree eviscerates a State's discretionary authority over its own program and budgets and forces state officials to reallocate state resources and funds.

Finally, the dynamics of institutional reform litigation differ from those of other cases. Scholars have noted that public officials sometimes consent to, or refrain from vigorously opposing, decrees that go well beyond what is required by federal law. See, e.g., McConnell, Why Hold Elections? Using Consent Decrees to Insulate Policies from Political Change, 1987 U. Chi. Legal Forum 295, 317 (noting that government officials may try to use consent decrees to "block ordinary avenues of political change" or to "sidestep political constraints"); Horowitz, Decreeing Organizational Change: Judicial Supervision of Public Institutions, 1983 Duke L.J. 1265, 1294–1295 ("'Nominal defendants [in institutional reform cases] are sometimes happy to be sued and happier still to lose"); R. Sandler & D. Schoenbrod, Democracy by Decree: What Happens When Courts Run Government 170 (2003) ("Government officials, who always operate under fiscal and political constraints, 'frequently win by losing' in institutional reform litigation (citation omitted)").

The Court of Appeals did not engage in the analysis just described. Rather than applying a flexible standard that seeks to return control to state and local officials as soon as a violation of federal law has been remedied, the Court of Appeals used a heightened standard that paid insufficient attention to federalism concerns. And rather than inquiring broadly into whether changed conditions in Nogales provided evidence of an ELL program that complied with the EEOA, the Court of Appeals concerned itself only with determining whether increased ELL funding complied with the original declaratory judgment order. The court erred on both counts."

Horne v. Flores received little media attention despite its relevance in California where a three-judge federal panel had ordered enormous expensive changes in prison health care management oblivious to a state teetering on bankruptcy. Complying with the 'institutional reform' ordered by the court will demand budget cuts unimaginable in the state. The *Horne v. Flores* case is also an alert to the 9th Circuit and other federal courts to the danger of federal intervention in state political issues. In the *Horne v. Flores* case the federal court monitored the school district for a decade.

Horne v. Flores is not just a solitary exception of federal interference in state issues. In *Fisher v. Tucson Unified School District* the federal district court monitored the Tucson Unified School District for thirty years, and the 9th Circuit was still dissatisfied. Despite the district court order approving a desegregation plan for Tucson schools, the 9th Circuit criticized the decision, reversed the district court, and retained jurisdiction. Subsequently the district court ordered the parties to agree on a Special Master-- to be paid by the School District.

Aside from federal intervention, this case illustrates another instance of federal courts ignoring state sovereignty. The amount of tax money spent in this case is enormous and will never end until the 9th Circuit exits. And the U.S. government also intervened in the case. At taxpayer expense.

The 9th Circuit sent the case back to the district court to comply with the Supreme Court order to erase the trial judge decision.

Arizona Christian School Tuition Organization v. Winn, 131 S.Ct. 1436 (2011). Reversing the 9th Circuit decision in 586 F.3d 649 (9th Cir. 2009). The First Amendment provides that Congress shall "pass no law respecting the establishment of a religion."

In drafting the First Amendment prohibiting the "establishment" of a national state church, the authors of the Constitution would never have anticipated the inordinate amount of litigation that would emerge over judicial interpretation of these few words in the text. Because all schools in 1787 were private, no one worried about public assistance to private schools. And the first ten amendments to the Constitution applied only to the national government, not the states. That has changed since the Supreme Court "incorporated" the First Amendment into state law.

Few would quarrel with a State program providing outright gifts of public funds to private schools. But several states have attempted to offer an option to parents of children who elect to attend private schools, in most cases, religious schools. Tax credits, vouchers, and other alternatives survived the Establishment Clause in a Supreme Court decision entitled *Zelman v. Simmons-Harris*. In the Zelman case the Court ruled that if the State offers vouchers to all school children who have an opportunity to participate, the program does not "establish" religion.

The Arizona legislature enacted a law offering parents an option to set up a detailed program allowing school children to participate in alternatives to public schools and simultaneously receive a tax credit. All children could participate in any school of their choice. The State did nothing more than offer parents an option they could elect for their children. The Arizona Supreme Court upheld the program, yet dissatisfied taxpayers filed a claim in district court alleging the Arizona program violated the Establishment Clause. The district court dismissed the case and the plaintiffs appealed to the 9th Circuit. Despite the similarity of the Arizona program to the voucher system approved by the Supreme Court in the *Zelman* decision, a three-judge panel of the 9th Circuit ruled the statute violated the Establishment Clause.

The 9th Circuit refused to rehear this case, confirming again the animus toward religion that exists in that circuit. The dissenting judge dissected the reasoning of the three-judge panel in an opening paragraph: "I dissent not only because *Winn* cannot be squared with the Supreme Court's mandate in *Zelman*, but also because the panel's holding casts a pall over comparable educational tax-credit schemes in states across the nation and could derail legislative efforts in four states within our circuit to create similar programs. In short, the panel's conclusion invalidates an increasingly popular method for providing school choice, jeopardizing the educational opportunities of hundreds of thousands of children nationwide."

As a judge in an unrelated court case noted, the *Winn* decision is biased against religion. The American people are not in danger of a theological jihad. Further, its decision overrules the Arizona Supreme Court in yet another example of disrespect to the shield of state sovereignty. Ten years after the Arizona Supreme Court upheld the legislation, a federal court of three unelected and tenured federal judges in the case scuttled the program.

The State of Arizona appealed the 9th Circuit decision and the Supreme Court reversed. The Court did so in an eloquent review of judicial authority often ignored by the 9th Circuit. "Few exercises of the judicial power are more likely to undermine public confidence in the neutrality and integrity of the Judiciary than one which casts the Court in the role of a Council of Revision, conferring on itself the power to invalidate laws at the behest of anyone who disagrees with them. In an era of frequent litigation, class actions, sweeping injunctions with prospective effect, and continuing jurisdiction to enforce judicial remedies, courts must be more careful to insist on the formal rules of [the right to file litigation] not less so."

This quotation reveals that not all the judges in the 9th Circuit are engaged in policy decisions and "political correctness." The Supreme "Court judicially imposed limitation served as an admonition to 9th Circuit judges who found the right to sue if someone was "offended." Barnes-Wallace v. City of San Diego).

B. Schools and Freedom of Speech
Harper v. Poway Unified School District, 549 U.S. 1262. (2007). Reversing the 9th Circuit decision in *Harper v. Poway*, 445 F.3d 1166 (9th Cir. 2006). Unfortunately, the Supreme Court has also Constitutionalized some of the most controversial issues involving education disputes, either under the First Amendment prohibiting public suppression of free speech, or by restricting religious expression in schools. Again, the Supreme Court of the

1960s and 1970s was responsible for creating the path to judicial interference subsequently trod by the 9th Circuit.

Because First Amendment jurisprudence on freedom of speech and freedom of religion is entangled with philosophical and religious issues, any attempt to sort out Supreme Court cases is fodder for another book. The materials in this text review 9th Circuit cases not only written on their own ground but as a legacy left by earlier Supreme Court cases. The 9th Circuit decision in *Harper v. Poway Unified School District*, a case subsequently reversed by the Supreme Court, illustrates an example.

Tyler Harper, a student at in the Poway district, wore a T-shirt to class expressing religious condemnation of homosexuality. School officials who had expressly approved a day of silence to respect gays, lesbians, and transgender pupils forbade Harper from wearing the sign and suspended him. He sought injunctive relief from the school decision in federal district court but the judge denied his claim. Harper appealed to the 9th Circuit.

In a split decision, the majority of judges ruled that the school officials who suspended Harper did not violate any Constitutional right Harper may have held. These judges engaged in a sociological discussion lamenting emotional damage incurred by students in the category condemned by the T-shirt. The three-judge panel did not find any constitutional right specifically applicable to all students. Rather, it found a right for those primarily offended by the T-shirt but not for other students. In other words, the new constitutional "right" applied only to those offended.

The dissenting judge cited the error of finding a constitutional right applicable to only some people but also noted the court record contained no evidence of any student complaints, no fights, no threats, and no disorder. The dissent comments on the Constitutional dimension of free speech highlighting our toleration of people to express distasteful views, but notes the school administration specifically approved a day of silence in the school, indirectly approving free speech in that context, but simultaneously squelching the opposition.

The majority decision of the three-judge panel in *Harper* is an example of the 9th Circuit concept of "social justice" rather than legal writing. In the current political debate over selection of federal judges, it is called "empathy" by some people. Here is the language of a judge in the majority confirming the right of school officials to suspend the student:

> "The dissent[ing judge] still doesn't get the message. Advising a young high school or grade school student while he is in class that he and other gays and lesbians are shameful, and that God disapproves of him, is not simply "unpleasant and offensive." It strikes at the very core of the young student's dignity and self-worth. Similarly, the example the (dissenting judge) offers, a T-shirt bearing the message, "Hitler Had the Right Idea on one side and 'Let's Finish the Job!' on the other, serves to intimidate and injure young Jewish students in the same way as would t-shirts worn by groups of white students bearing the message Hide Your Sisters The Blacks Are Coming.' Under the dissent's view, large numbers of majority students could wear such shirts to class on a daily basis, at least until the time minority members chose to fight back physically and disrupt the school."

Perhaps some of us are unaware of, or have forgotten, what it is like to be young, belong to a small minority group, and be subjected to verbal assaults and opprobrium while trying to get an education in a public school. Or, perhaps some are simply insensitive to the injury that public scorn and ridicule can cause young minority students. Or maybe some simply find it difficult to comprehend the extent of the injury attacks such as Harper's cause gay students. Whatever the reason for the dissent[ing judge's] blindness, it is surely not beyond the authority of local school boards to attempt to protect young minority students against verbal persecution, and the exercise of that authority by school boards is surely consistent with . . . protection of the right of individual students to be secure and to be let alone."

This language speaks for itself. Not a single citation to any case decided by any court, no legal analysis, only a personal opinion called "social justice." But this same judge would applaud a student wearing a t-shirt condemning the war in Iraq, ignoring students whose fathers had died in battle.

The Supreme Court granted a hearing but dismissed the case on procedural grounds. The Supreme Court returned the case to the 9th Circuit majority of judges who eagerly concluded the student had graduated and could no longer file litigation-a ruling not available when the 9th Circuit wants to avoid it. In addition, the court refused to award money damages to school officials who had suspended Harper. Apparently this 9th Circuit sociology decision survives in some quarters.

Morse (School Principal) v. Frederick, 127 S.Ct. 2618 (2007)

Reversing the 9th Circuit decision in 439 F.3d 1114 (9th Cir. 2006); returned to the district court in 499 F.3d 926 (9th Cir. 2007)

During a school-sponsored event held outside the school building itself, principal Deborah Morris approached a group of students watching a parade whose participants were celebrating the passage of the Olympic torch through the State of Alaska. One of the students displayed an unfurled banner proclaiming "Bong Hits for Jesus." The principal demanded the student cease displaying the banner. When he refused, the principal seized the banner and subsequently disciplined the student. Unsurprisingly, the student sued the school. How did the 9th Circuit approach this fact pattern after reaching the result in the Harper case?

The 9th Circuit panel reversed a district court judge who had dismissed the case. The panel not only found a violation of Frederick's First Amendment rights but refused to confer qualified immunity from civil litigation on the school principal because she acted contrary to "clearly established federal law." The State of Alaska sought review in the Supreme Court, and the Justices reversed the 9th Circuit. The Supreme Court summarized the 9th Circuit decision as follows:

"[P]roceeding on the basis that the banner expressed a positive sentiment about marijuana use, the [9th Circuit] nonetheless found a violation of Frederick's First Amendment rights because the school punished Frederick without demonstrating that his speech gave rise to a risk of substantial disruption. The [Ninth Circuit] further concluded that Frederick's right to display his banner was so 'clearly established' that a reasonable principal in Morse's position would have understood that her actions were unconstitutional, and that Morse was therefore not entitled to qualified immunity.

At least two interpretations of the words on the banner demonstrate that the sign advocated the use of illegal drugs. First, the phrase could be interpreted as an imperative: [Take] bong hits'. . . a message equivalent, as Ms. Morse explained in her declaration, to smoke marijuana' or 'use an illegal drug' Alternatively, the phrase could be viewed as celebrating drug use, 'bong hits [are a good thing], or "[we take] bong hits,' and we discern no meaningful distinction between celebrating illegal drug use in the midst of fellow students and outright advocacy or promotion.

School principals have a difficult job, and a vitally important one. When Frederick suddenly and unexpectedly unfurled his banner, Morse had to decide to act, or not act, on the spot. It was reasonable for her to conclude that the banner promoted illegal drug use in violation of established school policy, and that failing to act would send a powerful message to the students in her charge, including Frederick, about how serious the school was about the dangers of illegal drug use. The First Amendment does not require schools to tolerate at school events student expression that contributes to those dangers."

The Supreme Court, having concluded no First Amendment violation occurred, denied that the federal law was as "clearly established" as the 9th Circuit thought, and reversed the decision. This case emphasizes not only the governmental responsibility to provide public safety diluted by the 9th Circuit as demonstrated in Part I, but a failure to protect children from the obvious attempt to encourage the use of drugs. The 9th Circuit panel in the Harper case, so worried about the social implications harming children, forgot about all the implications of drug use in adolescents. The panel misrepresented the purpose of the banner, ignored reality, and was properly chastised by the Supreme Court in another reversal.

C. Schools and Race

Critics of public education in general abound, and issues of race continue to flood the courts at every level, from elementary schools to law schools. Once race enters the courtroom, the emotions submerge the logic, and the history of race relations in the United States does not permit easy resolution. From the beginning of *Brown v. Board of Education of Topeka, Kansas,* the seminal Supreme Court case declaring separate schools for black students unequal to white schools, to the most recent Supreme Court decision in *Parents Involved in Community Schools v. Seattle School District No. 1,* innumerable communities railed against compulsory busing. And federal courts were at the forefront of this issue.

Parents Involved in Community Schools v. Seattle School District No. 1, 551 U.S. 701 (2007)
Reversing the 9th Circuit decision in 395 F.3d 1168 (9th Cir 2003); en banc (full court); 426 F.3d 1162 (9th Cir. 2004)
The City of Seattle, Washington, never specifically endorsed segregated schools. No court ever issued a decree ordering the City to bus students, but black and white populations lived in separate geographic communities. Seattle undertook a study of the school population and decided the only

way to accomplish a diverse student community and its presumed benefits lay in identifying students by race and compelling all schools to achieve racial balance. Unsurprisingly, white parents rebelled and objected to a compulsory government endorsed race-based policy in another example of "structural reform." The parents sued the School District in district court and prevailed. The School District appealed.

On appeal to the 9th Circuit, a three-judge panel affirmed the trial court, but the full 9th Circuit reheard the case, reversed that decision and approved the School District racial preference policy. In its decision, the majority of judges reviewed the studies prepared by the school district in support of the project and accepted their conclusions without reservation. In a decision written more on sociological grounds than legal, the panel approved the school policy. Their decision is replete with citations to the Equal Protection Clause of the Fourteenth Amendment, and the appropriate level of judicial scrutiny required in evaluating public programs endorsing a racial quota.

The dissenting judges wrote that the court majority refused to acknowledge that public officials had enacted public policy based exclusively on race. The school district never denied this fact. The parents appealed to the Supreme Court. The Justices reversed, criticizing the School District, and indirectly the 9th Circuit, challenging any policy unequivocally based on racial grounds. In fact, all the Supreme Court decisions involving racial conflict repeatedly refuse to accept any policy based exclusively on race, including those rules that only mask a race-based decision. The Supreme Court wrote: "Classifying and assigning schoolchildren according to race is an extreme approach in light of the Court's jurisprudence and the Nation's history of using race [as a factor] in public schools, and requires more than an amorphous end to justify it."

Smith v. University of Washington, 392 F.3d 367 (9th Cir. 2004)
Six months after the 9th Circuit decision in *Parents Involved in Community Schools*, white students challenged the admissions policy at the University of

Washington Law School on substantially the same grounds as the *Parents* case. The 9th Circuit panel wrote its decision in *Smith v. University of Washington*, citing *Parents* as authority for the proposition that the University Law School bears the burden of demonstrating its consideration of race and ethnicity in its admissions was narrowly tailored to serve a compelling interest. "We must assume that it [Law School] acted in good faith . . . and defer to its educational judgments." This observation ignores the language used by the Supreme Court in *Parents*, reversing the 9th Circuit and condemning the use of race as criteria for admission to schools. The 9th Circuit's answer, paraphrasing: "we are not dealing with an elementary school as in *Parents*. This is a law school." Oh. (In 2014 the Supreme Court would have rejected this absurd decision).

The 9th Circuit also had "deferred" to the school district in *Parents* by simply invoking "social policy" coinciding with 9th Circuit philosophy, but did it "defer" to the School District in *Horne v. Flores*, holding the School District in thrall for ten years? A reading of the record in the trial court belies this excuse to "defer," and the decision in *Smith* defies Supreme Court precedent as written in *Parents*.

Times have changed. Minority students outnumber white students in elementary and secondary schools and the rationale for busing in large part no longer applies. But during this transition, the nation experienced anger from all sides. Litigation flooded the courts, and white parents fled their neighborhoods or sent their children to private schools. Whether the time span from *Brown v. Bd. of Education* to *Parents etc. v. Seattle* produced any positive result is in question. Regardless of the merits of complaints about schools, the underlying question is whether the court or the legislature should make educational decisions. Critics argue that the legislature has failed to do its job of educating black students on the same level that it does white students. Regardless of that argument, the Constitution forbids schools from enacting programs based on race or "racial preference."

D. Schools and Religion

Eklund v. Byron School District, 154 Fed. Appx.648 (9th Cir. Case)

In this case, Eklund alleged that the Byron School District engaged in extensive inculcation of seventh grade children who were told to memorize and recite Muslim practice, prayers, and to fast for a day. Unlike the cases seeking to abolish vestiges of Christianity in schools, the 9th Circuit disposed of this case in three paragraphs and buried their decision in an unpublished report.

The parents of Eklund alleged a number of Muslim practices taught in the school room of the Byron School District compelled seventh graders to react to a "course" favorably, even disallowing any criticism of the subject matter. Although masked as a secular course, the well-know fact is Muslims integrate their faith intimately with politics, and clerical dominance of Muslim countries is abhorrent to Americans who seek to avoid mixing the secular with religion in public schoolrooms. The reader can imagine whether the 9th Circuit would have reacted similarly to the Byron School District requiring school children being taught about the Incarnation, life of Jesus, his crucifixion, and resurrection. Or, assume the program endorsed fasting, reciting Christian prayers, and memorizing a passage from the Bible.

The 9th Circuit treated this case as a trifle and disposed of it despite its obvious illegality.

Trent v. Kent School District, 551 F.3d 850 (9th Cir. 2008)

As noted above, the First Amendment prohibiting an established church and confirming the right of every person to the "free exercise" of religion has caused the courts with endless grist for the judicial mill.

The Supreme Court has not been helpful, but recently has shown a more traditional viewpoint in allowing students in public schools to establish faith-based study or discussion groups. First Amendment law is unquestionably mired in legal paralysis and the restrictions between the role of public schools in regulating or forbidding-faith-based groups is unduly complex. But the 9th Circuit's anti-Christian bias is evident as noted above and in the next Chapter on Freedom of Religion.

More to the point is the *Trent v. Kent School District* case. The School District did not allow discrimination against homosexuals, women, or race and ethnicity, but excluded religious groups within its policy. The court record established an attempt by several students to participate in an after-school group requiring a commitment to morality and faith in Christ to conform their lives to that goal. Of course this quest was repugnant to the school and its administrative records unequivocally reflect the dilatory approach of its governing board to resolve a student request to meet on campus after school. By the time the board rejected the Truth group request the students who held leadership positions had graduated and the case had become moot. Compare this treatment with the summary disposition of parents who had objected to students mimicking Muslims.

Nurre v. Whitehead, 580 F.3d 1087 (9th Cir. 2009)

For several years, music students graduating from a Washington state high school played instruments during the graduation exercises of seniors. In 2005 the school received complaints (the court does not say how many) that one of the songs contained religious connotations. In 2006 the graduating seniors in the music department selected an instrumental version of "Ave Maria." The students who wanted to play "Ave Maria" thought the song best displayed their musical ability and was a "pretty piece."

According to the principal of the school, Carol Whitehead, she refused to approve the music on grounds of a potential violation of the First Amendment Establishment Clause. She also worried about complaints from parents. One of the students, Kathryn Nurre, sued the principal and the school district for violation of free speech and hostility to religion under the same Establishment Clause.

The 9th Circuit upheld the right of the principal, who held advanced degrees in education, to withhold performance of "Ave Maria" despite her previous unawareness of the title or the music. The three-judge, two-to-one majority panel cited the usual court cases on the Establishment Clause and ultimately denied the students' claims. According to the dissenting judge in *Truth*, the School District had allowed Adventists and Muslims to participate in after-school activities, but not Christians.

Being "offended" is now sufficient in 9th Circuit case law to establish "standing" (The right to sue). The ultimate resolution of the 9th Circuit decision confirmed the right of the principal to deny students playing an instrumental piece of medieval music without lyrics during a graduation ceremony. As noted in the dissenting opinion, the principal's concern with violating the Establishment Clause is now sufficient justification to invoke a court decision. So, worrying about a First Amendment violation is sufficient to confirm the rationale expressed by the principal. Refusing to allow students to play an instrumental version of "Ave Maria," without lyrics, a song undoubtedly foreign to the vast number of students at the high school, including the principal, defies comprehension.

Playing the instrumental version of "Ave Maria" is forbidden by the 9th Circuit, but how many students knew the English translation of the lyrics? Even the principal lacked knowledge of its Latin base. The song is a classic played regularly for centuries, and it continues to be sung. Not in Washington public schools, however. The First Amendment was never intended to outlaw this music, yet the Supreme Court declined to hear the case.

E. Schools and Sex

A number of commentators and writers have identified a "culture war" erupting in the United States pitting friends, neighbors, and total strangers against each other. The crux of the argument is located in defining the "status" of people according to race, gender, age, and ethnicity. In an earlier time, the roles of men and women in each of these categories were substantially defined. Women married, had children, and worked outside the home only under extreme circumstances. Minorities of either gender held low low-paying jobs, subsisted on welfare, and were held in disrespect.

The debate over the role of women and minorities continues today, but the general consensus, although not universal, is the importance of education in enabling all students to achieve their potential. This objective has engendered "affirmative action," essentially masking "political correctness" in the employment and commercial world, but the judicial equivalent of these terms applies to members of a "protected class." Whatever the characterization, public schools suffer from litigation engendered by race and gender issues. Because the Supreme Court incorporated the First Amendment applicable to the States, the federal courts and state courts - must confront First Amendment issues in public schools.

Aside from that, parents have challenged school districts for a variety of reasons, including mandatory dress codes, mandatory attendance, and compliance with scholastic requirements for academic achievement. More recently, schools have begun invoking subjects other than reading, writing, and arithmetic. Here is an example.

Fields v. Palmdale School District, 427 F.3d 1197 (9th Cir. 2005) [modified in 447 F.3d 1187 (9th Cir. 2006)]

In *Fields v. Palmdale School District,* the 9th Circuit described a "modern" subject for evaluation: a social science survey asking questions of a sexual nature to elementary school students.

The author of the survey, in her letter sent to parents, wrote of the school district's interest in children exposed to "violence." Nothing was said or implied about inquiries into their sexual activities. When parents discovered children were asked questions on that subject, they sued the school district for violation of their constitutional rights and the right of privacy. On appeal by the parents from the trial court denial of their Complaint, the 9th Circuit panel quoted the content of the informational letter submitted to the parents. The author of the letter failed to include a single word about questions on sexual intimacy. In the classroom, the subject of exposure to violence had changed. Whether the School District could permit the survey initially is one issue, misleading parents is another.

The author of the 9th Circuit opinion undertook a conventional review of relevant legal authorities and could not find any Due Process violations or right to privacy violations. Parents formerly sent their children to school to learn "reading, writing and arithmetic" and they obviously surrender a significant amount of time to the care of other adults. Unquestionably they expect the school to assure the safety and welfare of their children during school hours. They do not expect misrepresentations.

The court did concede its own judicial irrelevance in resolving curriculum issues and reminded parents the appropriate forum for redress of their grievances lies in the school-except when it doesn't, as in *Horne v. Flore* and *Parents Involved in Community Schools*. But judicial indifference to the misleading letter sent to parents, and the immaturity of elementary school students, differs sharply from 9th Circuit hostility to government displays of religious messages in schools. As documented in the succeeding chapter, the court has no objection to subjecting children to a test that may challenge the religious convictions of their family. None of the judges suggest their own expertise in education, and they recommend parents should seek redress from the school board, unless the school board makes a decision some 9th Circuit court judges agree as compatible with their philosophy.

Colleges and Universities provide the advanced education for children qualified to meet academic standards, and the educational level encourages the use of reason and analysis in solving a variety of problems. Adolescents at that age are exposed to sexual intimacy, but students in elementary schools have not achieved a level of maturity enabling them to intelligently answer questions on intimate issues. Yet the 9th Circuit panel ignores both the questionable value of the test to an immature audience and a letter from the author who misled parents to the extent of the survey.

Ultimately the American people should decide what kind of a country we should inhabit. Schools are a major training ground and exist to enable professional educators to teach basic subjects necessary for children to participate in a democratic society. Schools are not social science laboratories for the edification of sociologists. Schools temporarily take custody of children to impart expertise, not conduct social science studies.

F. Schools & the Pledge of Allegiance
Elk Grove Unified School District v. Newdow, 542 U.S. 1 (2004); *Newdow v. U.S. Congress,*
540 U.S. 962 (2003). Reversing the 9th Circuit decision in 328 F.3d 466 (9th Cir 2003).
The 9th Circuit decision: Seeking to cleanse the stain of the words "under God" in the Pledge of Allegiance, two judges of a three-judge panel of the 9th Circuit ordered school districts in western states to delete these two words in schoolroom settings. Congressional reaction was immediate and universal, though neither the Attorney General of California (Lockyer), who failed to participate in the appeal of the California case to the 9th Circuit, nor the Governor (Gray Davis), protested. A federal appellate court, ignoring the overwhelming majority of American people who regard the Pledge as a unifying and binding confirmation of allegiance to the United States, held that the two-word phrase "Under God" violated the First Amendment prohibiting a governmental "establishment of religion."

The 9th Circuit panel ostensibly distinguished prior contrary Supreme Court law to this decision and rejected the opposite conclusion reached by another federal appellate court in an identical case. Because neither the public nor Congress can intervene to change this "Constitutional" rule imposed by the 9th Circuit panel, other than through the tortuous process of a Constitutional Amendment, the only remedy is seeking review of the decision by the United States Supreme Court. The Attorney General of the United States - not the California Attorney General - did just that. In the same case, but under a different name, the Supreme Court reversed the 9th Circuit on procedural grounds and the case remained viable.

Not all 9th Circuit judges agreed with the majority decision in *Elk Grove*. In a stinging dissent, one judge said "it was wrong, very wrong - wrong because reciting the Pledge of Allegiance is simply not a 'religious act'. . . wrong as a matter of Supreme Court precedent properly understood, wrong as a matter of common sense." The last reason is the most compelling.

Acknowledgment of God appears in the Declaration of Independence, the Gettysburg Address, the national motto, and the national anthem (verse four). Do we now truncate reference to the equality of mankind in the Declaration of Independence that "all men are created equal, endowed by their Creator with certain unalienable rights?;" purge President Lincoln's reference that "this Nation, under God, shall have a new birth of freedom;" disable us from singing the fourth verse of the national anthem . . . or remove "and this be our national motto, in God is our trust" One can only shudder if the two federal judges were asked to rule on whether children living in the Union during the Civil War could sing the "Battle Hymn of the Republic" in school.

Setting aside the legal jargon that pervades the court opinion in *Elk Grove*, the judges ignore a public conviction held by millions of American people while simultaneously dismissing a simple expression of patriotism. For some people, the decision represents yet another judicial stake in the heart of those in the United States who seek to acknowledge the beneficence of God, but for most Americans the Pledge of allegiance confirms principles of liberty and justice for all. Invoking only two words, "under God," cannot possibly impose on the convictions of others or incrementally subvert the role of the state to the church. Another dissenting judge wrote: "it is difficult to detect any signs of incipient theocracy springing up since the Pledge was amended in 1954." The authors of the Constitution worried about the "tyranny of the majority." The 9th Circuit has reversed the polarity of this phrase into a tyranny of the "minority."

Pledging allegiance "to the flag of the United States of America" reflects a tangible symbol of solidarity confirmed by the words "and to the Republic for which it stands." The unifying phrase of "one Nation with liberty and justice for all" expresses a noble quest sought by legions of people deprived of their freedom in other countries who traveled or escaped to the United States. The Declaration of Independence, the Gettysburg Address, and the national anthem emanate from this theme and hardly resemble a call to religious domination or a jihad. The Supreme Court reversed the 9th Circuit on jurisdictional grounds, but Newdow filed another lawsuit (discussed next).

Newdow v. Rio Linda Union School District, 597 F.3d 1007 (9th Cir. 2010) After the Supreme Court dismissed the *Elk Grove* case on procedural grounds, other parties sued the Rio Linda Union School District. They alleged a California state statute permitting a teacher to lead students in a classroom reciting the Pledge of Allegiance violates the First Amendment prohibition of the "establishment" of religion under state sponsorship. The parties sought to enjoin the school district from reciting the Pledge of Allegiance containing the words "under God." The district court judge agreed with the earlier 9tht Circuit decision and issued an injunction (order) against the practice of reciting the Pledge of Allegiance in public schools. The plaintiffs appealed to the 9th Circuit.

In a brilliant scholarly decision, the 9th Circuit panel wrote this, in part: "The Supreme Court has agreed the Pledge is a 'patriotic exercise designed to foster national unity and pride.' Even the [dissenting judge in this *Rio Linda* case] agrees on this determinative point. '[T]he recitation of the Pledge both as originally written and as amended is a patriotic exercise. The question about which we disagree [with the dissenting judge] is whether this patriotic activity is turned into a religious activity because it includes words with religious meaning." The 9th Circuit panel who wrote the decision dismissed that form of "reasoning."

The 9th Circuit judge wrote further: "We hold that the Pledge of Allegiance does not violate the Establishment Clause [of the First Amendment] because Congress' ostensible and predominant purpose was to inspire patriotism and that the context of the Pledge - its wording as a whole, the preamble to the statute, and this nation's history - demonstrate that it is a predominantly patriotic exercise. For these reasons, the phrase 'one Nation under God' does not turn this patriotic exercise into a religious activity . . . Accordingly, we hold that California's statute requiring school districts to begin the school day with an appropriate patriotic exercise does not violate the Establishment Clause even though it permits teachers to lead students in recitation of the Pledge."

This decision, singularly atypical of many 9th Circuit decisions, is an exception to its general judicial practice and dismissive of the original decision in *Elk Grove* (reversed) ordering removal of the words "under God" from the Pledge of Allegiance. Not all judges of the 9th Circuit shared in the original *Elk Grove* decision - nine dissented - and many of the cases reviewed in Part I and Part II reflected their disagreement with "policy" decisions of other judges and the disparagement of state courts.

California Attorney General Brown made no appearance in support of the School District.

In a companion case, Newdow sought an injunction to prevent inscribing the national motto "In God We Trust" on coins. The 9th Circuit disposed of this case in an abbreviated decision.

CHAPTER 13

FREEDOM OF RELIGION

A vast gulf exists between "establishing a religion" and an expression of patriotism. We can readily understand the regrettable division of Christianity caused by religious differences in history, although in many cases the dividing parties were only masking political or nationalistic goals. The Constitution recognized the danger posed by a religion acting politically as evidenced by the flight of the Pilgrims to America, and the Elizabethan and Henry VIII relentless quest to eradicate Catholicism in England.

Subsequent to adoption of the Constitution, the authors realized that a governing document for the nation provided no protection from the abuses of English monarchs. Paradoxically, English citizens who fled to America immediately formed their own churches, confined to those who shared their convictions. When the First Congress drafted and enacted the Bill of Rights (first ten amendments to the Constitution), it reflected English history in general and religion in particular. The First Amendment protects the right to free exercise of religion and prohibits a national church.

As quoted in an earlier Chapter, the First Amendment provides, among other protection of rights, that "Congress shall make no law respecting the establishment of religion;" U.S. Constitution,. Amend. 1. The Amendment explicitly applies to Congress although the Supreme Court subsequently "incorporated" its language into the Due Process Clause of the Fourteenth

Amendment and made applicable to the states; *County of Allegheny v. ACLU.*

The First Amendment reflects the colonial experience with England when religious persecution spread throughout the country as English monarchs searched for dissenting Catholics, seized their property, and executed nonbelievers. For the Pilgrims, their flight to American resulted from exactly this kind of tyranny. Coupling religion with the secular state and its power of arrest and execution caused adherents of religion to seek shelter in the New World.

The Civil War Amendments imposed federal limitations on the states under the Fourteenth Amendment and its Due Process and Equal Protection Clauses. The Thirteenth, Fourteenth, and Fifteenth Amendments enacted by Congress intended to eliminate slavery and nothing else. None of these three Amendments applied to religion, free speech, assembly, or free press protected by the First Amendment, nor did anyone intend that goal. Southern states had fought for the right to disengage themselves from the Union and concurrently to permit slavery. The North refused to acknowledge any right to secession and simultaneously condemned the states that maintained slavery. The Civil War ended disagreement between the North and South but also opened a new chapter in federalism and the relationship between the state and federal government.

A. Public Property
Salazar v. Buono, 130 S.Ct. 1803 (2010)
Reversing the 9th Circuit in *Buono v. Kempthorne* (Secretary of the Interior) 527 F.3d 758 (9th Cir. 2008); *Buono v. Norton,* 371 F.3d 543 (9th Cir. 2004)
Although Protestants dominated the East Coast and Catholics explored the West Coast, in each case the role of religion permeated their worlds. Religion dominated European presence in the early formation of this country and its legacy is historically reflected in the names of cities and

towns throughout the United States. The simple Latin cross emerged as a familiar symbol of Protestant and Catholic churches commencing with the formation of the United States until today. Yet that symbol (Latin Cross) placed on public land decades ago continues to stir resentment, and today the cross has become a legal battlefield. Notably, the vast majority of cases are brought in federal courts, and the 9th Circuit entered the fray eagerly as evidenced by its decisions. This following excerpt from a 9th Circuit judge dissenting in *Buono v. Kempthorne* highlights the role of religion in American history:

> "Seventy-five years ago, the Veterans of Foreign Wars erected atop Sunrise Rock [located] in the Mojave National Preserve a memorial to veterans who died in World War I. The Memorial took the form of a cross near a wooden sign stating, 'The Cross, Erected in Memory of the Dead of All Wars and Erected 1934 by Members of Veterans of Foreign Wars.' The sign has since disappeared, and the cross has been replaced several times, most recently in 1998. Each incarnation of the memorial was created and installed by private citizens; there is no indication in the record that citizens ever received permission from the National Park Service."

The facts of *Buono v. Kempthorne* are essentially undisputed, although their interpretation is not, as evidenced by litigation between the parties spanning six years. Plaintiff Buono filed a Complaint in federal court alleging he traveled a road in the vicinity of the cross erected on public land and it offended him. According to the Complaint, the cross violated the First Amendment prohibiting the establishment of a religion. The U.S. district court judge agreed and issued its original injunction in 2004 commanding removal of the cross on First Amendment grounds. Congress replied by transferring the property to a private source, thereby escaping any Constitutional issue. [An appeal of that decision to the 9th Circuit followed]. The memorial has stood for seventy-five years to honor those who died in the service of their country. These men and women who traveled abroad and left their friends and family to fight a war on foreign soil are entitled to a symbol of their commitment. The cross compels no one to join any religious group, terrorizes no one, inflicts no harm on anyone other than being offended."

The case subsequently took a tortured judicial history. According to the 9th Circuit majority in *Buono v. Kempthorne*, decided in May 2008, this Congressional act of transferring the property amounted to a "sham transaction." The court held that Congress violated the First Amendment Establishment Clause, and affirmed the injunction issued by the district court ordering removal of the cross. In a disservice to the dead and simultaneously interring American history, the 9th Circuit deserves Congressional and national repudiation previously voiced when the court precluded the right of school children to include "under God" in the Pledge of Allegiance.

The quotation above from the dissenting opinion in *Buono* (joined by four other judges) signals determination by a majority of the 9th Circuit judges to eradicate religion from the public square no matter how tenuous the evidence and regardless of the public weal. As noted by the dissenting judges, the memorial has existed without a single complaint until 2002 when the American Civil Liberties Union elected to intervene on the grounds that the Latin cross violated the Establishment Clause of the First Amendment. An unadorned cross in the middle of a desert erected as a memorial hardly qualifies as "establishing a religion."

In Salazar (Secretary of the Interior) v. Buono the Supreme Court criticized the 9th Circuit for applying the wrong law. The only issue before the Supreme Court consisted of the Buono's attempt to expand the scope of the injunction the district court had originally issued. The facts, and the ultimate Supreme Court ruling, are not as important as the language used by the Court in its decision.

The Supreme Court chastised the district court and the 9th Circuit for ignoring the proper legal approach to the plaintiff's challenge to the erection and maintenance of a Latin cross on federal land. The Supreme Court majority applied its previous Establishment Law precedent. The first requirement to avoid a violation of the Establishment Clause requires a religious symbol to include a secular component. The Supreme Court said:

> "In this case, the cross did not attempt submission to any religion but was a memorial to soldiers who died in World War I . . . The cross is of course the preeminent symbol of Christianity . . . But the original reason for the placement of the cross was to commemorate American war dead and, particularly for those with searing memories of The Great War, the symbol that was selected, a plain unadorned white cross, no doubt evoked the unforgettable image of the white crosses, row on row, that marked the final resting places of so many American soldiers who fell in that conflict."

> "If Congress had done nothing [about the cross] the Government would have been required to take down the cross, which had stood on Sunrise Rock for nearly 70 years, and this removal would have been viewed by many as a sign of disrespect for the brave soldiers whom the cross was meant to honor. The demolition of this venerable, if unsophisticated, monument would also have been interpreted by some as an arresting symbol of a Government that is not neutral but hostile on matters of religion and is bent on eliminating from all public places and symbols any trace of our country's religious heritage."

The irony of this case is the sad fact that not a single national monument exists to honor those soldiers who died or were wounded in World War I; 16 U.S.C. § 431 (listing officially designated national memorials, including the National D-Day Memorial and the Vietnam Veterans Memorial). Research discloses no other national memorial honoring more than 300,000 American soldiers who were killed or wounded in World War I.

The Supreme Court said it succinctly: "But a Latin cross is not merely a reaffirmation of Christian beliefs. It is a symbol often used to honor and respect those whose heroic acts, noble contributions, and patient striving helped secure an honored place in history for this Nation and its people. Here, one Latin cross in the desert evokes far more than religion. It evokes thousands of small crosses in foreign fields marking the graves of Americans who fell in battles, battles whose tragedies are compounded if the fallen are forgotten."

The Supreme Court concluded the *Salazar v. Buono* case by citing a previous Supreme Court decision involving the Ten Commandments: "It is reasonable to interpret the congressional designation as giving recognition to the historical meaning that the cross had attained 40 years without legal challenge to a Ten Commandments display suggest[s] that the public visiting the [surrounding] grounds has considered the religious aspect of the tablets' message as part of what is a broader moral and historical message reflective of a cultural heritage."

The First Amendment has undergone significant revision in the last quarter century as federal courts in general, and the Supreme Court in particular, have attempted to harmonize the religious origins of the United States with the significant public interest in religion manifested throughout American history. In *Buono*, the 9th Circuit majority again continued its attempt to extirpate any trace of religion in the public square (or in this case, the desert) by compelling removal of a poignant memorial of men and woman who died for their country.

The language of the dissenting 9th Circuit judge in the original opinion that ordered removal of the cross is a scathing indictment of the majority decision who worry that an observer "would believe, at least suspect [italics in original], that the cross rests on public land . . . In three quarters of a century no one worried about it.

The 9th Circuit not only ignored Congressional approval transferring the land to a private party but contradicts this Supreme Court quotation in another case, *Corp. of the Presiding Bishop of the Church of Jesus Christ of Latter Day Saints v. Amos*: "There is ample room under the Establishment Clause for benevolent neutrality which will permit religious exercise to exist without sponsorship and without interference."

As noted below in the *Vasquez v. Los Angeles County* case (Next), a party cannot file a lawsuit in court unless it has "standing." This judicial doctrine requires a party filing a lawsuit to allege an injury caused by a party and subject to judicial redress. In *Buono*, the 9th Circuit permitted a person who complained about an unattended cross on public land in a desert to establish "standing" because he had to drive his vehicle out of his way to avoid the cross. Only in the 9th Circuit could this ludicrous argument prevail.

The 9th Circuit in *Buono* added another reversal to its voluminous record. The majority cited not a single Supreme Court case supporting its decision. The *Buono* case is not legal analysis. This is ideology.

The Latin Cross case was not over. The district court judge, in a thorough and concise decision, agreed the cross could continue to be erected on private land. The 9th Circuit reversed this decision three years later in *Trunk v. City of San Diego* and returned the case to the district court. The 9th Circuit panel in *Trunk* wrote that it had read the Supreme Court decision (reversing the 9th Circuit in *Buono*) and held it inapplicable. The Supreme Court reviewed the case on appeal from the 9th Circuit and held that the transfer to the district court meant no final judgment had been entered and therefore lacked jurisdiction. The case continues.

Attorney General Brown made no appearance in support of the City of San Diego.

Vasquez v. Los Angles County
487 F.3d 1246 (9th Cir. 2007)

The irony of this case is judicial disapproval of the cross depicted on the Los Angeles (translated in English as "The Angels") County seal. A diminutive cross, accompanied by other illustrations of California history had been used on the Los Angeles County seal for years without a single complaint. The reference to California history on the seal obviously depicted Catholic missionaries who founded numerous missions throughout the state. According to a Complaint filed in federal court by a dissident, this symbol "offended" him. Just as the Latin Cross erected in the desert "offended" a malcontent, that someone's "sensibilities" were offended by observing a tiny cross on the county seal deserved nothing more than an incredulous response. According to the 9th Circuit, this "offensiveness" endorses the right of a dissenter to file a lawsuit.

In purported response to this Complaint, the County removed the cross from the seal and replaced it. The political uproar eventually subsided and, unfazed, the 9th Circuit upheld the right to remove the cross purportedly by the County to avoid a lawsuit. Again, one of the central questions in the *Vasquez* dispute involved whether the plaintiff had the right to sue (i.e., in legal parlance "standing"). According to the 9th Circuit majority decision in *Vasquez*, a party ordinarily must have a "concrete" injury remediable by judicial redress, but the Establishment Clause "is primarily aimed at protecting non-economic interests of a spiritual nature as opposed to a physical or pecuniary nature."

The 9th Circuit panel in *Vasquez* wrote: the injury must be "caused by unwelcome direct contact with a religious display that appears to be endorsed by the state." The [Ninth Circuit] panel concedes that in some cases the injury is so abstract, tenuous, or indirect as not to give rise to "standing." The Supreme Court agreed with that description in an unrelated case: "The [requirement of 'standing'] is necessarily so, lest this court be converted into a vehicle for the vindication of the value interests of concerned bystanders." This doctrine represents precisely what *Vasquez* contends albeit from a reverse mirror. For years no one thought the seal "offensive" or "unwelcome." And most importantly, no one has ever alleged "coercion" into religious conviction by observing the seal.

What legally protected interest was involved in *Vasquez*? What "injury" occurred? *Vasquez* is obviously different from the usual complaint alleging government conduct fostering religion. *Vasquez* sought removal of a "revised non-religious symbol" in lieu of the cross. In other words, he alleged in a lawsuit that the removal of the cross on the seal disfavored religion.

Unfortunately the Supreme Court has not embraced the most obvious rationale for the Establishment Clause: coercion. The historical record is unambiguous that Henry VIII coerced the English people to accept the new religion and punished or executed them if they did not comply. Had that theory been selected by the Supreme Court, the vast majority of religious cases would disappear. Forcibly removing crèches from public squares to satisfy a handful of dissidents suffering not the slightest harm from the display, and removing a cherished and historic memorial of Christian history in the United States, deprives millions of people an opportunity to view a simple artistic format revered for centuries throughout the world and in the United States.

Community House, Inc. v. City of Boise, 490 F.3d 1041 (9th Cir. 2007)
The Supreme Court began its First Amendment Establishment Clause jurisprudence in an attempt to reconcile the potential conflict of "state and church."

The judicial ability to achieve a balance between state aid to parochial schools, religious services on public property, or religious symbols on public property, has been illusory. Numerous courts have struggled with the Ten Commandments in public buildings, Christmas crèches on public property, and a host of other conflicts of religious symbolism. In the last few years, the Supreme Court has softened its previous restrictions and recognized the "establishment of religion" nowhere suggests the danger - as one judge put it - of a theological jihad.

Note: in 2014 the Supreme Court imposed the correct relationship between state and church.

The *Community House, Inc. v. City of Boise* case illustrates a 9th Circuit oblivious to the civic role of religion in cities and states.

Innumerable churches provide homes for battered women, orphans, the homeless, and the disabled, often without regard to their religion. In some cases, the religious environment echoes throughout the facility but the social service clearly outweighs the religious factor. In *Community House, Inc. v. the City of Boise*, the City of Boise, Idaho, had an opportunity to shed the expense of maintaining its homeless shelter by leasing it to Boise Rescue Mission (BRM), a religious organization providing shelters for men, women, and children. Recognizing the need for separation of men and women in its facilities, BRM proposed allowing only men in the current shelter until it could build an alternative shelter for women.

Does this sound reasonable? Not according to the majority of judges (2-1) in the 9th Circuit panel writing its *Community House* decision. In an endless discussion of federal statutory and Constitutional law, these judges prohibited the BRM proposal and decided the plan violated the Establishment Clause on grounds that BRM held religious services in the facility albeit on a voluntary basis. The dissenting judge identifies the absurdity of that decision and emphasizes the absence of coercing anyone to enter the facility or attend religious services. In other words, a compassionate attempt to serve unfortunate people failed because of academic ivory tower writing.

The court reheard the decision, refused to reverse the panel decision, and returned the case to the trial court. In July, 2008 the trial court, wasting more time, issued additional orders.. No further record is available on the particular issues in this case.

B. Public Facilities

Barnes-Wallace v. City of San Diego, 551 F.3d 891 (9th Cir. 2008), on denying rehearing; 704 F.3d 2067 (9th Cir. 2012)
Alleging violation of the First Amendment Establishment Clause and the
California Constitution No Religious Preference Clause, a lesbian couple
and an agnostic sued the City of San Diego for leasing a portion of a public
park to the Boy Scouts.

According to their Complaint, both the couple had visited the park
and were "offended" by the City lease. They observed no religious symbols on the property, the Boy Scouts opened their facility to anyone who
wanted to use the land, and did not deny use of the facilities to anyone.

The district court dismissed the Complaint. The plaintiffs appealed to
the 9th Circuit, and a three-judge panel affirmed the dismissal on grounds
the plaintiffs suffered no "injury in fact" required for "standing" other
than psychological discomfort with the Boy Scout policy excluding homosexuals. Despite that decision, the three-judge panel decided to reconsider
its opinion and completely changed the result without explanation;. The
grounds: if the couple would have visited the property (which they never
did) they could arguably assert some form of injury. Other than that, their
injury consisted of an ideological disagreement, never a judicial ground for
"standing.

The dissenting judge wrote this:

> "Our court [the Ninth Circuit] promulgates an astonishing new
> rule of law for the nine Western States. Henceforth, a plaintiff
> who claims to feel offended by the mere thought of associating
> with people who hold different views has suffered a legally cogni-
> zable injury-in-fact. No other circuit has embraced this remarkable
> innovation, which contradicts nearly three decades of the Supreme
> Court's standing jurisprudence. In practical effect, the three-judge
> panel majority's unprecedented theory creates a new legal land-
> scape in which almost anyone who is offended by almost anything

has standing to air his or her displeasure in court. I must respectfully, but vigorously, dissent from our failure to rehear this case en
banc [full court)."].

This opening statement by the dissenting judge in the *Barnes-Wallace*
decision is astonishing not only for the vigor of its language but also for the
consequences of the majority decision. The 9th Circuit refused to rehear
the case despite the two unexplained inconsistent decisions, and refused
to change the ruling. Quoting the dissent in criticizing failure of the full
court to rehear the case, the judge wrote:

"Then, on rehearing (its original decision), the majority reversed itself
and adopted the theory it had initially rejected. It concluded that "the
Breens [other parties] and Barnes-Wallace have avoided [the Boy Scouts']
Camp Balboa and the Aquatic Center because they object to the Boy
Scouts' presence on, and control of, the land. They do not want to view
signs posted by the Boy Scouts or interact with the Boy Scouts' representatives in order to gain access to the facilities. Article III [of the Constitution]
requiring an 'injury-in-fact', according to the majority, was the Breens' and
the Barnes-Wallace ['offense'] at the Boy Scouts' exclusion, and publicly
expressed disapproval, of lesbians, atheists and agnostics, 'their aversion to
the facilities,' and their feelings of [unwelcomeness] there because of the
Boy Scouts' policies that discriminated against people like them." The 9th
Circuit panel satisfied itself that it had jurisdiction."

Aside from the issue of "standing (right to sue)," the three-judge
panel certified resolution of the merits of the allegations to the California
Supreme Court to decide the case under California law. The California
court declined. Accordingly, this case becomes precedent for 'standing'
and opens the door to anyone who is offended by the policies of a particular group." No other federal circuit court has adopted the rationale of
the three-judge panel in *Barnes-Wallace*. Unfortunately the Supreme Court
denied review. Apparently the dissenting judges are correct. "Emotional
offense" is sufficient to file a lawsuit.

Faith Center Church Evangelistic Ministries v. Glover, 462 F.3d 1194 (9th Cir. 2006). A dissent to the published decision written by eight 9th Circuit judges is published at 480 F.3d 891 (9th Cir. 2007).

No court has ever adopted the theory of "coercion of religious beliefs" when worrying about the use of public facilities to display religious symbols. Along with this aversion, public entities are forbidden from any reference to religious speech conducted on public property, including schools and libraries. *Faith Center Church Evangelistic Ministries v. Glover* is a perfect example of the restriction on religious speech as illustrated by 9th Circuit decisions Several dissenting judges commented that the majority reasoning is specious and masks a secularist ideology..

In the *Faith Center* case, the County of Contra Costa in California offered the use of public library facilities for a discussion of cultural and recreational activities. The pastor of Faith Center sought permission to conduct a religious discussion and a "worship service" at the library congruent with this policy. The county denied permission and refused to permit this group to meet at the library. On appeal to the 9th Circuit the judges also denied their request. Faith Center sought review in the Supreme Court of the 9th Circuit decision denying permission, but the Justices denied a hearing.

The difference between the majority and eight dissenting judges in *Faith Center* dramatically exposes the difficulty of navigating the difference between religious and nonreligious speech. Reasonable minds can differ whether the Supreme Court would allow Faith Center to meet at the public library, but the language of the 9th Circuit majority judges demonstrates their animus toward religion. According to the majority, the "mere" (word used in text) worship practice of Faith Center was suspect. This phrase is demeaning and dismissive in confirming the result the majority reaches.

CHAPTER 14

FREE SPEECH AND GOVERNMENT

A. Police

Chaker v. Crogan, 428 F.3d 1215 (9th Cir. 2005)

The Supreme Court has expanded its First Amendment decisions to a variety of topics. The Court has refused to strike child access to violent videos, permitted flag burning, and permitted nude dancing, all of which are irrelevant in discussing public discourse. The 9th Circuit has also embraced the First Amendment in several decisions, discussed below, but its zeal has created a serious breach of state sovereignty by judicially overruling California decisions on California law.

In *Chaker v. Crogan*, the California Supreme Court interpreted a California statute penalizing anyone who knowingly files a false complaint of police misconduct. After a jury convicted Chaker of this charge, he filed three petitions in California courts, all denied, and a habeas corpus petition in federal court also denied. Aside from the extensive cost of trial, appeal, petitions in state and federal court, the record established that Chaker had filed excessive petitions against police officers in other cases. California courts had been declared him a "vexatious litigant," a statutory confirmation of a person who abuses the judicial process.

None of this affected the 9th Circuit habeas corpus decision after the district court denied Chaker's petition. In an analysis that in effect overruled the California Supreme Court decision that had upheld the statute (*People v. Stanistreet*) the 9th Circuit ruled that the statute prohibits reporting false statements of police misconduct but ignores false reports supporting police officers. Assuming a citizen would knowingly file a false report supporting police officers, that the statute did not include this element is irrelevant at worst, or subject to legislative amendment at best. Not in the 9th Circuit. According to the panel, this omission constitutes "viewpoint discrimination," a doctrine prohibiting legislatures from selective prohibition of speech on certain topics. Because the statute only prohibited knowingly submitting false reports of police conduct, but not false reports supporting police conduct, the statute impermissibly applies to only one category.

That incredulous decision aside, the more crucial issue is the reversal of a criminal conviction of Chaker confirmed by the California Supreme Court in a similar case filed by a different party challenging the same statute. In other words, at the time of Chaker's latest complaint in federal court the California courts had already ruled the local statute enforceable. The 9th Circuit shunts aside California courts again and imposes its own will. The California Attorney General (Lockyer) apparently sought not review in the Supreme Court.

B. Employee Speech
City of San Diego v. Roe, 543 U.S. 77 (2004)
Reversing the 9th Circuit decision in *City of San Diego v. Roe*, 356 F.3d 1108 (9th Cir. 2004).
Employee complaints about management are endemic to their relationship with each other. When the employer is a public entity, as distinct from a private employer, the legal chemistry changes if the employee publicly complains about alleged management or misconduct.

The Supreme Court confronted the issue of public employee criticism of, or commentary on, conduct of the employer in *City of San Diego v.*

Roe. In earlier cases, the Supreme Court had distinguished the routine complaints of inter - office politics or grievances that would ordinarily be resolved in collective bargaining agreements or by intra - office complaint departments. But when employees speak out on matters of public concern, the Supreme Court acknowledges that their information could be valuable outside the workplace.

Distinctions between public and private speech cannot always be easily categorized, but the 9th Circuit judges completely lost track of rational thought when it decided *City of San Diego v. Roe.* The facts suggest that this case illustrates "cultural decay" as well as a judiciary impervious to common decency.

On the Internet, a police officer published himself masturbating in uniform. He advertised exotic toys, and identified himself as a member of law enforcement. When notified of this conduct, his supervisors conducted a hearing, and the City terminated his employment. The officer sued the City, arguing it had infringed on his Constitutional right of freedom of speech. That this lawsuit could even pass the first stage in litigation (pleading) is astonishing, but not in the 9th Circuit. According to that court, the officer was entitled to engage in this conduct as an element of free speech. The City sought reversal in the Supreme Court.

The 9th Circuit decision caused the Supreme Court in *City of San Diego v. Roe* to write that the only source for the 9th Circuit point of view consisted of 9th Circuit precedent, not Supreme Court law, and in a unanimous decision so dismissive of the 9th Circuit that the Justices did not even name the author of the opinion. The Court reversed on grounds the 9th Circuit had again ignored Supreme Court precedent in approving the absurdity to litigate this unfortunate incident.

Here is the decision of the Supreme Court: "We understand that police officers, like everyone else, make mistakes. Sometimes they abuse their authority, but the vast number of officers attempt to enforce the law and do their job within the boundaries of the law. That any officer would engage in the kind of conduct reviewed in this case and argue he did it on his own time is disgusting and a black mark against those who do not disgrace the Department." That the 9th Circuit would actually consider this case suitable for consideration speaks volumes about the authors of its decision.

C. Flags

When the Supreme Court approved of dissidents in the United States burning the American flag, the vast majority of the public expressed incredulity. The American flag has flown in public places, including courtrooms, for centuries. For the men and women who fought in two world wars, the symbolism of the flag is incomparable. The presence of the flag is pervasive and acknowledges the valor of the armed forces and the principles for which they fought. The flag flies in cemeteries for the deceased in war, and in hospitals for the wounded. It flies in the capitol in Washington and in every state of the union.

Songs have been written about the flag, the national anthem reveres its appearance in the "dawn's early light" and in the words "Oh, say does that star spangled banner yet wave." Literature is replete with stories of its role in American history. Of course, some people think the flag symbolizes nothing more than a piece of cloth depicting various colors and of no particular significance. In fact, despite the political, religious, and social differences among the American people, in time of war or threat of war they rally around the flag and proudly display it. No other banner, sign, or flag displays a comparable symbol.

In Santa Cruz, California, the Department of Transportation allowed the American flag to fly on overpasses to the freeway after the disastrous events of 9/11. No one complained, but dissenters had also placed a banner on the overpass criticizing the portent of war in Iraq. Someone removed that flag on two occasions and then, unsurprisingly, the dissenters filed a lawsuit in federal court alleging restrictions on free speech and their entitlement to show a "flag."

The average American would probably assume this lawsuit is "silly" or "outrageous" or might use other more pejorative characterizations. Not in the 9th Circuit, whose three-judge panel unanimously ordered the Department of Transportation to remove the flag unless other flags could be flown. According to the panel, permitting only the American flag and restricting other flags constituted "viewpoint discrimination" characterized above in the *Chaker* case. The government obviously requires a policy of neutrality and should not endorse competing public speech. But to disallow display of the American flag, to which we "pledge allegiance to the flag, . . and to the Republic for which it stands, one nation, indivisible, under God" . . . unless other flags can also fly is not "viewpoint discrimination." It is a repudiation of country. Is our pledge of allegiance to the flag only a naive slogan, or does the language stand for a principle?

Immediately the debate descends into all the iniquities imposed on people throughout American history. Critics forget the deaths of American armed forces personnel in two world wars fought to save other countries from dictatorship. National holidays memorialize their lives and those of their friends and families. Instead we hear a litany of complaints about race, gender, Vietnam, and Iraq. The flag signifies the commitment of the American people to a free country and is an incomparable symbol of our freedom, but not in the 9th Circuit. Unfortunately the defendant Department of Transportation tried to defend flying the American flag on statutory and other implausible grounds without a word about national unity in a time of attack. The court nods it head to the tragedy of 9/11 and simultaneously ignores the unanimous support of the American people comparable to the unanimity of the country in response to the Japanese attack on Pearl Harbor. The court launches into a rhetorical legal analysis ignoring any of the symbolism of the flag for the American people.

This case illustrates as much as any other the distance and disconnect of the 9th Circuit from the real world. By eliminating display of the flag with academic hairsplitting and refusing to acknowledge the incomparable display of its national unity, the court continues the balkanization of culture to assure that no principle of a unified people exists. This case mirrors numerous other 9th Circuit cases fraying the thread that weaves this county into one nation. Forbidding Christmas displays, prohibiting the Latin Cross, in effect frustrating religious symbols for Christmas and Easter, foreclosing and stultifying the convictions of millions of Americans while worrying about "offending" someone. You would think the American flag might be an exception.

CHAPTER 15

ESPIONAGE

Tenet (Director of CIA) v. Doe, 544 U.S. 1 (2005); Reversing the 9th Circuit decision in *Doe v. Tenet,* 329 F.3d 1135 (9th Cir. 2003).

Although not a "cultural" decision per se, *Doe v. Tenet* illustrates the 9th Circuit's complete disregard of Supreme Court decisions. The *Tenet* case, reflecting a judicial indifference to rules, is particularly appalling because of the damage the 9th Circuit would have done to national security had it not been reversed by the Supreme Court.

The backstory story begins in 1861 when President Lincoln privately and discretely agreed to pay a federal agent to spy on the Confederate army during the Civil War. When the war ended, the agent's estate (the agent, Totten, had subsequently died) sued the federal government alleging in *Tenet v. U.S.* that Lincoln failed to pay the amount agreed upon. The Supreme Court denied the claim on grounds the disclosure of such a contract would not only have jeopardized the agent's life during his tenure as a spy but also impaired national security of the government which must rely on this kind of service in times of war. Otherwise, every secret contract would be subject to disclosure and result in the consequent diplomatic injury in national and international relations. The Supreme Court denied payment. In addition to the *Totten* case, all federal courts have scrupulously followed this rule; *U.S. v. Reynolds.*

In *Doe v. Tenet* (real name of Doe not revealed) his estate alleged a similar contract between the spy (Doe) and the Central Intelligence Agency (CIA) and sought its enforcement. But in *Doe v. Tenet* the 9th Circuit panel held that the *Totten* Civil War case only applied to cases alleging breach of contract, and, if the allegations of Doe were accepted, a party could sue on a promise relied upon to his detriment (known in legal language as promissory estoppel). In addition, Doe's estate contended it could proceed with the lawsuit based on Doe's "liberty interest" of the Due Process Clause of the Fourteenth Amendment. The district court disagreed but on appeal the 9th Circuit agreed with Doe and allowed the case to go forward.

The Supreme Court granted review, and issued this decision:

> "We think the Court of Appeals was quite wrong in holding the former *Totten* [case] does not require dismissal of [Doe's] claims. That court [the Ninth Circuit] reasoned first that *Totten* developed merely a contract rule, prohibiting breach-of-contract claims seeking to enforce the terms of espionage agreements but not barring claims based on due process or estoppel theories. In fact, *Totten* was not so limited: '[P]ublic policy forbids the maintenance of any suit in a court of justice, the trial of which would inevitably lead to the disclosure of matters which the law itself regards as confidential. The secrecy which such contracts impose precludes any action for their enforcement.' No matter the clothing in which alleged spies dress their claims, Totten precludes judicial review in cases where success depends upon the existence of their secret espionage relationship with the Government."

> In a far closer case than this, we observed that if the 'precedent of this Court has direct application in a case, yet appears to rest on reasons rejected in some other line of decisions, the Court of Appeals should follow the case which directly controls, leaving to this Court the prerogative of overruling its own decisions.'"

The Supreme Court reversed the 9th Circuit unanimously, accompanied by another stern rebuke. The Supreme Court expressed dismay that the 9th Circuit's decision, if allowed, would have had a disastrous impact on national security, not in so many words, but a clear reproach to the 9th Circuit.

CHAPTER 16

INTERNATIONAL RELATIONS

Sosa v. Alvarez-Machain, 542 U.S. 692 (2004); Reversing the 9th Circuit decision in 331 F.3d 604 (9th Cir. 2004)

Anyone who thinks a court repeatedly denying immunity to public officers and dismissive of state court decisions is not anti-government should read this case. *Sosa v. Alvarez-Machain* is a civil case; not criminal; not prisoner's rights; not state sovereignty; but a case filed by a Mexican national against the United States. The Supreme Court thoroughly discredits the 9th Circuit's aberrant reasoning and reverses their decision.

In 1985 a U.S. Drug Enforcement Agency (DEA) agent was tortured and killed in Mexico. The DEA, believing Machain was responsible for the murder, secured his indictment in federal court, and the judge issued an arrest warrant. With the cooperation of Mexican nationals who detained Machain in Mexico, the DEA arranged to transport him to the United States, where federal agents placed him under arrest. Nevertheless, a jury acquitted him of murder.

Alvarez-Machain sued the DEA and the U.S government under two federal statues: the Alien Tort Claims Act, a statute limiting federal court jurisdiction, and the Federal Tort Claims Act, a statute providing for a money damages remedy against the federal government for negligence committed by one of its employees. The 9th Circuit, invoking a so-called "headquarters" rule, decided that although the federal statutes provided limited jurisdiction to recompense injuries occurring only in the United States, if the "planning" of an act occurred domestically the injury could provide jurisdiction for a remedy in money damages. The planning occurred in Washington D.C., DEA "headquarters," said the 9th Circuit panel, therefore the alien could sue and seek money damages in the United States.

This decision by 9th Circuit judges to allow an alien to sue for "planning" the detention of Machain was not unanimous. The majority judges' decision, characterized by the dissenting judges as a disquisition (forty-three footnotes), listed a variety of "human rights" violations." By citing only its own previous court decision as authority for conferring federal jurisdiction, the 9th Circuit invented a claim for violation of the "law of nations." In other words, in the absence of statutory or case law precedent from any source, the 9th Circuit majority approved of applying international law.

The Supreme Court unanimously reversed the 9th Circuit. The Justices dismissed the "headquarters" doctrine as an unbounded application of tort law (personal injury or death) allowing anyone injured in a foreign country to sue any America agents who planned, trained or organized an operation that resulted in an injury to someone. Although the Supreme Court decision is highly academic, the Justices severely restricted the right of parties to sue the U.S. government for the conduct of its agents in the United States for conduct that occurred outside U.S borders.

Supreme Court Justice Scalia has repeatedly argued against expanding federal jurisdiction with the admonition that we are a democracy, and the legislature drafts legislation. Congress does not invent claims and, for example . . . "would be appalled by the proposition that the American peoples' democratic adoption of the death penalty . . . could be judicially nullified because of the disapproving views of foreigners." He wrote: "It would be bad enough if there were some assurance that future perversions of perceived international norms into American law would be approved by the Court itself (though we know ourselves to be eminently reasonable), self-awareness of eminent reasonableness is not really a substitute for democratic election."

The animus of the 9th Circuit toward government as expressed in its *Doe v. Tenet* and *Sosa v. Alvarez-Machain* decisions is more than mere judicial interpretation. Both cases clearly repudiated Supreme Court precedent but, more dangerously, each jeopardized national security and perverted the law as identified by the dissenting 9th Circuit judges in both cases. The majority of the 9th Circuit judges are not engaged in judging, they are initiating policy based on their perception of the world.

CHAPTER 17

IMMUNITY FROM LITIGATION

U.S. v. Olson, 546 U.S. 43 (2005); Reversing the 9th Circuit decision in *U.S. v. Olson,* 362 F.3d 1236 (9th Cir. 2006).

Federal officials are entitled to "discretionary immunity" from civil litigation comparable to the immunity applicable to state officials for conduct occurring in the course of their duties. This doctrine applies under the federal Tort Claims Act, and in *U.S. v. Olson* the federal officials (mine inspectors) cited immunity against a charge by miners in a civil trial that inspectors had violated mine safety rules. The 9th Circuit denied the inspectors the defense of immunity, but on review by the Supreme Court the Justices unanimously held: "The Ninth Circuit's first premise is too broad and the second premise [for its decision] reads the Act too narrowly . . . The 9th Circuit should have looked to [cases decided in other courts] for an analogy." The Supreme Court reversed the decision and returned the case to the 9th Circuit. That court returned the case to the district court for further hearing. The district court dismissed the case. Miners appealed to the 9th Circuit.

Undeterred, the 9th Circuit reversed the district court decision again. Here is the circumvention of the Supreme Court decision written by the 9th Circuit panel in the *Olson* case after reversing the district court: "Plaintiffs [injured miners] also assert that the district court's reconsideration of discretionary immunity violated the rule of mandate [a court order] and the law of the case. The rule of mandate did not bar reconsideration because the Supreme Court's decision in [the first Olson case] did not expressly or impliedly resolve the issue [of discretionary immunity]. The law of the case doctrine ([the definitive rule in the litigation] is also inapplicable because the Supreme Court vacated our decision thereby depriving that decision of precedential effect." Returning the case to the district court, the judge dismissed the case.

In other words, when the Supreme Court reversed the original 9th Circuit decision it no longer became law. So the 9th Circuit could rewrite the same decision as the original case because its original case no longer existed as precedent and binding. What do you call this kind of deception?

Although this case does not involve a "cultural" decision, it serves as an example of the 9th Circuit's complete rejection of Supreme Court decisions and an arrogant disregard of precedent. The 9th Circuit's legal lingo is admittedly confusing, but it is not so much hairsplitting as a specious attempt by the 9th Circuit to impose its own policy.

CHAPTER 18

INTERNATIONAL LAW

Republic of Philippines v. Pimentel, 553 U.S. 851 (2008); Reversing the 9th Circuit decision in *Republic of Philippines v. Pimentel,* 464 F.3d 885 (9th Cir. 2006).

The Constitution vests federal courts with jurisdiction to resolve conflicts with foreign countries in civil litigation, but those cases are not within the scope of this text. Cases in this Chapter only reflect the relationship between the 9th Circuit and the Supreme Court. The underlying facts are not important because the issue is entirely a legal one. In this case involving former Philippine president Ferdinand Marcos, the Supreme Court initially described the underlying facts in the case, and then wrote,

> "We conclude the [Ninth Circuit] gave insufficient weight to the former sovereign status of the Republic and erred in reaching and discounting the merits of their claim. When the opinion of the Court of Appeals is consulted, the reader will find its quotations from Federal Rule 19 [a federal procedural rule] do not accord with its test as sought here.
>
> The Court of Appeals erred in not giving the necessary weight to the absent entities' assertion of sovereign immunity. The court in effect decided the merits of the Republic and the Commission's claims to the [country's] assets. Once it was recognized that those

claims were not frivolous, it was error for the Court of Appeals to address them on their merits when the required entities had been granted sovereign immunity. The court's consideration of the merits was itself an infringement on foreign sovereign immunity; and, in any event, its analysis was flawed."

The Supreme Court continues with its criticism of the 9th Circuit decision and ultimately reverses in a vote of 8-1, returning the case to that court.

Benitez v. Garcia, 419 F.Supp.2d 1234; 449 F.3d 971 (2006); 495 F.3d 640 (2007)

Ninth Circuit panel members will often rewrite their original opinion, sometimes several years later. Here is an example taken from a criminal case but involving international relations: Benitez was extradited (judicially ordered by one country to another sovereign country) from Venezuela to the United States, but the foreign court conditioned the extradition by imposing sentencing limits for Benitez in state court in the event of a guilty verdict or plea of guilty. After Benitez was convicted in state court, the judge denied the right of a foreign country to impose limits on his sentencing and sentenced Benitez in accord with state law.

Benitez sought review in district court (habeas corpus), and that court denied his petition. Benitez appealed to the 9th Circuit. The 9th Circuit reversed the district court and granted the petition. The 9th Circuit panel subsequently withdrew its decision and amended it. Later, in another decision on the same case, the original decision was withdrawn. The court wrote yet another decision, vacated the earlier decisions, and denied the petition.

In fairness, the only possible explanation is the subsequent Supreme Court decision in *Carey v. Musladin* (discussed in chapter 5) restricting the authority of federal courts of appeal in reversing state court decisions. The 9th Circuit decision said nothing about that.

CHAPTER 19

HOSPITALS

Oregon Advocacy Center v. Mink, 322 F.3d 1101 (9th Cir. 2003)

The Oregon Legislature enacted a statute to provide a pre trial program for identifying mentally deficient inmates detained in city or county jails awaiting trial. Upon that certification by a court, the statute required transfer of the inmate to a state operated facility within seven days. In a lawsuit filed by an inmate in district court, the federal judge ordered the counties and cities of the state to comply with the statute despite their objections that the inability to provide services to patients (inmates) made a seven-day deadline impossible to achieve until an open bed was available. The trial judge issued an injunction, rejecting the reality described by state officials, and the State of Oregon appealed. The 9th Circuit affirmed on the usual Due Process grounds used in eviscerating state law. Curiously, the Oregon Attorney General did not seek review in the Supreme Court.

No one contended that mentally impaired inmates should not receive treatment to determine their competency to stand trial. Aside from imposters and posers who pretend to be mentally incompetent to avoid trial, Oregon had provided a humane system, apparently insufficient for the 9th Circuit. But the principle issue is state sovereignty. The plaintiff inmates filed their lawsuit in federal court without affording Oregon courts any opportunity to interpret their own state law. Finessing state courts by invoking a Fourteenth Amendment Due Process violation, the 9th Circuit imposes its own Constitutional demand in interpreting the state law.

This decision is another case of federal interference ("structural reform") with states. The 9th Circuit dismissed the "federalism" issue in one paragraph. When the Fourteenth Amendment was enacted no one thought this kind of result was remotely possible.

CHAPTER 20

MILITARY

Winter v. Natural Resources Defense Council, 550 U.S. 7 (2008); Reversing the 9th Circuit decision in 518 F.3d 658 (9th Cir. 2008).

"To be prepared for war is one of the most effectual means of preserving peace." So said George Washington in his first Annual Address to Congress, more than two centuries ago. No case demonstrates the indifference to this statement than *Winter v. Natural Resources Defense Council.* The decision of the Supreme Court in this case is discussed in some detail to reveal the disservice the district court judge and the 9th Circuit imposed on the American people.

The *Winter* case is best described in this summary (edited) prepared by the Supreme Court:

> "Antisubmarine warfare is one of the Navy's highest priorities. The Navy's fleet faces a significant threat from modern diesel-electric submarines, which are extremely difficult to detect and track because they can operate almost silently. The most effective tool for identifying submerged diesel-electric submarines is active sonar, which emits pulses of sound underwater and then receives the acoustic waves that echo off the target. Active sonar is a complex technology, and sonar operators must undergo extensive training to become proficient in its use.

This case concerns the Navy's use of 'mid-frequency active' (MFA) sonar during integrated training exercises in the waters off Southern California (SoCal). In these exercises, ships, submarines, and aircraft train together as members of a 'strike group.' Due to the importance of antisubmarine warfare, a strike group may not be certified for deployment until it demonstrates proficiency in the use of active sonar to detect, track, and neutralize enemy submarines.

The SoCal waters contain at least thirty-seven species of marine mammals. The plaintiffs - groups and individuals devoted to the protection of marine mammals and ocean habitats- assert that MFA sonar causes serious injuries to these animals. The Navy disputes that claim, noting that MFA sonar training in SoCal waters has been conducted for forty years without a single documented sonar-related injury to any marine mammal."

The district court entered a preliminary injunction prohibiting the Navy from using MFA sonar during its training exercises, imposing six restrictions on the Navy's use of sonar. As relevant to this case, the injunction required the Navy to shut down MFA sonar when a marine mammal was spotted within 2, 200 yards of a vessel, and to power down sonar by six decibels during conditions known as 'surface ducting. The Navy moved to vacate the district court's preliminary injunction. The district court refused to do so, and the Court of Appeals affirmed. The Court of Appeals emphasized that any negative impact of the injunction on the Navy's training exercises was 'speculative,' and determined that the 2, 200-yard shutdown zone was unlikely to affect naval operations".

The Supreme Court ruled as follows:

"The preliminary injunction is vacated to the extent challenged by the Navy. The balance of equities and the public interest-which were barely addressed by the district court-tip strongly in favor of the Navy. The Navy's need to conduct realistic training with active sonar to respond to the threat posed by enemy submarines plainly outweighs the interests advanced by the plaintiffs.

Even if plaintiffs have demonstrated a likelihood of irreparable injury, such injury is outweighed by the public interest and the Navy's interest in effective, realistic training of its sailors. For the same reason, it is unnecessary to address the lower courts' holding that plaintiffs have established a likelihood of success on the merits.

Here, the record contains declarations from some of the Navy's most senior officers, all of whom underscored the threat posed by enemy submarines and the need for extensive sonar training to counter this threat. Those officers emphasized that realistic training cannot be accomplished under the two challenged restrictions imposed by the district court the 2, 200-yard shutdown zone and the power-down requirement during surface ducting conditions. The use of MFA sonar under realistic conditions during training exercises is clearly of the utmost importance to the Navy and the Nation. The Court . . . concludes that the balance of equities and consideration of the overall public interest tip strongly in favor of the Navy. The determination of where the public interest lies in this case does not strike the Court as a close question.

The district court did not give serious consideration to the balance of equities and the public interest. The Court of Appeals considered these factors and concluded that the Navy's concerns about the preliminary injunction were "speculative." The lower courts failed to properly defer to senior Navy officers' specific, predictive judgments about how the preliminary injunction would reduce the effectiveness of the Navy's SoCal training exercises."

The Court of Appeals concluded that the 2, 200 zone limit would not be overly burdensome because marine mammal sightings during training exercises are relatively rare. But regardless of the frequency of such sightings, the injunction will increase the radius of the shutdown zone from 200 to 2, 200 yards, which expands its surface area by a factor of over 100. Moreover, because training scenarios can take several days to develop, each additional shutdown can result in the loss of several days' worth of training. The Court of Appeals also concluded that the shutdown zone would not be overly burdensome because the Navy had shut down MFA sonar several times during prior exercises when marine mammals were spotted well beyond the Navy's self-imposed 200-yard zone. But the court ignored undisputed evidence that these voluntary shutdowns only occurred during tactically insignificant times."

The district court also abused its discretion by requiring the Navy to power down MFA sonar by six decibels during significant surface ducting conditions. When surface ducting occurs, active sonar becomes more useful near the surface, but less effective at greater depths. Diesel-electric submariners are trained to take advantage of these distortions to avoid being detected by sonar. The [9th Circuit] Court of Appeals concluded that the power-down requirement was reasonable because surface ducting occurs relatively rarely, and the Navy has previously certified strike groups that did not train under such conditions. This reasoning is backwards. Given that surface ducting is both rare and unpredictable, it is especially important for the Navy to be able to train under these conditions when they occur."

The Supreme Court reversed the decision of the 9th Circuit. Here is the reaction of the 9th Circuit to the Supreme Court reprimand when it received the decision: "We remand to the district court to comply with the United States Supreme Court decision in *Winter v. Natural Resources Defense Council*". Nothing said about a "reversal."

The *Winter* case is not only of national importance but another example of judicial irresponsibility. For a district court judge to override the testimony of naval officers who prepare for war and the defense of this country, and its decision confirmed by the 9th Circuit, is more than absurd. It is irresponsible. And dangerous.

Witt v. Department of the Air Force, 527 F.3d 806 (9th Cir. 2008); Rehearing denied, 548 F.3d 1264 (9th Cir. 2008)

Courts in general and the Supreme Court in particular recognize the different perspective the military brings to American life. Rights that civilians possess are markedly curtailed in the military in deference to the need for a unified command responsive to orders. Congress, after extensive Congressional hearings, enacted a "Don't Ask, Don't Tell" policy (subsequently reversed) concerning the issue of homosexuality in the military. The merits of that policy were contentious and the disagreements impassioned. On appeal, a 9th Circuit panel undertook a challenge to the law in which Air Force Major Witt admitted her homosexuality and her sexual relationship with another woman. After a military hearing, the commission filed a request to discharge her. Witt filed a lawsuit challenging the discharge on Constitutional grounds citing the Equal Protection and Due Process Clauses of the Fourteenth Amendment. The district court dismissed the case.

On appeal, the 9th Circuit panel reviewing a district court decision, denied the Equal Protection and procedural Due Process" grounds but launched into an expansive review of substantive Due Process. As the basis for their rule that Witt had stated a federal claim, the three-judge panel cited *Lawrence v. Texas*, a case written by the Supreme Court invalidating a Texas statute prohibiting prosecution of consensual sodomy. In

an excruciating lengthy and ineffective review of substantive Fourteenth
Amendment Due Process, the three-judge panel misinterpreted the
Lawrence case as explained in the opinion of the dissenting judges. The
panel reversed the district court which had dismissed the case, and sent it
back for development of the record. Presumably the Congressional record
and its extensive hearings and report did not satisfy the 9th Circuit panel.

In a dissenting opinion, several judges reminded the panel that the
Supreme Court had written critically about "substantive" Due Process.
Here is the language of their dissent:

> "To guide lower courts, the Supreme Court has explained its 'estab-
> lished method' for determining what counts as a fundamental
> right, nowhere more famously than when it reversed [a] previous
> [Ninth Circuit decision]. "First, we have regularly observed that
> the Due Process Clause specially protects those fundamental rights
> and liberties which are, objectively, deeply rooted in this Nation's
> history and tradition and implicit in the concept of ordered liberty,
> such that neither liberty nor justice would exist if they were sacri-
> ficed. Second, we have required in substantive-due-process cases
> a careful description of the asserted fundamental liberty interest.
> Our Nation's history, legal traditions, and practices thus provide
> the crucial guideposts for responsible decision making that direct
> and restrain our exposition of the Due Process Clause. As we stated
> recently . . . the Fourteenth Amendment forbids the government
> to infringe . . . no fundamental liberty interests at all, no matter
> what [due] process is provided, unless the infringement is narrowly
> tailored to serve a compelling state interest."

> "The [majority of Ninth Circuit judges] today do not once . . .
> describe homosexual sodomy as a 'fundamental right.' And, more
> importantly, gave no license to ignore our cautionary admonition
> [in the previous case] to hew closely to precedent in substantive due

process cases. In particular, the Supreme Court reminds us that [b]
y extending constitutional protection to an asserted right or liberty
interest, we, to a great extent, place the matter outside the arena
of public debate and legislative action. We must therefore exercise
the utmost care whenever we are asked to break new ground in
this field, lest the liberty protected by the Due Process Clause be
subtly transformed into the policy preferences of the Members of
this Court."

"The result of the panel's innovation, its remand to the district court to develop the record on an [statutorily] as-applied basis
flies in the face of both Congress' careful consideration and the
Supreme Court's emphasis on deference to military policies. Such
judicial adventurism lays the groundwork for a continuing series of
fact-bound challenges to the specific application of a law that Witt
only calls into constitutional question in the first place by stretch-
ing substantive due process beyond repair. I know no principle of
law or logic that justifies such a result.

No matter how strongly some of us may feel about the underlying issues in this case, the Supreme Court's precedents in substantive due process law compel not only our usual obedience, but also
our self-conscious restraint. We have no mandate to follow either
our reasons or our convictions down paths the Constitution and
the Court have left for Congress to chart. [The Supreme Court]
did not change that, nor did it provide a forum for lower courts to
measure the policy decisions of Congress against the circumstances
of a particular litigant."

Whatever we think of its merits, the 'Don't Ask, Don't Tell'
policy is not an outlying anachronism, but a considered legislative
judgment. If Congress now reconsiders it in the light of new devel-
opments or evidence, then it acts entirely within its constitutional

powers. But until Congress acts, the federal judiciary should not preempt its policy choices, and certainly not at the cost of tearing substantive due process law from the guideposts to which the Supreme Court has fastened it."

This analysis in a federal case is consistent with the 9th Circuit reversal of state courts, its invention of new rights, and imposing policy rather than law. The dissent is correct in asking: what is the trial court supposed to do? Congress has already held extensive hearings. But the most dangerous part of the 9th Circuit decision is the interference of the judiciary into policy decisions of Congress.

The *Witt* case is not the first case written by the 9th Circuit inventing use of the Due Process Clause to find a "liberty interest" or a "fundamental right." The dissent in *Witt* cited the 9th Circuit's previous case in *Washington v. Glucksberg*, a Supreme Court case reversing a 9th Circuit decision invalidating the Washington assisted suicide statute. The Supreme Court invokes the same censorious language of the 9th Circuit it has used in other cases.

This is how the dissent sums it up:

> "This is the first case in which a federal appellate court has allowed a member of the armed services to bring a substantive due process challenge to the congressionally enacted 'Don't Ask, Don't Tell' homosexual personnel policy for the military. With respect, I believe that our three-judge panel has erroneously reversed a district court order dismissing such suit and remanded for further factfinding under an unsanctioned and malleable standard of review.
>
> This case is far more than a harmless remand. The majority in this case claims to rest its decision on the Supreme Court's opinion in *Lawrence v. Texas*, which decriminalized private and consensual homosexual conduct. Instead, however, *Witt* contravenes Supreme Court precedent, including *Lawrence*, in the area of substantive

due process, creates a circuit split, and stretches the judicial power beyond its constitutional mandate. At the end of the day, *Witt* creates a forum in the judicial branch (rather than the political branches) to challenge the validity and the particular application of "Don't Ask, Don't Tell," even though such policy infringes no constitutional right. Since today's order denies rehearing of this problematic case by an en banc [full court] court, I must respectfully dissent."

Years later the Supreme Court indirectly sanctioned same-sex marriage in a reversal of a California Initiative mandating the role of marriage occurs only between a man and a woman. In a tax case, the Court also refused to enforce the federal counterpart of defining marriage (Defense of Marriage Act) signed by all members of Congress. Litigation continues on this issue.

CHAPTER 21

SEXUAL ORIENTATION

When the issues in court are race, gender, age, or disability, an observer of these cases notes that the parties and their supporters are often influenced by emotional perspectives regardless of the merits of a case. Congress responded to complaints of discriminatory treatment in these four categories, particularly in the context of employment, by enacting a series of statutes forbidding employers to use the "status" of an employee as an excuse to terminate or retaliate against that employee. Characterized as "civil rights," discrimination is often in the eye of the beholder, and one person can easily view the conduct of another differently. Juries must sort this out, but they too are governed by their own personal perspectives.

Unlike commercial cases judged by objective standards (e.g., product loss or failure of performance, service disruption, or countless other allegations that one person or entity breached the written contract of another), the civil rights statutes are governed by subjective perceptions often contained in personality disputes.

S.D. Myers, Inc. v. City and County of San Francisco, 336 F.3d 114 (9th Cir. 2003)

Most state public entities have passed comparable civil rights legislation, generally following federal law, but no governmental body has embraced "civil rights" as enthusiastically as San Francisco. Here is the language of its

City ordinance as of 2003: "All contracting agencies of the City . . . shall include in all contracts and property contracts . . . a provision obligating the contractor not to discriminate on the basis of the fact or perception of a person's race, color, creed, religion, national origin, ancestry, age, sex, sexual orientation, gender identity, domestic partner status, marital status, disability, or Acquired Immune Deficiency Syndrome or HIV status (AIDS/ HIV status) . . . against any employee of . . . such contractor and shall require such contractor to include a similar provision in all subcontracts executed or amended thereunder."

S.D. Myers, the plaintiff contractor, sued the City on grounds that California state law preempted this ordinance. The 9th Circuit managed to evade the argument in the *S.D. Meyers* case that state and federal laws preempt city ordinances. The court noted that contractor Myers had submitted a bid lower than that awarded to another contractor but he was denied the contract because he refused to abide by the ordinance. In other words, the city taxpayers paid more for a public project.

Presumably the City enacted this ordinance in an attempt to maintain a "level playing field" so that no one would be disqualified from bidding on public projects. Of course the "level playing field" ought to consider who can construct a project faster and cheaper than anyone else. Shouldn't the test be the cost to taxpayers?

CHAPTER 22

RACE

The legacy of slavery in the United States, abolished over a century ago, survives and continues to affect innumerable political, religious, and social issues. Education is foremost, though housing and employment are equally contentious. For some, race colors every component of American life and, in effect, the system endemically. For others, "political correctness" has run amok. The courts, including the Supreme Court, have confronted racial issues, and the same disagreement among the judges occurs as among the public. Although having decided several controversial racial issues, the Supreme Court has recently resisted overtures to impose quotas as a cognizable legal interest, particularly in education and employment.

Meyer v. Holley, 537 U.S. 280 (2003)
Reversing the 9th Circuit decision in *Holley v. Crank,* 258 F.3d 1127 (9th Cir. 2001).
Needless the say, the 9th Circuit is at the forefront of resolving racial issues in favor of those alleging discrimination conducted by various entities. In *Meyer v. Holley* the Supreme Court reversed the 9th Circuit in a real estate dispute between the parties. An interracial couple alleged the defendant real estate company (Holley) violated federal law by discriminating against them in the purchase of a house, and they subsequently filed a lawsuit. Unsuccessful in the district court, the couple appealed to the 9th Circuit on grounds the

owner of the company was "vicariously liable" (responsible for the actions of an agent or employee in the course of their work). The 9th Circuit agreed. The real estate company sought review in the Supreme Court.

In *Meyer v. Holley* the Supreme Court dismissed the 9th Circuit's "misunderstanding" of basic California law.The Justices wrote: "Finally, we have found no convincing argument in support of the Ninth Circuit's decision to apply nontraditional vicarious liability (agents) on principles (employers)-a decision that respondents [the couple] do not defend and in fact concede is incorrect . . ."

Underlying the 9th Circuit decision was a "social duty" (whatever that means) the court imposed on the real estate company. The court ignored the words of the relevant federal statute and basic common law. The Supreme Court reversed the 9th Circuit and returned the case for further proceedings. Without any reference to the reversal of its decision by the Supreme Court, and undeterred, the 9th Circuit reheard the case and found "vicarious liability" again in conjunction with other reasons for not dismissing the case; *Holley v. Crank*. Six months later, without any explanation, the court rewrote the opinion again, reversing the district court dismissal of the case and permitting the couple to amend their Complaint. No further action was taken in the case.

Lindsey v. SLT Los Angeles, 447 F.3d 1138 (9th Cir. 2006), amended decision
A federal statute (42 U.S.C. § 1981) prohibits discriminatory treatment of individuals on grounds of race in contractual relationships. The Supreme Court invented a three-part test to determine whether a contractor had discriminated against an employee (or other contracting party) on grounds of race. First, the contractor must allege a prima facie (simple recital of facts) case alleging discriminatory treatment; second, the defendant (contractor) must prove it had a legitimate nondiscriminatory reason for its

adverse employment action; and third, the employee must prove the reason asserted by the contractor is a pretext to its discriminatory effect.

This test almost guarantees a jury trial in every case because the employee thinks the contractor decision to suspend, terminate, or reprimand is discriminatory, and the contractor counters by explaining the employee's unacceptable conduct that led to its decision imposing a penalty or discharge. Under this rationale, companies began instituting "human relations" departments to respond to employee complaints, but the parties frequently ended in litigation because the perceptions of each side differed dramatically. Most jurors are, or were, formerly employees and tend to favor these parties against the deep pockets of contractors. These cases and employment cases.have dominated in state and federal courts, sometimes justified, sometimes vindictive.

The federal statute is not limited to discriminatory treatment in contracting or employment. The statute also applies to interference with "contractual relations" attributable to racial discrimination. The burden to justify alleged negative action service establishments (e.g., hotels, restaurants and other public places) is substantial. For example, in *Lindsey v. SLT Los Angeles*, the aggrieved parties sued the hotel SLT on grounds it had failed to provide the correct banquet room and instead had provided it to another group. Miffed and disappointed, the African American parties filed a lawsuit against the hotel. At the trial, the hotel personnel testified the plaintiffs failed to deposit reservation funds in a timely manner; the plaintiffs testified the hotel had assured them of a particular room to accommodate the crowd.

It is difficult to imagine that a contractual dispute with conflicting testimony on this issue should be the subject of a lawsuit. The district court agreed and dismissed the case. The parties appealed.

The 9th Circuit applied the same burden burden-shifting standard the Supreme Court developed in contract and employment cases and concluded the case should go to trial. So, a jury must sit through a case to determine whether the hotel had engaged in racial discrimination. The *Lindsey* case allows any minority group to complain of mistreatment and file a lawsuit forcing the service provider to expend time and money on frivolous litigation when the evidence is entirely circumstantial and in conflict. The statute should be reserved for more obvious cases of discrimination.

McDonald v. Domino's Pizza, 126 S.Ct.124 (2000)
Reversing the 9th Circuit decision in *McDonald v. Domino's Pizza,* 107 Fed Appx. 18.
As noted in the *Lindsey* case above, among the many statutes that address racial discrimination, federal law protects the equal right of "[a]ll persons within the jurisdiction of the United States to make and enforce contracts without respect to race." The statute currently defines "make and enforce contracts" to include "the making, performance, modification, and termination of contracts, and the enjoyment of all benefits, privileges, terms, and conditions of the contractual relationship." This statute is vague, ambiguous, and susceptible to any kind of litigation filed by a dissatisfied person.

In *McDonald v. Domino's Pizza* the 9th Circuit upheld the right of McDonald, the black contractor, to sue under this statute for damages allegedly attributable to the conduct of Domino's Pizza agents in breaching a contract he had negotiated on behalf of a corporation of which he was the sole owner. The parties who negotiated and signed the contact did so under their respective corporate names, not their individual names. The law has always distinguished between a corporation as a separate entity from those who manage it or who act on its behalf. This basic law of "agency" (of one who is authorized to act on behalf of another) applies to contracts imposing liability on the corporate entity if an agent wrongfully acts on its behalf. In other words, the corporation is liable for the wrongful or negligent acts of its agents committed during the course and scope of their employment.

In his lawsuit, McDonald convinced the 9th Circuit to ignore this basic rule, but the Supreme Court did not agree. The Court wrote: "When the

Civil Rights Act of 1866 was drafted, it was well known that '[i]n general a mere agent, who has no beneficial interest in a contract which he has made on behalf of his principal (owner), cannot support an action (lawsuit) thereon."

In other words, McDonald signed a contract on behalf of the corporation, not himself, and therefore could only sue in the name of the corporation. Having sought to enforce the contract himself under the Section 1981 statute instead of the corporation, he cannot maintain the litigation and the Supreme Court reversed the 9th Circuit.

Incidentally, the 9th Circuit had buried its original decision in this case in an unpublished report relying on a case it had previously decided; *Gomez v. Alexian Bros. Hospital*. Obviously the *Gomez* case was also wrongly decided.

Committee Concerning Community Improvement v. City of Modesto, 583 F.3d 690 (9th Cir. 2009)
Race is unequivocally the issue in this case. Plaintiffs alleged the City of Modesto and the County of Stanislaus in California intentionally discriminated against specific residential home areas predominantly occupied by Latinos. According to the Complaint filed in federal court, certain public entities failed to provide sewers and infrastructure to Latino households in cities not annexed to the City of Modesto, California. Defendants city and county responded by introducing evidence of tax sharing disputes between each other preventing any agreement on which entity should build first. The district court ruled in favor of the City and the Latino plaintiffs appealed.

The 9th Circuit panel spent endless pages explaining the difficulties of annexing an unincorporated area into the city. Because the experts for both sides disagreed on the correct interpretation of records and studies of the area, the defendants City and County objected, but the court permitted the Latinos to go forward with the lawsuit. In addition to filing their case under federal and California state statutes, the Latinos cited the Equal Protection Clause of the Fourteenth Amendment as one of the grounds for the lawsuit. Only in the 9th Circuit could such an extension of the Fourteenth Amendment survive.

But more importantly, Latinos allege that police response time to calls from residents of majority Latino areas were longer than those in white areas. By less than one minute. Despite the absurd difference of less than one minute, the court panel held, "This court cannot agree that as a matter of law, the difference of one minute be characterized as not making a 'meaningful difference' when one is waiting . . . for law enforcement or emergency personnel to arrive." This statement clashes with reality and is incomprehensible. "One minute" is a "meaningful difference? Any jury will would dispose of this contention in the same amount of time.

The 9th Circuit returned the case to the district court judge who made additional findings but conducted no further judicial proceedings. The most disturbing element of this decision is evidence of another federal court interfering with two public agencies and oblivious to budget constraints, tax issues, transportation and a host of other municipal issues confronting city and county governments. *Modesto* is a spin-off of "institutional reform" condemned by the Supreme Court in *Horne v. Flores*.

This case has been endlessly rewritten. In 2010 a federal district court wrote the last opinion on a procedural issue and as o 2014 remains in the pleading (allegation of facts) stage.

CHAPTER 23

ABORTION

Invalidating the criminal law of every state prohibiting abortion, the Supreme Court in 1973 decided *Roe v. Wade*, upholding the right of a woman to abort a fetus within the first trimester of pregnancy. Few issues in contemporary American life have invoked more passionate debate than this decision conferring a "right of privacy" on women.

The arguments between the protagonists for each side consist of a mixed bag, frequently based on a subjective evaluation of abortion but attempting to validate the position by posing objective arguments. From a legal perspective, critics argue that the Supreme Court seriously breached the role of the judiciary in revoking statutory prohibition of abortion extant in every state. In addition, those who saw a judicial decision usurping the legislative role of enacting legislation, contended the Supreme Court subverted the separation of powers between judge and legislature, and committed a serious breach of that principle.

Other legal challengers to the abortion decision decry the judicial invocation of a "right of privacy" to justify their decision, a term nowhere found in the text of the Constitution or the Bill of Rights. Indeed the decision lacked any Constitutional textual basis, but the Supreme Court discovered a Fourteenth Amendment "liberty interest" in the right of a woman to terminate a pregnancy. Nowhere in the Court decision do the Justices address the right of the people in a democratic society to decide the issue of abortion. Once the court "Constitutionalized" the right to abortion, no one could change the decision short of the almost impossible task of amending the Constitution.

From the perspective of religion, critics railed against the termination of a viable fetus that, if allowed to survive until term, would become transformed into a human being. The option of obliterating a potential human being qualified as anathema to religious men and women who continue their demands for elimination of a right to abort.

For those who agreed with the right of a woman to abort a fetus, the Supreme Court decision signified "liberation." for a woman who could unilaterally elect to discontinue pregnancy. In an age when women were emerging from a perceived second-class status, their decision to abort enabled them to decide resolution of the issue independently. In some quarters this Supreme Court decision "empowered" women.

This Chapter in the text does not attempt to adopt any of these conflicting perspectives *per se* but includes the abortion cases to reflect the disparate views of well intentioned people regardless of their argument. Abortion is included to reflect the cultural clash that exists not only in court but in a myriad of principles that govern people's lives. Abortion is an issue consistent with other decisions of the 9th Circuit whose judges impose policy preferences by invoking a Constitutional principle to justify their decisions. In other words, cases decided by the 9th Circuit on other issues are identical in masking policy in Constitutional clothing. Previous chapters have attempted to establish this thesis.

Eleven years after *Roe v. Wade* the 9th Circuit invalidated an Idaho statute limiting abortion in *Wasden v. Planned Parenthood of Idaho*. Two years later, in *Planned Parenthood Federation of America, Inc. v. Gonzales*, the 9th Circuit repeated its rejection of a federal statute enacted by Congress regulating "partial birth abortions." A description of this practice is gruesome and horrifying, consisting of surgically ripping out a fetus in the third trimester of pregnancy and smashing parts of the body in extraction. Yet the 9th Circuit invalidated the Congressionally enacted federal statute.

The Supreme Court reversed the 9th Circuit in *Gonzales v. Carhart* (a companion case from another federal circuit court on the same issue). After a horrifying description of the process, the Supreme Court agreed that Congress could regulate doctors who performed "partial birth" abortions. The majority decision of the Supreme Court in *Gonzales* only rearranged the abortion debate, and Justice Kennedy openly said just that to abortion proponents who challenge state statutes limiting abortion on procedural grounds. The Supreme Court in *Gonzales* rejected a Constitutional challenge only to the language of the statute, not its application to a specific set of facts. Framed in Constitutional language, abortion proponents can challenge individual cases based upon the facts presented at trial. This rationale ensures a continuous series of challenges to any statute regulating abortion based on the specific evidence in each case.

Despite Supreme Court approval of the federal statute in the *Gonzales* decision and rejection of the 9th Circuit analysis, deeper issues underlie the case. In *Roe v. Wade*, the seminal decision on abortion, the Supreme Court constitutionally justified abortion as a "right of privacy" protected by the Fourteenth Amendment. Apparently Supreme Court Associate Justice Goldberg abandoned that perspective . . . In *Gonzales*, she wrote: "[L]egal challenges to restrict abortion procedures do not need to vindicate some generalized notion of privacy, rather they center on an a woman's autonomy to determine her life's course and thus to enjoy equal citizenship status." This philosophic rhapsodizing does not address the abortion issue *per se*, but refers to judicial policy making absent any legal foundation, uncorroborated in any statute or case law, and an example of 9th Circuit rationale even in some members of the Supreme Court.

CONCLUSION

This text has reviewed and summarized innumerable cases written by the 9th Circuit Court of Appeals reversed by the Supreme Court. Despite the 9th Circuit record breaking number of reversals, some of its members continue to impose policy, not the law, on the people of western states. Repeatedly reversing death penalty cases previously affirmed by state supreme courts has cost the state and federal courts an incalculable sum. Ninth Circuit decisions account for the backlog of cases in California courts, yet no one will call attention to this reason for exorbitant cost and delay. In the 2011–12 term of the Supreme Court the justices reversed four major death penalty case decided by 9th Circuit judges, and simultaneously insisted the 9th Circuit defer to state court judgments. The years 2013 and 2014 are no different.

In the early days of the Constitutional Convention its supporters assured members that the judiciary retained little power. That naïveté has been rejected, and some members of the 9th Circuit have obliterated any semblance of judicial restraint. The court is an unofficial legislature imposing its philosophy on the people within its jurisdiction.

Printed in Great Britain
by Amazon